JEFF JOHNS

Jet Lag Junkie

Unfiltered Tales of a Compulsive Wanderer

Library of Congress Control Number: 2024917637

First edition

ISBN: 979-8-218-49704-0

This book was professionally typeset on Reedsy.
Find out more at reedsy.com

To my girls – may our adventures never end.

Contents

Acknowledgments

For anyone who has ever asked me "How was your trip?", this book is the long answer. And none of this would have been possible without the support of several important people in my life.

Chief among them is my wife Anne, who looked me dead in my eye and told me to write it, followed by my patient family and friends who let me live it, and the support of even more patient editors. Specifically, Sheila Johns, my dear mother, who took on the herculean task of copy-editing this manuscript in record time to ensure that my story was told clearly, with a fierce dedication to keeping my voice. Additional thanks to Megan Close, Scott Carnahan, and Kaitlyn Caldwell who worked tirelessly to review my early drafts and provided critical feedback and support over the last many years and endless versions of this book. They've all done their best to turn my ramblings into a tale as adventurous as I remember it being, and hopefully, more coherent than it was while I was living it.

I've worked diligently to reconstruct all timelines, locations, dates, names, and historical facts. Any inaccuracies are my own.

'Jet Lag Junkie' is imperfect, raw, and reads like a journal, for all I ever wanted to be was a storyteller.

Introduction

"Adventure is allowing the unexpected to happen to you."
– Richard Aldington

Salt Lake City, Utah, USA, 1995

There's no stranger feeling than four-inch thick plush, neon green carpet between your toes -and in a bathroom no less. It's something I never quite got used to. The small glass cups by the sink had neon green horse riding scenes etched into them, the toilet seat was also covered in green carpet, and even the hand soap was the same blinding shade - a color that should only be used for movie theater candy and children's toys.

I spent a lot of time in that bathroom, just sitting on the floor peering at the contents of an old cupboard, lost in a state of wonder I'd never known and didn't understand.

I first remember summer visits to my grandparents in the early 1990s, down the steep, see-through staircase below the sprawling Salt Lake City home. My sister and I would often sleep on the giant, sunken couch, basking in the static of a thick curved TV screen, feeling excited and a bit scared of the dark in that big empty basement. The childhood bedrooms of my aunts and uncles, untouched since they moved on to college in the 1970s, held a museum-like quality. I never remember walking into them, only peering through the door, gazing at the portraits of each one painted and hung above the perfectly made beds.

All of the triumphs and struggles of their time in those rooms now sat silent, still, frozen. Their younger years were well behind them, and mine were all ahead. With so many portraits of once youthful relatives and others long gone dotting the walls, it was hard not to feel watched, or to turn around and see if I was alone, to quickly look behind each door I opened.

As the last beams were nailed into place in this big house, the neon green shag carpet freshly laid on the bathroom floor, a man had just walked on the moon for the first time, the Olympic Games in Munich had not gone as planned, and a fellow named Manson was causing a lot of trouble in California. Nearly three decades later as I sat in that same basement, untouched for a generation, Nintendo 64 was all the rage, Atlanta was preparing for a memorable Summer Olympic games themselves, and the world was starting to panic about mad cow disease.

But for me, a chunky elementary school kid clinging to every pop culture trend I could find, the American Dream was alive and well. I was happy, healthy, and had all I needed from life in the good 'ole U S of A. The whole country seemed to be happy, too. Business was booming, there was steady job creation, rising productivity, low inflation, a surging stock market, and a balanced budget. Life was good.

Sure, I couldn't focus my mind to save my life and had the attention span of a gnat, but it kept life interesting, and my creative mind would run on overdrive during every waking moment. I assumed that all children had the same mind I did and that struggling to pay attention to the smallest task was nearly impossible for everyone. But my life ahead looked smooth from my sheltered perspective, with boundless opportunities, and a path filled with freedoms and conveniences lay before me, undiscovered. After all, I didn't know this was the American Dream. This was just life, the only way I knew it. And for a time, during these summers in my grandparent's basement, it would remain smooth sailing – at least until I headed off for college.

That basement held countless darkened hallways and hidden rooms – a woodworking shop for my grandfather down an endless and dark corridor, a summer kitchen full of a thousand trinkets, jars filled with buttons, infinite spools of yarn of every color, canned peaches, pears, and plums. An ancient fridge humming in the corner held my grandfather's soda, which I fearfully stole each and every summer. I'd gulp the last drop just hoping I wouldn't get caught, the citrus bubbles stinging my nose as I watched the hall for faint shadows approaching.

But what I remember most is that bathroom with the long green neon carpet.

As curious as a field mouse, I opened all the drawers and cupboard doors I could find in that little bathroom. And that is where I found my treasure map.

I don't remember how many years' worth of National Geographic magazines were stacked in the bathroom cupboard, but it was far more than I could read in a lifetime. My head turned sideways in fascination to see the issue month and year stamped and fading on the spine, many so far in the past that it felt like I'd stumbled on a time machine.

So many copies were piling up that if one more issue arrived in the mail, it just might not fit. Their bright yellow covers were endless, some pristine and bright as the sun, others tattered and torn, faded from years of existence.

September '63, April '79, December '85 – I stared at them for ages before grabbing one that was awash with swirls of luminous stars covering its half-hidden page. Soaking in the striking images on the cover, I read whatever words I could understand - "Lost Worlds", "Ancient Cities", "Never before seen...". My eyes grew bigger with the turn of every page.

Some stories told of crumbling pyramids, others featured colorful alien insects, the vastness of ancient deserts, and new worlds I'd never heard of. Each issue slightly creased from where Granna had read it before closing the cupboard downstairs in the bathroom with the four-inch neon green plush carpet.

It was as if these wondrous treasures had been left specifically for me, little breadcrumbs to spark my imagination when I found them. I was frozen, calm, in a complete state of attention, a rare and captivating experience for me. Time didn't just slow down, it downright stopped, as my eyes methodically absorbed every single detail in those rich images.

Sitting on the bathroom floor, toes curling in the long carpet, I was transported around the world, to scenes and places I couldn't process, but one particular image always stuck with me - a tall explorer with a huge bushy beard and a safari cap who looked like my grandfather, snow white hair, a stern and serious face. Flanked by tribesmen from a far-off continent, they all stared at the camera as if caught in the middle of a riveting discovery.

'Where are they? What are they talking about? What have they discovered!'

Getting lost in that image, envisioning the adventures that led to that moment, right there on the bathroom floor with the neon green plush carpet - that is where my love for travel was born. I longed to be the explorer with the bushy beard. I longed to dive into those pictures and experience both the calm and excitement that I felt in looking at them.

4

Exploring the Sahara Desert, trekking up Himalayan peaks, being detained in Tajikistan, held at gunpoint in gambling dens, and climbing lost pyramids - all adventures too sensational for me to imagine at the time, much less believe that I'd experience for myself one day.

The fantasy of living these experiences was one thing, but having the self-confidence to head out into the world and chase them, to take a great leap into the unknown and trust that the world would catch me, was another thing altogether.

I had my treasure map now. I just needed to learn how to read it.

First, however, I'd have to drop out of college, get fired from my first job, and find myself held against my will at an airport in a country I'd never heard of on the other side of the world.

1

Learn to Read People: Dreaming of Being Locked Up Abroad

"You must not lose faith in humanity. Humanity is an ocean; if a few drops of the ocean are dirty, the ocean does not become dirty."
– Mahatma Gandhi

Dushanbe, Tajikistan. June 2016

I can still remember the blank stare Anne and I gave the flashing monitor in Terminal 2 at the Dubai International Airport. Terminal 2 is not the fancy Emirates terminal in Dubai. Instead of flights to Paris, London, or Tokyo, there are flights to Baghdad, Addis Ababa, and Jaipur. Most of the airlines are local to the Gulf, originating in countries you've only seen on a map if you've heard of them at all. "What is Somon Air?" we said out loud, almost simultaneously. It's a rare occasion I come across a capital city or airline name I don't recognize, but Tajikistan has both.

In all my travels, I'd never come across anything about Tajikistan, but here we were, boarding a flight three hours northeast of Dubai into the heart of Central Asia bound for Dushanbe, its capital city. This is when I could focus the most – as my mind stopped darting around like lightning stuck in a bottle when I boarded a plane to a country I knew absolutely nothing about, where everything was new and my only goal was problem-solving the next five minutes.

The summer heat of Dubai is at its peak in July, and it has long stopped being fun or a novelty. All thoughts are on escaping to somewhere, anywhere cooler. Months of oppressive heat are already behind and months more are still ahead before it finally cools off toward the middle of October. The humidity hits like a punch in the face when you step outside, and the thick air soaks up the last of your energy before lunch rolls around. Anne and I had been dating for about a year and a half, and sitting in our small Dubai apartment, the warm tile floor covered in endless dust beneath our feet, blistering heat permeating the large sliding glass doors surrounding our living room, we began dreaming of escaping for the upcoming long weekend. A quick search while hovering over the kitchen counter and Tajikistan popped up. "*Tajikistan?*" I thought.

'*How am I going to sell this?*'

"Tell me one interesting thing about Tajikistan, one thing we can do there, and I'm in." Anne chimed from the bedroom half-jokingly, knowing I'd jump on the opportunity.

'*Challenge accepted.*'

I'd typed "Where is Tajikistan?" before she could finish speaking. Bordering Afghanistan, China, Kyrgyzstan, and Uzbekistan, Tajikistan is known for its rugged mountains, if anything at all. Telling Anne that in addition, Tajikistan had the world's largest flagpole didn't quite sell it as quickly as I'd hoped, but there we were at the airport nonetheless.

Calling my travel style erratic was an understatement, and while the excitement of jumping into the complete unknown is how I'd come to best navigate the world, I was constantly nervous that Anne wouldn't be able to tolerate it. But she hadn't given up.

'How on earth did I convince this beautiful French girl to travel the world with me?'

I like to think my unending American enthusiasm convinced her to take the chance - both on me and on many of our shared adventures – like chasing after a puppy through an ice cream shop at 30,000 feet in the air.

Stepping off the plane in the middle of the night in Dushanbe, we sleepily stumbled down the heavily air-conditioned empty corridor towards immigration. Blinking fluorescent tubes on the ceiling panels seemingly guiding our way. Long-since arrived and departed flights flashing names like Kam Air and Ural Airlines paired with cities like Almaty, Kabul or Chelyabinsk followed us as we walked. Little did we know I would find myself back in these dark, empty halls in less than 48 hours, held against my will.

Sighing with exhaustion, we were soon faced with the harsh reality that the airport had no ATMs and they didn't take UAE dirham, the local currency in Dubai, at immigration.

'You win this round, Travel Gods. Time to put some problem-solving skills to the test.'

Approaching a cracked plexiglass window, I interrupted the sleep of what seemed to be the only man working in the airport. Multiple layers of green and brown, some resembling an official military uniform, others hand-me-down sweaters, lined his thick frame. A faded gold watch band hugged his chubby wrist, dark black hairs covering the knuckles on each and every finger. A droopy mustache escaping the corners of his mouth, was all that was visible under the brim of his army-green beret. I imagined his stale breath reeking of cheap cigarettes and cheaper beer, but Tajikistan is a 98% Muslim country, so I wasn't sure of anything other than that he probably hadn't smiled since the Clinton Administration.

Holding my breath, I tapped the rickety window, which creaked enough to rouse the officer. Assuming we were local Tajiks returning home, he didn't even bother looking up before reaching out his hand to accept our documents. Upon realizing we were actually tourists, he was utterly unfazed at our predicament and ushered us out of his sight until we had the right bills to pay for our entrance visa. Explaining through broken language and hand gestures that we didn't, and couldn't, manifest his local currency no matter how long we stood there, he stewed in his badly worn swiveling chair for what seemed like hours before begrudgingly pocketing the small bills we had on hand - a few Dirham, a folded dollar bill, a few Euro coins as well - the contents of whatever we could scrape up from the bottom of our backpacks after so many travels. "Very important - keep for exit." he said, slapping the entry paper in our passports and sliding them back to me. It was 3 am, and the airport terminal was utterly deserted but we were in. Welcome to Tajikistan.

Met with a silent blanket of darkness covering the Arrivals terminal exit, no cars buzzed by and no locals shuffled about in the dark, only dim lights in the distance and a cool breeze passing through the dead of night. We paused for a moment, took a breath, looked at each other, closed our eyes, and smiled.

'Ok...now what?'

Flashing a smile that was impossible not to return, with her streaking blond and brunette hair, an eclectic wardrobe only a European woman could pull off without looking disheveled, the glow of her golden Mediterranean tan escaping between layers of spandex, checkered scarfs, and an Adidas track jacked that would make Joseph's technicolor dreamcoat blush, Anne's eyes said it all, "You got us here, so this one is on you, buddy."

Slowly, one of the dim lights in the distance crept closer. A sputtering exhaust came with it, and a dusty mustard hatchback with one working headlight approached us at the airport entrance. Unsure whether friend or foe, his warm smile confirmed my boyish optimism, and when he offered us a ride to our hotel, we didn't bat an eye as he really was our only hope. Backpacks hastily thrown in the trunk, we bounced over the exit speed bump and sputtered down the main road into the sleeping city.

"Ha! Take that. Told ya it would work out!"

Passing dark, obscured government buildings along the way, I had no idea at that moment how close I'd get to ending up held in one of them in the coming days.

The two single beds pushed together were comfortable enough, and we sped through the last ten minutes of the sparse hotel breakfast the next morning - local sweet rolls, pourable tangy yogurts, and sliced cheeses. After all we'd been through just hours prior at the airport, our first mission was to find cash. None of our bank cards worked at any ATM we tried. The local machines took four-digit pins only, and our cards were six, so we failed every time. We only had a weekend to explore Tajikistan, and at this rate, we wouldn't be able to do much, so we called our bank for help. "Tajikistan? Can you spell that? Do you mean Afghanistan?" the teller sheepishly responded.

'Thanks for nothing.'

Abdul was young, energetic, and clearly had both his morning coffee and a great night's sleep - two things any traveler hopes for in a front desk clerk. His eyes sparkled with kindness behind his large round glasses and pressed white collared shirt as we approached. "How can I help you sir?" he happily spat out, excited to speak English to us after overhearing our frustrated phone call with the bank. Explaining our cash conundrum, he motioned to a boy sitting by the hotel entrance. Abdul passed along the message in Tajik, and the boy waved for us to follow him out the door into a fast-approaching old model minivan with his friend inside. From one bank to the next, ATM to ATM, we had no luck. Local pop music blaring, Anne and I could only look at each other and smile. We were trusting Tajikistan to show us the way, led by the guidance of our new friend Abdul with the help of his two friends, who couldn't have been more than 20. Finding, at last, a small, dilapidated Western Union in a rundown grocery store that was willing to sell us Tajik somoni, we finally had a wad of cash in our pocket —our golden ticket to exploring for the weekend.

Returning to the hotel, Abdul eagerly greeted us and was so excited that we were there simply to see Tajikistan that he took the day off work, jumped in the passenger seat with us, and planned an entire itinerary on the spot for us to see all we could around the capital city. He'd only ever welcomed rich Saudi businessmen looking to party or retired German hikers heading into the Fann Mountains to grow their sandal tans - never excited tourists just looking to discover his country, and he couldn't contain his joy.

Hours after arriving at a cold and unwelcoming immigration terminal in the middle of the night, we sat grinning ear to ear as we sped down the road out of the city center with a new friend, to explore his country, his culture, his world. "Tajikistan is a Muslim country now" Abdul explained, "and although the majority religion is Islam, our national language is Farsi, and we use the Cyrillic alphabet." A collage of cultures had evidently remained after the end of the Soviet rule - perhaps the most unique mix we'd ever come across.

Pulling off the paved highway onto a coffee-colored dusty road, we explored the ancient city and fort of Hisar, on the banks of the Khanaka river - a city dating back to Cyrus the Great, King of Persia, in 600 BC. Heading for the mountains, we swerved up stunning, winding roads that hugging -hugged the crystal clear river's edge on our way up the Fann Mountain range. We passed by endless, sprawling summer homes dotting the valley, homes that held the stories and memories of countless generations – silent and unknown to us until this moment. Snow-capped peaks revealed themselves as we climbed higher. The river slowly faded away, man-made buildings vanished, and we were left with stunning views fading into infinity. As Robin Williams once said about Alaska, "It's not the end of the world but you could see it from here."

At Abdul's signal, the driver pulled into a gravel patch on the side of the road. Awash with stones and rocks in every shade of gray, it was hard to see where the earth ended and the mountain behind began, as both sheltered in the shade from the hot summer sun. The empty lot was dotted with faded wooden boxes - white, yellow, blue, and green. An outdated Soviet trailer contained even more, stacked on top of each other, paint chipping away into the wind. Gravel crunching beneath our feet, a humble man with a shy smile approached. "Salom!" I waved, relying on my own smile to show our friendly intentions better than my weak attempt at speaking Tajik.

"This man is a bee farmer - the best in Tajikistan," Abdul eagerly explained to us. This was his bee farm, his workshop, his office - not a roadside stand to sell his goods. He had no golden jars of honey on display and no Instagram handle, but he was more than happy to pry open one of the boxes, wave away the buzzing bees surrounding them, and proudly dip a thin wooden stick into the side, scraping the edges of the box and revealing its dripping treasure. It was the freshest honey we ever tasted –bee pollen served to us like fine caviar on a teaspoon. "The best for a strong heart, inflammation, and antioxidants." Shaking hands and waving goodbye, Anne yelped and started dashing zig-zag across the gravel, swatting at her yoga pants. You can't enjoy fresh honey without a bee sting... Anne was the last to laugh, but soon we were all giggling, and at that moment any language or cultural barrier completely evaporated - sharing an experience every child can relate to.

Winding our way back down the valley towards Dushanbe, our conversation returned to Tajikistan's turbulent history. Clashing between Soviet rule and Islamic pressure from neighboring Afghanistan, the tensions culminated in a bloody civil war between 1992 and 1997. Over 1.2 million Tajiks were left displaced, and the country was left in absolute devastation, the economy in disarray, infrastructure demolished, and government services abandoned with most of the population subsiding on international handouts and aid.

"Afghanistan has a big problem with Islamic extremists." Abdul continued. To combat this, Tajikistan introduced a highly controversial mandate to avoid the same fate within their borders - both beard and hijab (a Muslim woman's headscarf) bans were forcibly imposed around the country, especially within Dushanbe. While the government denied that a ban was in place, police encounters on the street painted a very different picture. The women could continue to wear the traditional dress, the abaya, but black was no longer allowed, as it was deemed to be too extreme –only colorful abayas would be permitted, and there would be no hijab. The men could still grow short facial hair, but anything longer was no longer permitted – and completely cleanly shaven if you wanted a passport.

Traffic picked up on the outskirts of Dushanbe as we approached, and bouncing from stop light to stop light, we soaked in all we'd experienced - our thoughts enough to fill the air with no more need for conversation. Passing soviet monuments, towering Slavic structures, crumbling museums, and outdated city parks, we meandered through the city center. And we passed that famed flagpole, which Abdul proudly told us was "the second largest flagpole in the world!" only behind Saudi Arabia. "Ha!" Anne was quick to blurt out with a chuckle and a flash of her smile that I could never get enough of.

Our stomachs were growling, and the late afternoon sun was long across Rudaki Park as we pulled onto the curb and said goodbye to both Abdul and our trusty driver. We'd walk home from here we told them, doing what we do best; wandering aimlessly through an unknown city as evening fell. We never saw the French or American Embassies in Tajikistan that day, but we found the one other establishment you'll find in any country on earth - an Irish pub.

Grabbing an outside table, flanked with local brews and a monumental platter of fire-roasted meats from who knows what, we were quick to make friends. Our adventurous day turned into a riotous evening filled with laughter and mostly nonverbal communication with the locals any traveler knows so well. A warm smile and a gung-ho attitude can go a long way when you're far from home. Pausing from the action, I stepped into the bathroom and found myself face to face with poorly constructed topless cutouts of famous actresses glued to the wall above the urinal. The edges were peeled and picked at by someone wanting a souvenir, the good people of Public Pub quick to glue them back in place. The awkward tilted head of Mila Kunis staring back at me atop some other woman's naked body. I was caught in the moment between pop culture pranks and the sordid history of this country fresh in my mind. The meat was overcooked, the weissbier was flat and watered down but to us, it tasted like champagne.

I couldn't help but chuckle – what an adventure.

* * *

There came a point in every weekend adventure Anne and I took from Dubai, usually around 7 pm on a Saturday, when we both acknowledged that our overnight flight was due to leave in a few hours, with work waiting for us hours after landing, and it was time to start heading to the airport. Fumbling around in our backpacks as we walked into the same terminal we'd emerged from 48 hours earlier, Anne was quick to throw her passport in one hand, arrival visa and paperwork in the other, but I wasn't quite so lucky.

I found my passport easy enough, as it's always in the same spot. But as I continued to fish in the middle pocket of my backpack, I could not locate the small inserted immigration paper that the hairy-knuckled officer had resentfully shoved in between the pages of my passport a few nights earlier. "Very important – keep for exit, " his words echoed in my mind.

'I'll just let them know, they'll see the stamp in my passport and understand.'

"I'll be right back" I half muttered under my breath as I handed Anne my bag. Still flipping through my passport pages, I approached a gun-wielding security officer and with hand gestures, revealed my predicament, sure that a warm smile was all that was needed to remedy the situation. I'd been through passport controls in more countries than I could count, a necessary nuisance of travel that was never fun but never an event either. Swiping my passport out of my hand before I could offer it to him, he motioned for me to follow, and within a second, I was being escorted to the next building over, with Anne left standing alone in utter confusion.

Out the back door we went, across a dimly lit sidewalk, into a secondary building, and up a dark staircase to an endless hallway that reminded me of my grandparent's basement. As stale cigarette smoke filled my nostrils and I tried to process what was happening, I glanced back and saw two additional guards following at a short but constant distance. It was all happening too quickly. The weissbier turned stale in my belly. My mind was electric but calm. One step at a time. I had to focus.

I have never seen a single lightbulb just hanging from a wire like the one above this guy's desk, it looked like a cartoon. I had to blink to believe what my eyes were seeing after being whisked from the hall and into the middle office of the dark second floor. Whoever he was, he looked important, the same multi-layered green and brown military-style uniform I'd become familiar with at this airport but with one big difference - this officer was sporting a lot more metals, pins, and stripes, and he was not excited to see me. He wore a different hat than the other officers, pointy at different ends. The faded patches sewn to his forest green uniform lapels held high rank despite their age.

Placing his cigarette on the desk, burning tip dangling off the edge, thin trails of smoke racing to the dim light above, he motioned for me to look at his computer screen, an invitation to approach and stand shoulder to shoulder. An old Windows monitor, one any 90's kid knows too well, displayed a crude translation website running Internet Explorer 95.

'It's 2016 man, time to update your system.'

I instantly didn't take him as seriously as I should have because of his ancient tech —the same way I just can't take police sirens in Europe seriously either, because they just sound too funny.

But my amusement was short-lived.

"You will stay here and go to Monday court." the screen generated in English as he started typing. I instantly realized the gravity of the situation I thought was quite innocent just minutes prior. I started to worry that my birthright American enthusiasm would struggle to translate through a typing program. Usually, the golden retriever puppy when I travel, the hairs on my neck started to stand on end. Feeling like I may need to be more of a pitbull to get out of this one, I remained calm, my mind both racing and completely blank.

I spent countless lazy afternoons in college glued to my couch watching reruns of "Locked Up Abroad" fantasizing about being featured in an episode someday a thrilling story I was sure I'd have been able to wiggle out of and proudly regale to friends after returning home unscathed. The allure of a travel adventure was like no other in providing yet another detour to growing up and finding a career. Now, sitting here in a darkened and damp holding cell of a government office, I wanted absolutely no part of it. A hero's journey this most definitely was not.

'I bet you never experienced anything like this, Dad! But maybe that's for the better...'

I tried to argue, to plead my case, but it was hopeless - any nuance was erased immediately in the poor translation on the dull monitor before us. Reaching down and patting my jeans, I felt my wallet in my front pocket. I pulled it out and slowly flipped it open on the cheap laminate desk. Fingers shaking, I spread out all the remaining Somoni bills I had so they peeked above the crease and were visible to everyone in the room while keeping my eyes fixed straight ahead. Proceeding to type further onto his yellow-stained keyboard, I nudged the wallet in his direction intending that he would understand it was meant to be a bribe.

I've coughed up my fair share of pay-offs while traveling, but for the most part, they felt like friendly kickbacks, a little thank you, and ways to open doors otherwise closed - nothing sinister. There was no escaping the reality of this one, however. It was a bribe plain and simple —and of a military police captain. My heart pounded at the thought of the repercussions if I misjudged, came on too strong, or not strong enough - and I couldn't stop thinking of Anne caught in the crossfire. I'd seen those episodes of Locked Up Abroad spin out of control, one small mishap snowballing into establishing my new residency at the local jail, spending all my time learning Tajik.

My mind was a hollow shell as he stared at my meager offering while inhaling a thin, endless gulp of his cigarette and placing it down once again. Glancing at the officer who brought me in, he whispered a string of words as smoke escaped his lips with a smile like he was saying the punchline to a well-known joke. Everyone smiled but me.

Leaning down, he began typing again as I eagerly watched

the computer screen translating each character in real-time - transfixed on the outcome. Words like "bear" or "tablecloth" would flash for a split second before settling into their rough translation, unable to predict his thoughts well enough. When he stopped, a grin filled his face like he was presenting a finished work of art to an adoring audience but I laughed out loud when I saw the translation of what he'd typed. His grin evaporated instantly.

I'll never forget what I saw on that screen. And I'll never forget my instant impulse to reach into my pocket and take a picture of it before immediately stopping myself from quite literally attempting to document a crime in a dimly lit room with a post-Soviet officer who was not my biggest fan.

'This would make the dumbest episode of Locked Up Abroad yet...'

Because of how hard I was laughing inside while simultaneously panicking, as my mind raced to plot my next move, the words on that hazy, pixelated monitor were burned into my brain:

"You show me your pussy, I'll show you mine."

Obviously not exactly what he'd intended to say, but I understood well enough what he was suggesting...

What he didn't know was that Anne and I were experts at travel efficiency, especially with seldom-used foreign currency, which meant our remaining cash was perfectly accounted for down to nearly the last note, save for the return taxi fare to the airport and the last pint. In that barely lit room, it was clear that the wadded-up low-value notes must have looked much more impressive than their actual value would have justified.

'No turning back now, I've bribed a military police officer.'

I nodded and tried to exude an air of confidence in response to his subtle nod back, like a begrudging proud father who doesn't

19

know how to show love, with the last bit of cigarette smoke dancing in the light as it trailed up the wall to the single, hanging light bulb, straining to illuminate us both.

After an uncomfortably long pause, he took the entire crumpled contents of my wallet in a hurried fistful, including the $1 American bill and all the coins, and dialed the officer in Passport Control #4, to give him my details. It was only after he hung up that he realized the bills I had offered only amounted to pocket change, not even enough to buy himself tea at the end of his shift. Within an instant, I was being ushered out, frustrated words exchanged between all involved, a waste of everyone's time, my heart racing with every second as I moved away from that little room, each step one closer to the light and to Anne. Back down the dark stairs, across the path to the airport terminal where Anne, was frantically waving my 'lost' arrival card in her hand as she saw me approaching.

Like the peanut butter to my jelly, she obviously knew exactly where to find that document if I'd have just given her a second, but I was too proud and flustered to lean on her for help, preferring to act stoic and smug, like I had it all figured out. The paper had been in my bag the entire time. She fished it out moments after I'd disappeared in utter confusion at how I'd vanished so fast. And she had lived her own silent hell during every minute I was gone, imagining the worst.

'*Was he arrested? Kidnapped? Disappeared?*'

"I'll explain everything on the plane" I whispered into her ear as I held her tight and moved us towards security. Approaching Passport Booth #4 as instructed, I could feel my chest tightening and my heart was pounding. This was the point in every episode of '*Locked Up Abroad*' when something inevitably went wrong – but no matter how panicked I should have been, I felt strangely calm, because for once, I was fully focused on the present moment.

'*Thwap.*'

The customs officer met my gaze with a pause that said it all as I hastily laid my passport on the counter. A loud smack of the departure stamp and I was through without a word exchanged. Sitting anxiously at the gate, my eyes darted at every movement in the terminal, sure that I would be detained again just out of principle. I felt like Ben Affleck at the end of Argo waiting for the plane to take off, my breath held until all wheels were off the ground, visions of angry immigration officers storming the plane and removing me for attempting the weakest bribe of all time.

"The things we do, love." Anne said to me with a sigh under her breath, the plane wheels finally tucking closed beneath us as we lifted into the dark night air and headed for Afghan airspace. "The things we do." I whispered back as I rested my head on various layers of her earth-toned scarf and smelled the familiar scent of her lotion that now felt like home.

'*I have to marry this girl.*'

* * *

I learned a lot on that trip. I learned about a country I knew nothing about, its history, culture, nature, and its second-largest flagpole. But I was also confronted with the reality that the way I'd taught myself to harness my own mind could be reckless and erratic and could lead me down pathways I didn't intend – pathways I'd survived going down alone thus far, but pathways I couldn't inflict on Anne going forward.

And I learned the value of knowing how to read people, whether trusting the local front desk clerk at a hotel in a city I had never been before, getting in his car and sharing a spontaneous day together exploring his home, or reading the situation, and body language, of a grumpy military officer who'd pulled the night shift. Travel heightens all of your senses, and while sight, smell, and taste are often thought of first, feeling and instinct are the senses most bound to save you on your adventures. For me, they became the bedrock for how I navigated the world, how I navigated my life. Learn to read them, to develop them, and to trust them beyond anything else. You never know when you may need to rely on them for your life.

Most importantly, I learned that 'if you show them yours, they'll show you theirs'. Abdul welcomed us with open arms, the smile on his face never decreasing as he proudly showed us his home, his country, his world. That is how I'll always remember Tajikistan.

And I hope that crusty immigration officer thinks of me often and remembers the worst bribe of his life.

Embracing the unknown may be risky, but it has its own rewards. It's the connection I seek, not the danger.

2

Know What You're Chasing: A Fringe Religion, Alternative Education & A Plan

*"Being a great father is like shaving. No matter how good
you shaved today, you have to do it again tomorrow."*
- Reed Markham

Bethesda, Maryland, USA, 1995

I remember the crisp fall mornings and the sticky humid summer evenings in Washington, D.C. the most. The smell of fall leaves in October and freshly cut grass in August are burned into my mind - my sense of smell connecting me tightly to years otherwise fading in many other ways. But that particular morning was different. It was downright cold, which meant that while I waited for my Dad to drive me to school, I was pacing the sidewalk looking for a small twig to put between my lips and pretend to smoke.

It was cold enough to see my breath, but I hid my exhales so my Mom wouldn't have to see her 10-year-old smoking foliage from the front window. I don't remember seeing a single person ever smoke in front of me, so I must have seen it on TV and thought it was cool. The Marlboro Man was all the rage in those years. Or maybe I saw it on one of those National Geographic pages in the bathroom with the neon green carpet.

That was the first time I remember trying to be cool - really trying to replicate something I'd seen, absorbed somewhere, and stored in my subconscious, trying it out for myself to see how it felt. I felt like a fraud, but man, it felt cool to try. And it wouldn't be the last time I tried smoking something to be cool.

"Dad?" I muttered sheepishly as we barreled up our suburban street, our cold breath still swirling in front of us in the chilly morning. The small twig now snapped as I rubbed it between my fingers and picked at it with nails that were bitten bare. I'd wanted to ask the question for days, and now I'd committed but was almost too shy. "Yeah, Bud?" he responded instantly with a grin. "Can boys fart out of their... penises?" The smile spread larger across his face, already imagining telling the other doctors what his 10-year-old son had asked him on the ride to school that morning.

"We're just not built that way, Bud." he said without missing a beat, slowing down a bit as he flicked on the blinker and exited our quiet neighborhood for the beltway circling Washington, D.C.

I grew up with the best Dad in the world. I still have the best Dad in the world and have had for every minute in between. But that doesn't mean we haven't had our differences along the way, because while I was spending my school days in one bubble, my Dad was pulling me in another direction– the only one he knew, each Sunday.

During the week, I was off to the Washington Waldorf School, a thirty-minute drive each morning and afternoon across the sprawling Washington, D.C. suburbs. Waldorf education is based on the educational philosophy of Rudolf Steiner, the founder of anthroposophy, who affirmed that "Our highest endeavor must be to develop free human beings who are able of themselves to impart purpose and direction to their lives." Its educational style is holistic and human-centered, intended to develop students' intellectual, artistic, and practical skills, with a focus on imagination and creativity. In addition to mastering the usual academics, my educational environment included songs about gnomes and fairies, the movements and gestures of eurythmy, verses and poetry, beeswax modeling, watercolor painting and drawing, puppetry and marionettes.

That's right, I was a hippie kid –well, at least half of me was.

My school was unique and always felt like a very protective environment I stepped into every morning - like a cocoon filled with soft colors, familiar faces, rounded edges, and the knowledge that nothing was going to harm me that day from the outside world. The Waldorf community was nothing but warm, welcoming, and supportive, but I was keenly aware from a young age that it was alternative and thought by some to be radical - and that made me feel different, separate, and weird from as early as I can remember. To compact this, I was aware that my mind was different as well. While the children around me seemed able to focus, at least enough to hear a complete question and formulate a response, my mind was often fractured between multiple thoughts before the teacher could finish speaking, and I often panicked that I hadn't heard the question.

The entire school, from kindergarten through 12th grade, had less than 300 students at a time when the local public high schools had upwards of 1,500 kids roaming the halls. Public school students could easily get lost in the mix, and skip class if they wanted to, but for me, this would have been impossible. My teachers were akin to extended parents, many teaching siblings and generations of previous students in the same building, the same classrooms, and the same wooden desks. Every teacher knew the name of each student in the entire school, their brothers and sisters, parents – and personalities.

The neighborhood kids went to the local elementary, middle, and high schools, which resulted in very few similarities I shared with them. They may have known who the Eurythmics were, but they sure didn't know what eurythmy was. They all watched Sports Center on ESPN each afternoon after school, stuffing Chips Ahoy cookies into their mouths, while I was lucky to get an organic alternative (don't try carob if you're ever given the chance) and our TV was smaller than a dinner plate, fake wood paneling on the sides, and covered with a dull orange play cloth most of the time. No surprise that the Waldorf community was huge into healthy eating and organic food, years before Whole Foods made it popular (and more expensive). Waldorf education shied away from technology in the early developmental years as well, which meant a whole lot of make-believe instead.

Waldorf education has its reasons for delaying the teaching of reading, the use of technology, and the introduction of text-books for the students, but what wasn't taught in reading and writing during those earliest years was more than compensated for by teaching us how to listen by the example of teachers who deeply listened themselves. While I couldn't listen to save my life, I always knew that someone was listening to *me* whenever I had the courage and focus to share a thought.

While I was keenly aware that my reading and writing skills

were behind the other neighborhood kids, I never felt that I wasn't being heard or that the adults in my life weren't truly listening to me. One of the central pillars of Waldorf education is the practice of a single-class teacher accompanying the same group of students from 1st through 8th grade. For my lucky group of kids, that teacher was Jack Petrash, Mr P. for short. This single teacher fosters and balances the educational needs of the class and the individual students from childhood to adolescence by bringing consistency, trust, and a nurturing environment within which each student can flourish and become confident in their own individuality.

Mr. P. was devout in his dedication to ensuring that every single student felt heard when they spoke and that he was truly listening, no matter what ideas came out of our young minds. His intense eyebrows were intimidating beyond belief and made me feel like he was peering deep into my soul, into pockets of my mind that I was not even aware existed yet. Classrooms had no screens, computers, tablets, or loudspeakers. No plastic-printed charts or graphs hung on the walls, and no mass-printed textbooks on the desks. We just talked, sang, danced, drew, and listened. The world was ours – we just had to create it.

Mr. P. hand-designed nearly everything in the classroom, from the detailed chalk drawings recounting epic Norse myths on the blackboard to the months of the year on the wall, each hand-drawn with care. We each painted name tags for our desks and hand-wrote our own textbooks based on Mr. P.'s drawings on the blackboard - from 1st through 8th grade.

Sitting alone at my desk during recess one particularly crisp autumn day, I felt dejected and frustrated. Mr. P. had asked me to stay in my chair when the other children went out to play. I had been acting up, causing a distraction, not doing my work, and it was causing the other students to do the same. "Jeffrey, please stay here for a minute and talk to me.", Mr. Petrash said calmly as the other children clambered to grab their jackets and head into the increasingly cool October morning. "You haven't been able to pay attention today," he said, as he quietly pulled a tiny desk chair up to mine, lowering himself to my eye level. "What is going on?" he said with focus and kindness.

The room was still. The room I sat in every morning, every day, was quiet. The beautiful chalk drawings on the board, which usually felt alive, were motionless, and the desks usually filled with fidgeting students were empty and frozen. The warmth of the orange and rose-colored walls made me feel safe, but being the center of attention was uncomfortable. "I just can't focus," I said quietly. As my words pierced an intimidating silence, his eyes focused squarely on mine so that I couldn't look away. "Just breathe, Jeffrey, just slow down and breathe, and the focus will come."

What I didn't know at the time, what we wouldn't fully confirm until high school, was that I was in the early years of dealing with attention deficit hyperactivity disorder, or ADHD, which turned my developing mind into a spinning dial, totally and completely unable to be calm, to think clearly, to set upon a task, and complete it. No matter how badly I tried to answer a question in class, I could rarely stick to a single train of thought long enough to form a coherent answer. More often than not, my mind was a hive of activity when I was being taught and a silent and blank canvas when I was trying to answer a question.

But with the calming presence of Mr. P and the soothing walls within the Waldorf School, I felt like I had someone on my side to help me through, even when I was too young to tell the difference between a medical condition and the confusion and anxiety that comes with simply existing at that age.

While the outside world and the neighborhood kids were busy with Disney cartoons, pop tarts, and pop music, I was oblivious to them all, and it easily could have been 1895 in that classroom, rather than 1995. At least for the first few years. If America was a bubble, protected and separate from the outside world, I lived in a bubble within a bubble - well, two, actually.

While Waldorf education was supporting me to understand my true individual self, deeply listening to me, and teaching me to listen to others, that was just one half of my reality. There was another half of my life, in the same household, pushing me in the complete opposite direction. This feeling, this other bubble of my upbringing, felt strict, rigid, and sterile - and it begged me to conform.

Both of my parents were raised as devout Mormons, my father in Salt Lake City, Utah, and my mother in Los Angeles, CA, with eleven kids between their two families. My parents grew up in their own bubbles too. For my father, everything he needed was at an arms reach within his bubble, and nothing else was real beyond the vast snow-capped Wasatch Mountains circling his entire existence in the Salt Lake Valley. If I felt like I was growing up in a bubble within a bubble, Mormon Utah in the 1950s was a bubble on a different planet.

Married in the Mormon Temple in 1979, my Dad was certain he'd raise a flock of Mormon children together with my mother, and we'd all live happily ever after in the same protective religious environment in which he'd been raised. After all, no other vision of family or life existed for him.

But by the mid-1980s when I came around, they'd moved to Washington, D.C. and a few years after my sister was born, my mother chose a different spiritual path to follow - a decision we were mostly oblivious to until she stopped coming to church with us each Sunday.

While my Dad was a conservative-voting traditional doctor, my Mother was a liberal Democrat, drinking soy milk and eating kale decades before anyone knew what either was. While their marriage was happy and our home was nothing but loving, their opposing ideologies could not have pulled me further in different directions at the same time.

One bubble had to pop.

While ADHD was barely on the map in the early 1990s and little was understood about it, it was thought to be a genetic condition and had nothing to do with the environment in which a child was raised However, decades later, new research reveals insights that support the theory that parenting choices and environmental makeup in the early years can be a driving factor in the development of ADHD in young minds.

I grew up censoring the world from my Dad, feeling the need to protect him from things I felt he didn't understand or might offend him. I rarely wanted to have friends over to our house for fear they'd say something innocent that he'd judge as distasteful. And he wasn't intimidating or scary – quite the opposite. He was innocent, and I just wanted to protect that. I developed an increasing understanding during my confusing teen years that while my father may have disapproved of many things, they were no doubt things the church had dictated, so he may never have had the opportunity to learn these lessons in the real world for himself.

While I'd hear from other friends' Dads about their war stories from Vietnam or nights in college that ended in the drunk tank, I didn't have these from my Dad. To me, my father's life from middle school through to married life had just been a clean slate, with no big life lessons, no wild nights with hard truths. The population of Utah in 1950 was 98% white and over 75% Mormon, and every family had a perfect cookie-cutter version of the Mormon American Dream. If all the edges were rounded and smudges cleaned from the daily life he saw growing up, how was he supposed to know there was anything else out there?

But I was growing up outside of Washington, D.C. in the 1980s – a far cry from the idyllic stereotypes of 1950s Utah, and I was well aware of the big world out there. I knew there was more to discover, experiences to be had, both good and bad, and stories I would need to go out and chase myself if I ever wanted to share them with kids of my own one day.

I longed for advice from my Dad about the things I was facing in my 1990s teenage life. Perspective on pretty girls, perspective on peer pressure, pints, pills, powders, and plants.

So when I turned 14, I finally told my Dad I'd decided to stop going to the Mormon church with him, as the conservative religious beliefs were clashing too loudly with my free-spirited and creative upbringing at the Waldorf School.

Attending both regularly was like living with a foot in each world, and there started to be a lot of questions that just couldn't be answered.

POP! One bubble was gone.

And so before I learned to drive, graduated high school, or ever boarded a plane alone, I had my mind made up. I would do everything my Dad had not, everything I would need to have the perspective and point of view I felt he lacked, even if it meant getting lost, hurt, in trouble, or ending up somewhere I could never have dreamed of. If the National Geographic magazines were my treasure map, this decision was my first roll of the dice.

For once, my mind was clear on something, a direction

forward, even if it couldn't focus at all on how to get there.

Part way through that same sophomore year of high school, I went to see a doctor who confessed to my mother in hushed tones that I was one of the most extreme cases of ADHD he had seen and was adamant I be prescribed Ritalin. While my mother resisted, the idea of pharmaceuticals being the solution to her sons' restless, unfocused mind making her stomach churn, she was willing to give it a shot – for one week. Seven days later, as I sat behind my newly tidied desk, she gently asked me how the drugs were making me feel. Staring blankly ahead, I responded, "I can focus much better, but the magic is gone." And that was it, the pills went down the toilet, and we never spoke of them again.

It was now my job to master my own mind, to learn to be calm, to think clearly, to dream big, to process my thoughts creatively, and to determine how to leverage my brain to my benefit instead of erasing it to a dull hum with pills.

I knew I needed to take the plunge, head off, and seek the experiences I was determined to find, the experiences I was so convinced would help me make sense of the world. But something was holding me back – a feeling I couldn't quite put my finger on. I didn't want to face it, but it was ripping me in two, as I was caught between the panic of knowing I needed to break free into the world and the complete lack of ability, focus, and calm to know how to do it in a responsible way

'This is going to be a lot harder than I thought.'

With the unfailing support of my teachers and parents who believed in me, I managed to graduate from high school in good order, and then it was time for college. Moving 2,600 miles from Maryland to California, I embraced being wild and free more than your average college freshman away from their parent's house for the first time. I had never snuck out my bedroom window growing up, never got in trouble, never was arrested or served detention at school, but when I went off to college, I made up for it in spades. My decision to try everything my Dad hadn't was aimed at experiencing the big world out there, getting lost in foreign cities, eating exotic foods, and meeting mysterious strangers – but first, I'd have to try everything a wild college dorm could offer, and that took me a couple of years.

I was game for anything and everything. I met new friends from all over the country, was exposed to different perspectives, and felt a modest degree of encouragement that I'd found a community outside of the bubbles of my sheltered upbringing. I also ate absolutely anything and everything. A chunky kid sneaking cans of soda in his grandparent's basement in elementary school quickly turned into an overweight and self-conscious college freshman. I was desperate to be the explorer with the bushy white beard, but my confidence was plummeting while everything was speeding up around me. However, my metabolism wasn't speeding up at all, and thanks to an abundance of pints and plants, neither was my mind. The darting thoughts in my brain evaporated, and a dullness I had never experienced overcame my creative mind. While one side of my brain was relieved and the fatigue of overthinking finally calmed, the other half knew this wasn't my full self, and I longed to break free.

'How do I start? Where do I go? What if I'm too scared to do it alone?'

During these confusing college years, my ADHD took the passenger seat of my life while excess was clutching the wheel, a combination that was fueled by fun nights but left me exhausted, unhealthy, and my education more erratic than a flailing balloon

33

outside a used car dealership. I couldn't shake the feeling that I needed to start fresh and begin again. This time would be different, I told myself. But while I was becoming more and more aware of how my brain worked, I would remain a slave to it for years to come. So no, this time wouldn't be different. I just needed to do it in a different place, I'd tell myself, while holding out hope that a change of scenery would change my brain chemistry, without having to do any of the hard work to master it.

Little did I know that a natural disaster only weeks away was about to give me the chance to face my fears. The world itself was going to push me to take that leap and give me the opportunity to trust that it would teach me the lessons I so badly needed to learn - 8,700 miles (14,000 km) across the globe in the Indian Ocean.

3

Plunge into the Unknown: "Can You Even Find Thailand on a Map?"

"If you are trying to eliminate all risks from your life, what you're actually doing is eliminating all possibilities from your life."
-Edward Snowden

Chicago O'Hare Airport/Dublin, Ireland. December 2004

The benches were freezing, that's what I remember the most. They must have been the most uncomfortable airport seats in the world. I was wearing thick oversized jeans and can still feel the cold metal seeping through to my thighs as I sat down, eyes fixed on the blurry news coverage flashing on the hanging TV across the hall.

The volume wasn't loud enough to hear, but the subtitles were on, making the highlighted numbers all the more shocking. 80,000...115,000... 150,000 dead. The figures were growing out of control as the news was streaming in. I couldn't look away although I couldn't really grasp what I was looking at either. This was the type of disaster I'd only read about in history books.

The result of a 9.1 magnitude earthquake striking off the tip of Sumatra in Western Indonesia, this would be the largest natural disaster of the 21st century. It was December 26, 2004, Boxing Day, and a massive tsunami had just struck South East Asia, early on the morning after Christmas. Affecting some 14 countries, over the course of mere hours, it would kill over 230,000 people.

My family was lining up at the gate across the hall to board our flight but I couldn't move, eyes transfixed on the screen. Christmas break in my sophomore year of college was underway and we were on a layover in Chicago en route to Dublin, Ireland to celebrate New Year's together when the news of the Tsunami found me on the airport TV screens.

Eyes frozen on the chunky pixels of the rounded screens, I felt a helpless tug in my chest. It was as if the tsunami had struck within running distance, and I'd be in a full sprint to get there to assess the damage and help however I could – fear of the unknown be damned. But this was unfolding on the other side of the globe, most killed in countries like Thailand and Indonesia, in cities I'd never heard of like Banda Aceh, Khao Lak and Tamil Nadu.

I didn't know anything about these exotic locations except, perhaps, for the random picture of a beach scene or Buddha statue I may have seen on those pages of the National Geographic magazines in the bathroom with the green, shag carpet. But, in an instant, I was transported into them, falling into another world my mind couldn't comprehend but felt compelled to get to. I was filled with a calm and focus I'd rarely known while dreaming of landing in a disaster zone. The juxtaposition was jarring and confusing to me, but I had to follow it.

One of the last to board the plane, I was in a trance as I walked down the cold tunnel, mind racing as I sat uncomfortably in a tiny seat for the seven-hour overnight flight to the Irish capital. I didn't sleep a wink that night. My mind was already in Thailand, wherever that was.

'Is this the feeling I've been waiting for? Is this focus? Is this purpose?'

Within hours of landing in Dublin, I was in an internet cafe down a dark set of steps in a back alley of the city center, searching for any information I could find beyond the horrific news clips I'd seen in Chicago that were still looping in my head. News moved slower then—no iPhones yet, YouTube and Twitter didn't exist and Facebook was still being run out of a dorm at Harvard. Google was rudimentary and glitchy as I frantically searched for anything I could find.

"Are you seeing what is happening in Thailand and feel unable to help?"

Click!

'Yes!'

I gasped under my breath as I eagerly clicked through the simple pages of the website, thrown together with just enough basic information to get the point across. "Can I use the printer?" I asked the bored attendant, oblivious to the swells of excitement and nervousness competing within me.

Clutching printouts of every webpage I could find, I marched back to the hotel and presented all the information to my parents right then and there. "It's just a small group of volunteers, nothing official yet, but they need help." I stammered. A handful of expats and tourists who had been on the popular Southern Thai island of Phuket when the tsunami hit were doing all they could with the clean-up and recovery and they could use extra hands. The website they'd put together functioned more like a missing dog sign stapled to a telephone pole in cyberspace, but it was the last line of the page that stuck with me.

"We are based out of the second floor of a hotel in Bangtao, Phuket, Thailand, and have free rooms and meals provided for anyone who can show up and volunteer with us. Email Dave for more info."

I was in. Whatever little direction I had left in me at that point, as I was fumbling my way through college, realigned in that moment, and all arrows pointed in the same direction to a small island nearly 9,000 miles across the globe. I didn't know who Dave was, but he was about to know me.

By the next morning, I amazingly had my parents' blessing, and I had emailed my college advisor and laid out my plan for him. Requesting a semester off from school mere days before the second half of my sophomore year should have started, his surprising response came quickly and clearly.

"Freakin' go for it, dude!" he said, and that was all I needed – the planning started immediately. For the first time in my life, I had drive, and for the first time in my life, the excitement of what came next was greater than the fear of the unknown that accompanied it. While my ADHD had caused any glimmer of excitement or interest I had previously shown to fade faster than the flick of a lighter, this flame was burning a lot brighter, and everyone in my orbit could see it.

While my Dad had served a mission for the Mormon church in Cusco, Peru for two years at the age of 18, my first trip solo was going to be a little different. Mormon missionaries usually don't get a say in where they serve, a white envelope arriving in the mail telling them where they're being sent. If it means learning a foreign language, they are sent to the Mission Training Center in

Provo, Utah, and have a matter of weeks to learn a new language and master the skills of going door to door to convert strangers to a religion many have not heard of. No woman within an arm's length, no internet, TV, music other than hymns, no drinking, smoking, movies, or activities other than focusing on the goal at hand - converting others to Mormonism, only allowed to call home on Mother's Day and Christmas morning. As a Mormon missionary, my Dad wasn't permitted to fully explore the world like he was prepared to support me in doing, and while I wasn't taking it for granted, the opportunity wasn't going to go wasted either.

After returning to California from Ireland, it took a few weeks to sort out the details –phone calls between my dad and the volunteer team to assess their legitimacy and a few pricks at the doctor's office to vaccinate me for things like Yellow Fever and Japanese B Encephalitis. By early March 2005, I was sitting alone, Bone Thugs N' Harmony's "Change the World" on repeat from a bright red diskman clutched in my sweaty palm, in a deserted airport terminal, waiting to board my flight from Taipei to Phuket. I'd bit my nails down to the stubs on the first flight from Los Angeles and was only halfway there, and some had even drawn blood. My mind was a fidgety mess.

'What am I doing here? Maybe this was a mistake...'

So intent on running away from my life, I was more comfortable being terrified and alone on one side of the world than being terrified and at home on the other. But neither felt comfortable, and there was no direction to go but forward.

Phuket, Thailand. March 2005

The frigid airplane air was quickly replaced with the humidity

39

of the other side of the world as I wiped sweat off my pink forehead feeling a level of heat I had never known. Staring blankly at the ATM in the Arrivals terminal, I had absolutely no idea how much local currency to withdraw.

'What is a baht?'

In all my excitement, I hadn't even thought to research currency exchange rates or what the Thai currency even was. One thousand baht? 10,000? Was that about $20 USD? It seemed like too many zeroes, but clicking the most worn-out button, the dusty, yellow ATM machine spat out a wad of colorful bills that I hurriedly stuffed in my pocket.

Stepping outside, I simply jumped in the first taxi I saw, pretending to look confident and comfortable when I was anything but. Too shy to attempt a conversation, I held up the name "Bangtao Beach" poorly written, smudged, and sweaty, on a crumpled piece of paper, and we were off.

'Travel Gods, take us away!'

Turning off the paved road, we bumped over deep sunken holes in the makeshift road, while a brown mist of churning dust rose behind us as we made our way south from the airport to the beachside village of Bangtao. The devastation increased drastically as we approached the coast: misplaced debris, washed-out automobiles, bathtubs, and motorbikes, dead trees stripped of their greenery and sprawled across the earth like bleached elephant bones on the Sahara.

The destruction of Bangtao was complete. Sixteen hours earlier, I had been laughing with my friends as we drove through gridlock traffic in Los Angeles to LAX smoking joints, and now I was sitting in awe, passing through a completely washed-out Thai village with near endless damage surrounding me. The gutted ground-level shops, restaurants, and homes sat in stark contrast to the world just above them – apartments, hotel rooms, and balconies on the second floor, untouched by the madness that had swirled below, where entire shops filled with raging water up to their ceilings, violently mixing their contents like a blender, sucking out everything in sight and leaving the innards exposed and broken across the landscape.

Vibrant fabrics from tailor shops lay twisted and gripping everything in their midst, instantly unfurled and spread across vast areas – some stretching for fifty, sixty feet. Bright yellows, blues, and sharp reds connected random objects where roads once stood, street poles to kitchen tables, car tires to tree trunks. A natural massacre had occurred – nature, violent and unconscious – receding back into the ocean nearly as fast as she had suddenly emerged from it.

The taxi, sputtering to a stop, barrelled over a piece of debris, jolting me back to the present. I had arrived. Four months earlier, I was too scared to think about traveling anywhere solo, and now here I was, alone, in the tiny village of Bangtao I had read about in that internet cafe in Dublin.

'*Time to face the unknown.*'

Opening the door, I grabbed my backpack and suitcase and walked down a small alley, searching for anyone who looked like me. My mind was clear, calm, and focused on the only things that mattered – finding friends, food, and shelter.

'*Where is Dave?*'

Emerging from behind a drab yellow wall, the alley expanded into an open-air room, previously a hotel restaurant of some sort, I presumed by the various bits of mismatched furniture sprinkled around the concrete floor. There was not a soul in sight. Total silence met me, save for the insects chirping incessantly in the surrounding trees – a constant frequency my brain would be quick to tune out.

I knew I was in the right place though, as a huge whiteboard in the corner had information in English—updates, daily schedules, and volunteer names, including my own, as an expected new arrival. Sweaty, exhausted, and overwhelmed, I put down my bags and decided to wait for someone to show up. Spotting a blue plastic chair in the corner I plopped down my tired frame, and no sooner than I had exhaled, I heard truck tires on gravel getting closer and the chatter of voices which sounded familiar, possibly accented English, but I couldn't make out from where.

The truck stopped somewhere out of my sight, and my heart began to race - not with fear, but with excitement for what would meet me. As dusty boots and sweat-soaked volunteers rounded the corner, they were welcomed by the view of a very large American college dropout, dressed for a frat party and covered in sweat stains from simply sitting in the Thai heat, eagerly awaiting their arrival from their makeshift clubhouse.

"SNAP!"

No sooner had the group stumbled in and made eye contact with me than I felt one of the back legs of the chair give way as I stood to greet them. In an instant, all 300lbs of me was flattened on the ground - baggy camo cargo shorts covered in dust, bright green skater shoes heels up, obnoxiously large fake aviators strewn across the floor. This was the start of my Bangtao story, my next life chapter, as vulnerable and embarrassing as any meaningful life experience should be.

'Well at least I'll have one story for my kids, and I've only been here an hour!'

Over the coming days and weeks, I was given a crash course in humanity and a reality check on the privilege of my existence. Working in the beating hot sun, with daily temperatures soaring above 100F and humidity leaving me dripping wet before break-fast, I quickly found myself out of the protective bubble I was so aware of growing up walking the gentle halls of the Waldorf School and of the restrictive confines of the Mormon Church.

* * *

The main road in Bangtao slowly snaked its way through the village, large debris pushed to the side so basic life could resume when the waters settled. Simple Thai huts and unassuming open-air cafes and boutique hotel lobbies standing in total peace just a couple weeks prior, filled with the happy laughter and relaxation of tourists enjoying their holiday, now stood hollow and empty. Arriving at a battered field lined with debris, I joined a handful of volunteers to begin clearing a plot as best we could, revealing a cracked and displaced foundation below.

I would spend much of the coming weeks in this field with the same small group – a friendly pub owner from Ireland, a newlywed couple from England, and a prickly chain-smoking Canadian cowboy - all feeling the same pull to Bangtao. As different as we all were, we shared a common focus each morning - to help. Our tasks were simple, even if they came with endless sweat and exhaustion. We had to help people, clean debris, build shelter, find water, and eat food. The daily life could not have been more simple, more straightforward, and more calming for my mind, which was completely at ease each day.

As the days passed, I began to notice the same Thai man strolling by us, staying longer and moving closer as we started to smile at each other each morning. We interacted only with simple gestures and body language, recognizing the basic humanity in each other. All we were told before starting work at the site was that it had been a small fish shop, just 100 feet or so from the waves crashing on the hot sand, just beyond the low-hanging palm fronds, many of which were now strewn across the ground. The destruction was so complete that we'd never have known, based on the utter chaos that surrounded us, that this had been any type of shop, let alone a once thriving small family business.

Day by day, we continued work – clearing debris, untangling the life that had been here before us, hauling, sweeping, digging, laying a new foundation, and carting in loads of wood to erect the skeleton of a new structure. We began to share meals together with the locals, too, often eating fresh squid straight from the sea while squatting as the Thai do. Cooking over a simple fire and chopping crudely with a machete on a spare piece of plywood, we began hearing more about the area and the heartbreaking stories of the people in this small and unassuming corner of the world. And we learned more about the man we had come to recognize each day as well.

Not only had he been the owner of the small fish shop that was completely lost, but he had also lost his mother, his wife, and his young daughter that day - all gone in less than an hour. One minute he was displaying freshly caught fish on quickly melting ice in the hot early morning sun, and in the next, life as he knew it was violently ripped from his hands.

I had arrived in Thailand with a return ticket to Los Angeles three weeks later, but ultimately, I wouldn't leave there for nearly three months, so invigorated by the volunteer work, the electrifying experiences I was having, and the deep value and purpose I felt in being there. For the first time in my life, I felt like what I was doing was having a real impact, but in reality, any impact I had on the kind people of Thailand was minuscule compared to the impact they were having on me.

What I also realized in those first weeks was that being alone, in a country and culture I knew nothing about, the perennial outside stranger, focused my mind on just the essentials: work, eating, drinking, shelter, and sleep. Every other thought was quieted in my brain, which brought me much-needed peace, as I only focused on the important daily tasks at hand.

I was greeted daily by smiling locals, many of whom had just lost everything in their lives, from the roofs over their heads to their closest family members. Still, they welcomed me warmly into their community and offered me cool water when it was hot and a helping hand when I needed one, too. One woman in particular, Nok, took me under her wing, treated me like one of her own children, and cooked the best garlic pork in the world. She had been quick to rush out and find medicine for me when I was particularly ill one morning. "Nok!" I said, upon seeing her a couple of hours later, "I feel totally fine, what did you give me?" She paused, and a sheepish smile flashed on her face. "Birth control."

'Ha! The kindness of strangers. There's another story.'

It was during these months in Thailand that I first realized that *things* don't make people happy; people make people happy. I realized that collecting laughs and memories was more important than collecting material things and that if these Thai people could be so happy with so little, I should be able to be as well. Arriving in Thailand from Los Angeles couldn't have highlighted a more striking contrast between material wealth and what makes people happy. Where I had been living in a cookie-cutter house in a cookie-cutter neighborhood with shiny new cars sitting in most driveways, neighbors remaining strangers for years. Here, everyone was outside, sharing everything, warm to everyone, collecting nothing but quality time and experiencing life together.

'Be still, my capitalist heart. You know not what you want.'

What I did know was that I wanted a career and life with the meaning and happiness I saw in these people. And there was something else I found in Thailand – a small thread that I thought could lead me closer to my path, so I started to follow it. Because it was during these first weeks in Phuket that I started to fall in love with photography, a love affair that would profoundly change the direction of my life, just not how I ever expected.

* * *

With the unrelenting sun covering nearly everything in sight, I took a quick break from hammering nails on the new siding of our little fish shop and ducked under the shade of a nearby palm tree one afternoon. Resting my back against its giraffe-like trunk, I gazed down the sandy path in front of me leading to the sea and saw a man sitting on the bow of a beached and battered Thai long-tail boat. His silhouette contrasted boldly in front of the bright blue sea. I took out my small digital camera, all three megapixels of it, and snapped a quick photo before the battery died, the longtail boat lying across the bottom of the frame, the figure of this man looking out across the sea from right to left – glistening, calm waters stretching as far as the eye could see in front of him with nothing but a hot breeze moving through the frame. The moment begged me to capture it, a rare moment of calm and quiet in a shattered landscape. A rare moment of reflection and processing where I was in the world. And in 1/100 of a second, it was mine, captured for eternity, still and calm. With the gentle press of a shutter, I had paused the world around me.

Looking at the scenes in front of my eyes every day, I realized the impact that a picture could have, the way visual storytelling could convey an emotion and a place all without saying a single word - frozen in millions of tiny pixels.

I thought back to those National Geographic magazines in the basement bathroom with the neon green, plush carpet and realized for the first time that I was standing in one, surrounded by the sights and colors that had once seemed so foreign to me, peeking out from behind their glossy pages. It would be a couple more years before I could grow a real beard, but I finally felt like I was becoming the explorer.

It wasn't until I returned to California weeks later and looked at my images on a large screen that I realized the man in the image sitting on his longtail boat was the man who had lost his entire family - the man for whom we were building the new shop. I wondered what he was thinking while staring out at the calm waters of Bangtao Bay that had violently taken his entire family, changing his life story forever. A picture is truly worth a thousand words and in this single frame, I realized the power that images have, not only catching a fraction of a second, but truly pausing time, pausing my thoughts, and the swirling chaos in my brain.

* * *

A lot of what travel teaches us is about letting go, taking the leap, jumping into the unknown - replacing your environment and all its parts for a chance at what happens next. Astronauts often talk about the most impactful part of flying into space, and it isn't launching off through the stratosphere. It isn't traveling 17,500mph through the vastness of space either, but rather it is peeking out one of the small, rounded windows of the space shuttle and seeing the small blue dot we all call home.

I cannot imagine the profound silence that comes over your soul when looking down on a tiny ball where the memories, lives, achievements, tragedies, and triumphs of every single person who has ever lived have happened. I can only imagine the all-encompassing feeling of oneness in seeing that we all truly live together. Boundaries between countries are invisible; race, religion, and gender all pale in comparison to our connective human tissue.

What looking down on planet Earth gives astronauts in a glance, travel gives in pebbles distributed over time. Handed out like treasure for those curious enough to look for them, such experiences slowly accumulate into an overflowing basket of empathy, understanding, and love, for those with an open mind.

It would take until the end of my junior year at the University of Redlands before I called it quits, dropping out and moving back home to my parent's basement in Maryland to reassess my life at age 22. Only 15% of people with ADHD complete a four-year degree at a university, and I was quickly becoming a statistic after trying to dive back into the traditional academic environment after the raw life experiences I had lived and had begun to document.

I had a loose direction now, but no idea how to get there, and after nine months of walking dogs every day in the neighborhood where I'd grown up, I was eager to take the first step towards it. Picking up strangers' dogs shit day in and day out is exactly as rewarding as you might imagine. Following the only thread I had to hold on to, my newfound understanding of the power of images and the calm that I experienced looking through that tiny viewfinder, led me back to Southern California to a small visual arts school, the Brooks Institute of Photography.

In the Spring of 2007, my Dad and I loaded all my stuff in my beat-up Chevy Malibu and headed west, driving from Silver Spring, Maryland to Ventura, California in just over four days. We connected a lot on that drive, forty hours of driving, just father and son. Religion was still the great dividing wall between us, the hot topic we both thought about in silence and only gently poked. While our relationship was healing after my tense college years, my own grappling with religion and the trauma it had caused during my upbringing sat heavy with me in the passenger seat. Travel was a bond that my dad and I would always share, and soon it would be the spark that helped me sort through my views on religion too. Another breadcrumb on my treasure map, another impactful story to add to my collection.

I still didn't know exactly what I wanted to do with my life, but getting a degree in Visual Journalism would offer me a way to share the stories I came across - and it meant I could keep traveling, maybe even get paid by National Geographic or Lonely Planet one day. But most importantly, it allowed me to pause the world, both around and within, if just for a fraction of a second. This was my golden ticket.

I was going to tell stories with pictures, or at least that was my goal.

4

Continue to Seek Understanding: Don't Be An Asshole

"The two most important days in your life are the day you are born and the day you find out why." - *Mark Twain*

Silver Spring, Maryland, USA, 1999

Building up the courage to tell my Dad I was no longer going to go to the Mormon church with him took me months, but as soon as I had managed it, I turned my back on religion entirely. No more church on Sundays, no more morning prayers, no more living by the archaic and hollow rules I felt the church was putting forth - I was done buying what they were selling. It broke my Dad's heart, and it broke mine too, but I could no longer play the part. He was trying so hard to pass down some of the guiding principles that had helped him navigate his life, but I wasn't interested to hear or accept those principles, and I was years from being able to separate the morals themselves from the scriptures from which he extracted them.

I came to view the restrictions of religion as a middle finger directly in the face of the most beautiful gift in the world—the consciousness and opportunity to live a full life, to make all the mistakes, to learn from them, and to discover your higher self through the ups and downs. *'Isn't that why we're all here?'*

Existing is confusing, but trying to figure out the meaning of it all through religion makes as much sense to me as cleaning your dishes before you eat dinner to save time afterward. Joe Rogan put it best when he said, "If you ever start taking things too seriously, just remember that we are talking monkeys on an organic spaceship flying through the universe."

I rejected religion from those early teenage years not only in my personal life, but for the division it had caused in the world. From the Spanish Inquisition to al-Qaeda, to the harm done by Catholic priests to the persecution of Jews in WWII, and the endless tension between Israel and Palestine - religion, either through hate or obsession, was the common denominator of them all. The Mormons were heavily persecuted too, pushed, chased, tarred and feathered out of every community they were a part of. Earlier yet, the Native Americans in my own backyard were systematically removed from their ancestral homelands by our Protestant government clinging to their own manmade beliefs in destiny and God - to set up a country where freedom to believe in whatever you wished could flourish. Beyond ironic.

No longer content to blindly accept what any book, religious leader, or crowd had to preach, I had to figure out religion on my own.

Chennai, India. November 2008

As our Cathay Pacific flight started making the descent into Chennai International Airport on the eastern coast of Southern India, I knew I would leave as a different person than who I was when I landed, but I didn't yet know how. While I guessed such a process of transformation would have been sparked by an increased understanding of Indian culture, Hindi, Hindu, and Hanuman, I certainly didn't think it would also include a deeper understanding of God.

Simply put, India is one of the most overwhelming places on earth. It is a surreal feeling to be floating in a human stew of over one billion people, all on their own journeys. And the language, the very letters, were as far from familiar as could be.

I was one year into my studies at the Brooks Institute and had signed up for the upcoming international documentary trip before I even knew where it was going, eager to recreate the magic I'd felt in Thailand – and with better photographic skills to tell the stories I'd find.

Being surrounded by Buddhists in Thailand three years earlier had inspired a shift in my perception of religion. Something had started to make sense - it was the calmness, I think. Buddhism wasn't like the other religions I'd been exposed to. Seeing how the entire culture welcomed me and seemed to enjoy the little things without the controlling fear of God above them was a breath of fresh air for me. Buddhism just made sense; it was simple.

And here I was again, in a country with a religion that felt different from what I grew up with. Nearly 80% of the Indian population identifies as Hindu, so the separation between religion and culture is nearly impossible, but again, there was that calmness. Principals like dharma and karma guided those I met, and a sense of quiet resolve and kindness followed them,

53

as well. It seemed so simple.

'Don't be an asshole.'How did religion ever get more complicated than that?'

A close friend and fellow student Alana and I were in Bangalore filming various interviews and scenes for our project a few weeks into the trip, discussing our stories over masala dosa in the morning and a cup of chai at night, but chasing our separate characters during the day. She was following up with a local Indian dance teacher and conducting an interview at her small studio on the outskirts of the city, far removed from the gridlock and rush hour madness that gripped Bangalore.

Reviewing her footage later that night, as she logged the tapes without headphones, I'll never forget what I overheard. It echoed in my mind, and I instantly asked her to replay it. Explaining the culture of dance in India and the role that religion and God played in the movements that had been passed down from generation to generation, the teacher simply said, as if it was an obvious afterthought: "God is love, right?"

'God IS love.'

And right there, at that moment, when I heard those three little words, religion made sense to me for the very first time in my life. Something just clicked into place. God wasn't a man in the clouds. God wasn't the great chess master of the skies, plotting out billions of moves and judging us at the Pearly Gates - puppets in his celestial board game. No, God was love; it *was* that simple.

God was simply the act of love. God was taking care of ourselves, taking care of each other - God was our higher selves. God was that moment we helped a stranger, that moment we broke a bad habit. God was calling your Mother and telling her how much you loved her. God was donating blood, volunteering at a food shelter, holding the door open for a pregnant woman, paying the toll for the car behind you, being a 1% better version of yourself each day, or at least trying to. That was God.

God wasn't complicated; it didn't need to be. God was simply the three letters that symbolize the act of doing good in the world, for yourself, and for others. Three letters that through diverging interpretation, have dominated our world and destroyed countries, cultures, and communities for eons of time.

I don't remember a single other thing that the dance teacher said in that interview or if we ever even used that clip in the documentary. Alana may not even remember filming it, but I'll never forget it.

I've struggled nearly my entire life to understand my relationship with religion. It poked its confusing head into my childhood at way too early an age. But I was old enough to see its glaring inconsistencies and to know I shouldn't be having to deal with them yet. Paradoxically, the simple answer was right there in front of me the whole time.

Don't be an asshole. Why did it ever get more complicated than that?

It got more complicated than that because, it turns out, some people *are* assholes.

5

Don't be an Idiot: Never Gamble in Malaysia

"I take it back. You're not stupid. But damn, you are insane."
– Maya Rodale

Kuala Lumpur, Malaysia. February 2008

"Hey, where did you get your shoes, mate?", an unfamiliar voice somewhere behind me said with a local accent, sharply piercing the bubble of anonymity in which I was sure I had been walking. I'll never forget his voice because the question stood out as so odd, and "mate" wasn't something I was expecting to hear from a local in Malaysia. I was wandering alone around a large, green park at the base of the Petronas Towers in the bustling capital of Malaysia. No one knew me here, and my shoes were nothing more than beaten, dusty skater shoes. But although I may have been exploring a new country, I was in the habit of walking with the pace and confidence of someone who knew where he was going - a protective cloak I used to blend in –and which had just failed.

Brooks Institute operated on a year-round schedule with seven weeks on, one week off. This meant that if I planned it right, I could make it to Bangladesh and back before classes resumed again. I arrived in Kuala Lumpur from Los Angeles at about noon on a Tuesday, but my plane to Dhaka did not leave until almost 11 that night. I was once again jumping across the world to chase another disaster, volunteering with the same group I worked with in Thailand–this time, heading for Bangladesh, after a deadly cyclone had ravaged much of the country. Following the thread I discovered in Thailand, photography and volunteer work had become an obsession, almost a drug.

I had such a long layover that the airline gave me a voucher for the premium lounge with free drinks, excellent food, and hot showers. But this was my first experience in Malaysia, and there was no way I was going to spend the time I had sitting with other Westerners in a classy lounge eating egg salad and drinking pints of imported Carlsberg. I had to get lost–I couldn't help myself. I had intentionally picked the flight option with the longest layover. What they thought was a major inconvenience was a scheduled opportunity for adventure - another stop on my treasure map.

Immigration was smooth as silk, which was quite unexpected, and within a few minutes, I was on the train to KL Sentral, the main transportation hub in the city, a new stamp in my passport with the whole day yet to reveal itself to me. I followed the crowds and got off where they did, only wearing a backpack, a giant grin, and old skater shoes. After traversing a series of tunnels and walkways, I was spit out into a crowded modern mall. If you have never been to Southeast Asia, there is really no way to explain the malls there – they are massive and sprawling.

Lucky for me, I was trying to get lost, so mission accomplished. However, this mall felt too much like malls in the USA. I was looking for something different. Searching for the nearest exit door, I stepped outside and looked up, the humid hot air hitting my face like a sucker punch. I was standing at the base of the Petronas Towers, once the tallest buildings in the world at over 1,483ft (450m) in height, their 88 dizzying stories looming high above me.

I'd seen these towers splashed across the pages of National Geographic magazines when they were first built in 1993 (no doubt with my toes lost in neon green plush carpet…), but I hardly recognized them from this angle.

With my camera attached to my wrist, I snapped pictures I'd never look at again and continued walking through the park in front of me, the hot humid breeze enveloping my face with every step as a moist glaze of sweat gathered on my forehead before the cool AC of the mall had escaped my ankles. Tourists and locals wandered and relaxed in the shade of nearby tropical plants and trees surrounding me. Bright red hibiscus were in full bloom, their perfect yellow pistils dotted around me like tropical gumdrops. I walked with a sense of purpose and direction but with no destination other than forward. Passing a small gazebo, I nodded at the locals, aiming to exude confidence and my adventurous spirit. I wanted them to feel like I belonged here, and I wanted to feel like I belonged there, too.

"Hey, where did you get your shoes, mate?"

The two young Malaysians beckoned me towards them, half hidden in the sharp contrast of the shade, obscured behind giant elephant ear leafs. I couldn't imagine why they wanted to ask about my shoes which were utterly plain and well-worn.

'Maybe they recognize the logo?'

When I mentioned that both my shoes and I had flown in from California, they got visibly excited. "So, my friend, Obama or Clinton?"

'What?'

The blinding sun and oppressive humidity reminded me of summers in Maryland, but in Malaysia, it was just beginning to be Spring, early 2008, about six months before the US presidential elections later that year.

'How do they know who Clinton and Obama are?'

One of them asked a lot of questions about Orange County, because his sister was soon to depart Malaysia to live there as a nurse, or so I was led to believe. He invited me to join them at his family home, an impromptu visit, just a short drive through the city. He thought I might be able to answer some of the questions she might have, if I would oblige. I was instantly swept up in the moment.

'Could I be helpful to his family? I am an expert in California and the US, how ironic. Ahh, the magic of travel!'

Here was a spontaneous gift the Travel Gods were giving me - the right time, the right place, taking a leap into a new adventure. This seemed to be a most obvious breadcrumb to follow.

I paused for a half second, but a minute later, I was stuffing myself and my backpack into a taxi with my two new friends, and we sped down the bustling streets away from the Petronas Towers fading into the congested skyline behind us. We drove through traffic-filled streets busy with bicycles and young children selling newspapers, lottery tickets, and energy drinks. We seemed to be driving in circles. Actually, I was quite certain we were.

'There's that giant building with the faded yellow billboard again...Didn't we just pass that a minute ago?'

As I listened to one of the men yelling at a variety of people on his cell phone, I had to chuckle at the story I would surely have to tell in a few hours. I just didn't yet know how it would end.

After entering through a chain link gate and looping around what looked like a vacant factory, we finally slowed to a stop in front of a small row of two-story houses. Each home had a gated driveway, most looked empty, and a majority of them contained skinny, unhealthy canines, barking furiously as we passed. I didn't realize until the car stopped how tightly I'd been clutching my backpack on my lap. As I walked into the house, the corner unit in a row of seven or eight of those faded brown townhomes, I was informed that the ladies, including the young nurse, had gone to the hospital to visit their grandmother, who had been rushed there for emergency surgery.

'Ok...this is getting weirder. Maybe this isn't a story I'll tell my kids one day...'

A scene that had felt only somewhat eerie with the factory, metal gates, and barking dogs, quickly became unnerving with no women in sight, the idea that their calming presence would keep me calm, too. In reality, I was quite alone with eight Malaysian men, and a stranger to them all.

I was told to sit on the couch in the living room and watch the terrible early 90s action film playing on their small TV set as we waited for the nurse to return. However, I knew she never would, as she most likely never existed in the first place....

'What are they going to try and do to me?

The living room had only a small couch, a glass coffee table, a blaring television, and a shrine to Buddha—something seen in almost every home in Southeast Asia. This is where I met

Otto, who was sat transfixed in front of the glitching TV, hardly glancing up when I walked in.

Otto looked different than the young men who had brought me here. He had lighter skin and looked more Chinese than Malaysian or Thai. He had a scar above his lip that slightly deformed one nostril, and he was chunky, unlike the others, with a face as round as a fishbowl. And he only had one eye—or at least that is what the eye patch over his right eye would suggest.

'That's a face that has seen a thing or two.'

We didn't have much of a conversation at first. Otto, pointing to the TV, would laugh as a gang of intruders shot up a pool hall in one scene, finger guns blasting all over the living room and giggling to himself as spittle danced in the static glow that illuminated half his face. I smiled and nodded my head, playing along.

He was overly eager to brag that he worked at a local casino and, muting the TV in the background, started telling me about a woman from Brunei who he referred to only as "The Madam". The third wife of a rich oil Sheik who frequented his card table, she was addicted to gambling, "sometimes losing over a million dollars a night", he recounted. My eyes widened as he spoke, the characters he word-painted increasing in grandeur by the moment. His one eye was now squarely focused on just me.

'Where is this going?'

Otto ushered me into the kitchen, instructing me to sit on a hot metal chair, as plates were handed out to the other men and me. We ate a meal of rice, boiled chicken, and charbroiled fish stuffed with vegetables and a dense corn mush of some sort, all served cold. I ate a small portion before I realized that maybe I shouldn't be so eager to eat these strangers' food, my camera bag resting on my leg so I could always feel its presence. I'll never forget looking down at the square mesh lid covering the fish, flies eagerly buzzing around its edges, as I wondered what I had gotten myself into.

'Have I gone too far? Was this a mistake?'

After the meal, Otto asked me into his "office, a darkened room just opposite the table where we'd eaten. I had thought the door was a closet, but as he pried it open, I saw that it was as thick as a bank vault and consisted of one small metal table, four cold metal folding chairs, a small, dirty glass ashtray, a large rusted gray filing cabinet, and exactly no windows. The only light came from a small light bulb hidden behind a once-white plastic panel, now filled almost entirely with dead insects dotting the edges. I slowly entered the room, hesitantly, as the energy in the air turned truly dark for the first time since I'd come into the house. I had been anxious since I arrived, though the mood with the guys had been jovial, but now they had vanished. It was just Otto and me.

The dim yellow light, the rotten rusty walls, and the smell of stale cigarette smoke made me feel like I was in a scene from a cheap horror film. Something just felt off, but I couldn't quite figure out what was happening. Otto walked in, nodded to someone out of sight, and then closed and locked the heavy steel door. Now it felt *very* off.

'This feels like a doomsday murder bunker...'

My eyes darted around the edges of the room trying to log any additional details I could gather while I could. My mind was slow, methodical, and organized.

'How come I couldn't have this level of focus in algebra class?'

I was told to sit down on the far side of the table and move close to the wall. The gnawing feeling that I was out of place and alone grew steadily, but the cold slab of cement against my shoulder at least removed the feeling that someone, or something, was behind me. The two young men I met in the park had been gracious to me, but now, sitting in a closed room with Otto, things felt very different. Otto reached into his pocket, pulled out a tattered pack of menthol cigarettes, and lit one up, the string of wispy smoke rising above the scar on his face as straight as an arrow, no breeze to knock it off course. He reached into the cabinet behind him and pulled out a well-worn deck of cards, a tray of faded poker chips, and a pen and paper. Quickly opening and closing a second drawer he exposed a small black handgun, snatched it quickly and placed it on his lap. I didn't need to look to confirm it was pointing directly at my groin under the table.

I knew I was supposed to see it, but I still couldn't figure out why.

'What is the plan here, what have I put in motion?'

Instructing me how to play blackjack, Otto made it a point to write down everything he told me, including drawing a diagram of the two of us sitting at the table along with arrows connecting other people and names. He was meticulous, like he'd done this a dozen times before. He wrote out the rules down to the very last point, along with the name of the Madam; "Miss Asis Abad," he said with a faint snarl in his gravelly voice.

Then he started moving the cards quickly between his fingers, 9 of clubs, Jack of hearts, 3 of a kind, 2 pairs, cards moving faster than I could keep track.

'Is he showing off? Am I supposed to follow this? I don't like where this is going.'

Reminding me that he had originally met the Madam at the local casino where he was a dealer, he started to show me how to cheat. "Remember, I control everything, I am like God." He was telling me his secrets, some of them at least, how to beat the system, and how to work in tandem with the dealer to cheat an unsuspecting player.

'He wants us to scam the Madam. But surely I'm the one getting scammed... but how?'

He showed me a number of hand gestures that would tell me what cards the other person had, along with what card was next in his deck. A flick of the wrist, a tap of the finger, the slight bending of a card with his thumb - all secrets to help me see through the game as we played. He explained that if we worked as a team in the high-end room at his casino, which had no cameras, Otto, the scar-faced cyclops, and the heavy-set bewildered American could turn $1,000 into $800,000 in 15 minutes.

'That is impossible, this guy is full of shit.'

I acted very impressed and told him that he was the best dealer I had ever seen, hoping the accolades would satisfy him and not further reveal that I had no idea how to play poker. Beyond that, I was growing increasingly nervous about my immediate future.

We'd split the earnings, Otto said, each walking away with almost half a million dollars in less than the time it had taken me to drive to his house. Checking my watch, it was 5:15 pm, my flight left in less than six hours, and I had no idea where I was, let alone how far away from the airport we were. Regardless, I had no intention of going to any casino with him.

'How do I get myself out of this? I just need to get back to that crowded mall.'

Madam Asis Abad had promised Otto 3% of her winnings the night before, Otto continued, about $5,000, but she had only given him $300. He called her a bitch and told me that if he ever saw her again, he would kill her.

'All right Otto, a bit dramatic, buddy.'

The Madam, he'd told me, was so addicted to gambling that she would play anyone, anywhere.

BANG! BANG!

Suddenly collapsing the awkward silence between Otto and me came a jolting and aggressive pounding on the heavy door. Quickly gathering the scattered cards on the table into a pile, Otto lit another cigarette and stood up to unlock the door, once more, flying through the guidelines of the little scheme he'd been teaching me as he approached the deadbolt. Like an act of magic, he effortlessly slid three crispy $100 bills into my shirt pocket as he passed me.

"Your opening bet," he said. "Watch for my sign".

Two more steps to the door and finally opening its heavy frame, in walked a woman who I could only assume was Madam Asis Abad.

'Oh my God, she exists.'

She was average height, heavy set, and wore a dark blue pantsuit. She had short black hair framing her face, gold wide-rimmed, rose-tinted glasses, charcoal skin, elaborate gold jewelry, and a black purse under her arm. She wore the makeup of a 20-year-old but had to be pushing 60.

I was completely unsure how to act, and my mind was frozen.

'What is happening? Who is this woman?'

I had only been half listening to Otto the whole time because of his terrible English, with the thought of my impending doom playing on the screen of my mind, but in a flash, it all became real. I was snapped back into the moment and keenly aware I was being played, set up and positioned to fall into some sort of trap, but I still just could not figure out how. I quickly began thinking of a way out, of excuses for why I had to leave in the hope that the young men would drive me back to the park where we'd met, with no questions asked. I grabbed my phone to make a fake phone call, but the Madam was already sitting across from me, and Otto was asking me how long I could play – hoping that I would say "only 15 minutes", as I had been instructed.

I looked into the Madam's eyes and saw – nothing. I could see her eyes clearly enough, but there was nothing there. They were black and cruel. Never breaking eye contact, she reached into her purse and grabbed a wad of $10,000 cash, dropping it on the table with a thud. I had never seen so much money in my life and was completely frozen, with no idea what my next move should be. Otto grabbed the roll of bills and sniffed them like a dog smelling a raw steak, while a look of desperation flashed through his one good eye. Thoughts were racing through my mind, and my heart was pumping fast– amazingly, not out of fear, but with the excitement of someone watching a movie and not knowing what would come next. My mind was nearly blank. I felt like I was witnessing myself from above, unable to intervene in any way–only a passenger in the scene playing out before me. The cards were being dealt onto the table even before I could snap back to the moment, the crisp snap of Otto's fingers against each one as he dealt them out.

Thwap... thwap... THWAP...

Otto, sitting shoulder to shoulder with me, a bead of sweat slowly escaping from the worn edge of his eye patch, tapped my foot under the table, informing me to ask him for another card. Fearing the Madam would know we were in cahoots and spot the wad of cash in my breast pocket, I tapped back.

'I am 100% being played here – I've been set up from the time I was in that park. But what's the scam?!'

I put no money down, I didn't have any USD on me anyway, and I hadn't taken the time to stop and get Malaysian ringgit from an ATM. The only money I had were the bills Otto had put into my own pocket. Were they expecting me to have cash in my backpack—cash I'd be willing to use to bet against the Madam? How were she and Otto connected, and what was the con they were running on me? Was I about to be swindled out of the $300 and then taken to a bank, forced to take out my own money to pay off a mounting debt?

As my mind plotted all scenarios, I felt my camera bag at my feet and, as subtly as I could, fumbled to open the main zipper without looking. I felt the round edges of my flip phone, my thumb racing to locate the worn plastic power button. "So my friend, Obama or Clinton?" I flashed back to the comment in the park and thought I just might be able to use it, though it was a long shot. With the American election only a few months away, Barack Obama had become a global name, the first African American candidate nominated by a major U.S. party, and I could use this to my advantage. Obama was traveling all over the world making appearances - why not Malaysia?

Glancing down into the dark pocket of my backpack for a split second, I could see the dim green light reflecting off my fingers as the screen of my phone lit up. Knowing the buttons like the back of my hand, I continued stalling with Otto and the Madame, drawing out the growing tension around how I would play my hand. Otto had finished dealing the cards as I was scrabbling around in my backpack, my eyes fixed on the Madame—with hers and Otto's fixed on min.

'Left, left, down. Click. Down, down, right, Click.'

No longer able to hold out on making a move, I suddenly heard the sweet tones sounding from the phone inside my bag. Having successfully found the ringtone option, the digital melody played for all to hear, just as if I were receiving a call. I acted surprised, flustered even, that a phone call would interrupt our high-stakes game. "Hello?" I said, my brow concentrated and serious as I lifted it to my ear.

I quickly stood up, backpack in hand, and indicated that I had to take the important call. Pointing to the heavy door, I mimicked the movement of a key while staring at Otto, my eyes telling him I was serious. Prying open the heavy door, I rushed into the light of the living room and tried to walk outside into the open air of the driveway, but the thick iron screen had been padlocked. Otto rushed out of the back room with a look of disbelief on his face, upset that I was trying to leave but too caught off guard to say anything.

"Absolutely. Now?" I said with utter conviction into the silent plastic of my phone. "I can be there, but I'll need to leave right now." Pretending in earnest to listen to someone on the other end, I then told Otto that my partner from the Obama campaign had just arrived at the airport in KL, much earlier than expected, and he was calling with an urgent update about a mandatory last-minute meeting.

'I don't even think Obama is coming here. This plan will never work—they'll never believe me.'

I had to convince them that I was actually an important person, that I worked for the campaign of a possibly soon-to-be US President, and that someone would be looking for me.

I was gambling with the hope that even a loose connection to a trending US political figure, and that I might be someone important—too important to get involved in their petty scam, would be my saving grace. Sure, I'd been set up— a target from the second I walked into that park with my dumbass skater shoes, but I wasn't worth the risk anymore. Thinking back to the multiple cell phone calls in the car, I realized that my acceptance of their invitation had set off a chain of events between these strange men, Otto and the Madame - all players in a dirty game to capture the innocent, doughy-eyed American tourist who'd just been caught in their web.

"Otto, my friend, I absolutely need to get back downtown immediately. There has been a change of schedule, and I have an all-staff meeting in 45-minutes. If I am not there, it will be a big problem." Although I was hearing myself lie through my teeth, Otto, now distressed and frustrated, ushered me back into the darkened room to inform the Madame that I would not be able to stay and play. This time, I didn't enter the room but kept one foot firmly planted outside the door frame. From the moment I'd faked the phone call the Madame had not moved an inch. The young men who had driven me there appeared out of nowhere, and suddenly, movement and noise returned to the house. They unlocked the gate and started the car in the driveway, dogs furiously barking on either side of me, my backpack still slung over my shoulder.

Never happier to be stuffed into the backseat of a tiny car, I tried to keep a serious expression as Otto closed the door behind me, only reaching in the open window to take the $300 out of my breast pocket as the car started to reverse, and never making eye contact with me again. Without saying a word, he turned around and walked away with a look of defeat in his posture, closing the heavy gate behind him with a bang, like a fisherman who'd reeled in a giant bass and then had the line snap at the last second.

The Petronas Towers grew larger on the horizon with every turn, and my eyes fixated on them as we approached the city center. The adrenaline in my system pumping harder with every passing car, unsure of exactly what had just happened nor how it had all ended so quickly, I felt compelled to touch my limbs and guts to check for bullet holes.

'*Ha–the giant building with the faded yellow billboard.*'

I never thought I'd be so happy to see that sight again. Throughout the drive, I had been relentlessly checking my pockets and backpack, convinced that something had been taken from me, but only my innocence and travel naivety were missing now.

Lost in thought as my mind replayed every second of the last hours, the car slowed at the entrance of the giant mall hidden in the shadows of the Petronas Towers looming above. The two friendly young men who had started this whole adventure hours earlier in that park didn't even turn around as I climbed out.

"Hey," I said with a grin, my feet and belongings safely out of the car, back on safe ground. "Foot Locker. I got my shoes at Foot Locker." Shutting the door harder than was needed, blood rushed through my whole body as the giant glass mall doors opening to welcome me back to the familiar, sensation tingling in my fingertips with each step.

That was it. It was all over, as if it hadn't ever happened at all. I didn't turn back, only moving forward into the light, into the crowds, into the noise of the busy mall on a Tuesday evening. Once the sliding doors had closed behind me, the sweet feeling of frigid AC swirling again around my ankles, I hurried into the center of the crowd and just stopped. I was safe, I was whole. I paused, looked around, and was filled with gratitude and disbelief. Standing between a luxury chocolate store and an artisan stall selling colorful scented candles, I smiled to myself.

'*Today isn't the day you get Locked Up Abroad, dude!*'

What the scam was all about, I can only guess. I assume they were going to cheat me out of money one way or another, and I'd have ended up emptying an ATM for them, or carrying falsified documents, or delivering a well-wrapped package of opium, but I'll never know. What I do know is that I will never forget Otto and his eye patch, his cackle as he watched that fuzzy TV, or his desperate pleas to be my puppet master. And I'll never forget the darkness of Madame Asis Abad and the vacant blackness of her eyes that I felt in that cement room on the outskirts of Kuala Lumpur on a layover from Los Angeles to Bangladesh.

What I now know is that no matter the adventure, no matter the excitement you may feel, and no matter the situation, don't be an idiot. On this day, on this sunny, unassuming hot spring day in Malaysia, I had been an idiot. I had gone too far, not listened to my gut, got too involved, and could have ended up in a truly terrible situation that could have changed the course of my life forever- because it turns out that some people *are* assholes.

As I walked back through the corridors of that endless mall, I thought about my family. I thought about my caring parents and my loving little sister, an eerie feeling trailing me at the thought that I may have put our tight bond in jeopardy that day. My sister was just starting college, her greatest adventures ahead of her, but it made me think about my parents' childhoods, too.

'What lives had they lived? What crazy adventures, if any, have they had along the way?

I have met every travel adventure with an open sense of trust and with the deep belief that all people are good, or have good-ness within them, just as my father taught me. Unfortunately, neither enthusiasm nor unending belief in the good makes it true all the time, and no traveler should ever lose their ability to tell the difference. On this day, I almost had. I went to the brink, to the edge of the light in the world, and took a glance behind the curtain to the dark side.

Never lose the ability to discern light from dark. Never stop listening to your gut, as it is rarely wrong. Never ignore your instinct, and never lack the confidence to walk away from two strangers in a park who ask you about your shoes – even if you're confident it's a new experience your Dad never had.

My senses were sharp, my gut and intuition now firing on all cylinders, and as I left Malaysia on an overnight flight to Bangladesh a few hours later, I had no idea how much I'd need them in the coming days. Nor did I know how much more overwhelming the sights, sounds, and feelings I would experience there would be.

6

Know When to Laugh: Lost in an Unending Sea of Humanity

"Not until we are lost do we begin to understand ourselves."
-Henry David Thoreau

Dhaka, Bangladesh. March 2008

After I volunteered in Thailand, disaster-chasing sort of became my identity, and when I started at Brooks Institute, it was my only real direction, the only thing I felt I did that provided value. This work gave my life that little bit of meaning I needed more than just "Yea, that guy travels." The experiences I had had volunteering after natural disasters in the US, the Philippines, and Thailand were some of the most impactful of my life, each coming right at the time when I needed them the most. I still didn't believe in the traditional meaning of God, but after my adventures in Malaysia, I needed a positive human connection to resurrect my faith in people.

In early 2008, less than a year into my schooling in Ventura, CA, a typhoon blasted through South Western Bangladesh. It left over 4,500 dead – more lives lost than on 9/11 – although I hadn't even seen it come across the news. Groggy and hungover one Saturday morning, I woke up to a link dropped in a Facebook message from an old volunteer buddy. "Hey man, you seen this yet? Thinking of going?"

'Hell yes, I am'.

When it was over, Cyclone Sidr caused over $1 billion in damages to the struggling country, which sustained winds over 240 mph (380 kph) and waves over fifteen feet tall (4.5m). The tidal surge contaminated the drinking water, all electricity was wiped out in the low-lying agricultural areas, and roads and waterways became an impassable stew of thick mud and rancid water. It was the second massive natural disaster Bangladesh had seen in twelve months, and I had to get there.

I'd never been to a Muslim country before this trip, and I had no idea that Bangladesh even was one until I started reading updates from the volunteers who were already on the ground. When I stepped off the plane into the dimly lit, outdated airport in Dhaka that March night, the Muslim men and women, wearing their traditional conservative clothing, couldn't take their eyes off the worn, Western traveler three times their size. I felt like I had been transported to the Mos Eisley Cantina in Star Wars. Landing on Tatooine would have felt more familiar than Bangladesh was to me that night.

The heaviest I ever weighed was 312 pounds, and it was right around this time, too, so I definitely stood out in the crowd as I sheepishly stepped onto the passport control line. In the US, I was a big guy in a sea of big guys. Here I was a Goliath amongst Lilliputians, and I felt every pair of eyes following me.

I was dressed like an absolute idiot, too. Bright oversized blue t-shirt with some obnoxious logo plastered on the front, thick silver chain on my neck, flat-brimmed hat tilted sideways on my head - and those damn skater shoes that had nearly gotten me kidnapped in Malaysia the day before.

'Read the room, dude –jeez.'

I towered over everyone in the Arrivals hall, my fake diamond earrings reflecting the faint lights behind the dusty ceiling fan blades struggling to turn above. Emerging into the unfamiliar, dark Dhaka night, the ink smudged on the fresh passport stamp as I stuffed it quickly into my back pocket. Straight to a waiting cab, the first one to wave me over. "Hotel?" I asked sheepishly as if it was an absurd question to ask a taxi driver at an airport. Jumping out a short drive later as the taxi pointed to a half-open door across a busy street, I roused the sleeping receptionist and thanked the Travel Gods he had an empty room for me.

I didn't sleep much that night–too exhausted to rest, too anxious to relax, too jet-lagged to know what time it was. Otto and the Madame took more mental space than I'd intended to allow them. Here I was on the hamster wheel I'd created for myself, perpetuating the legend I invented for my life as an explorer–a life of adventure that often left me feeling numb and paralyzed. I had no idea I'd fallen asleep until I woke up a few hours later.

The room was silent. Faint morning light seeped through the worn, rust-colored drapes that were just a bit too small to cover the window. I didn't want to move, to face the outside world, or do anything other than order room service and watch TV all day. Except there was no room service, no TV, and nothing to do but get going and problem-solve my next challenge. I was happy imagining the myths of my travels passed around my friends back home, but on this day I didn't want to be the one living them.

It took me two days of searching in Dhaka before I found the completely hidden ticket office for "The Rocket", an ancient paddle steamer that has been taking locals up and down the mighty Meghna River for over 100 years. The central waterway of the country, the Meghna River, winds its way from Northern Bangladesh 165 miles (264 km) south until it empties into the Bay of Bengal. During the monsoon season each year, this massive river bulges at the seams and floods the surrounding areas, providing many farmers with the water their crops need to get them through the year. Twenty-five percent of the entire country is less than one meter above sea level, making Bangladesh one of the most susceptible to rising sea levels and climate change.

Arriving at the Sadarghat Ferry Terminal the next morning, it was total chaos. Over 300 boats and ferries arrive and depart here every single hour—one of the busiest ferry ports in the world. Boarding 'The Rocket', I was unaware that it was a 19-hour ferry ride to Reyenda, the tiny village I was attempting to find, and that it would be one of the longest rides of my life. I only had the handwritten village name scribbled on a piece of paper in Bengali. My hope was dwindling that I'd ever arrive there.

With only a backpack and a small handheld suitcase, I gingerly boarded the ferry, stepping across rickety wooden planks that barely remained in place between the concrete slab on the shore and the worn, paint-chipped side of the boat. Showing my ticket to a wild-eyed local man with skin the color of rich soil and a beard dyed bright sunset orange, I was escorted to my quarters—a room the size of a broom closet with a tiny bunk, a dimly lit hanging bulb, and yellow-stained sheets, with a small open window as my only hope for circulating air.

Thud! Thud! "Sir, hello?"

A hard pounding at the door two hours into the journey, and I was jolted out of a snooze. I was ushered out to the hallway - a long, dark corridor flickered with faint lights, a well-worn burgundy carpet the color of spilled wine extended into the darkness. In the middle of that corridor stood a single small wooden table with a single small wooden chair. Awkwardly seating myself in that chair, I beckoned for the two gentlemen standing by to join me so I wouldn't be so impossibly alone and uncomfortable. They politely declined. I was served locally caught fish, long-since warm steamed vegetables, a heaping plate of rice, and boiled eggs covered in a sticky brown sauce.

'Is this food clean? Were the vegetables washed? Where are all the hoards of people I boarded with?'

I blankly stared down the eery, dark, and silent hallway. Small doors to other cabins dotted the edges, but only mine was in use. Picking up the smudged silverware, I ate in a daze.

'Where have I ended up this time...and where am I going?'

Eating more than intended, I quietly walked down the hallway out onto the deserted deck and down a rusty, squeaking staircase to the deck below that was strewn with endless luggage, bags piled on the entire deck from bow to stern. But the floors weren't only filled with suitcases. The further I walked down the stairs, the more voices I heard. The entire deck was covered in people, and families, all huddled together. Some were sleeping on their bags, some under, some had laid out clothes to eat on, some to sleep on. Some were sleeping sitting up and some were simply staring at me staring at them. I'd intended to buy a regular ticket for a ride I assumed would be an hour, two tops. Instead, here I was feeling on display and elitist emerging from a stately, premium-class suite that most of these people would never see. Again, the world was slapping me in the face with my own entitlement.

Returning to the dark and quiet hallway, I felt guilty, exposed, and deeply aware of my privilege as I sat in my first-class room in a vast empty hallway of empty first-class rooms hovering above a sea of bodies less fortunate than I. Laying on those yellow sheets and turning off the flickering light bulb, my mind raced as I realized once again that the act of travel was again my greatest teacher. Everything is relative. Everything needs perspective.

I didn't sleep well that night, but another THUD! THUD! "Sir, hello?" on my door snapped me out of something resembling sleep some twelve hours later, the captain stopping the boat to let me off on the cloudy river banks. No arrival terminal, no dock, and no buildings in sight. Only a wooden board just strong enough to bear my monstrous weight connecting the ferry and the slippery earth it clung to. My shoes soaked in deep red mud to the heels, I watched the giant ferry slowly shrink away down the muddy brown river as it carried on its journey. I was certain I was in the wrong place as the piece of paper crinkled in my hand offered me no clues about where to go next.

No cell phone, no internet, not a single person in sight, let alone anyone as out of place as I felt, I did what any other sane traveler would do. I laughed out loud, hoisted my backpack over my shoulders, and started walking down the only path available towards the smoke I could see slowly rising through the wind-beaten trees in the distance. I must have looked like a lunatic, hands brushing the long river reeds on either side of me as I went along my way grinning like a gigantic happy baby.

This is what I traveled for—the totally inexplicable ecstasy of being on a true adventure. But my inner dialogue was starting to piece together my situation as well. The realization that I could disappear, be held hostage, or drown, and not a single person I knew would be within thousands of miles was utterly liberating. Not because I wanted any of those things—far from it—but because in modern life, between bed, couch, TV, office chair, and driver's seat - this feeling wasn't remotely possible. I'd never felt more alive than trudging down that muddy path, with grasses as tall as I was blowing on both sides of me in the southern fringes of Bangladesh.

Primal instincts came to the forefront of my mind, to the edges of my gut. What in the world I was doing here I didn't know, but I'd followed a feeling, and I knew that if nothing else, it would have an interesting ending.

'Stay alert. Play it safe, dude. Remember Otto.'

As I rounded the final bend in the dusty path, the mud starting to cake off my ankles, I saw the formations of a tiny village. A dirt town square surrounded by shanty huts and stalls, you could barely call them homes or storefronts. Merely structures stood before me. This wasn't a city, certainly not a town, and barely a village, but certainly an outpost of some sort. There was life here, and I was about to step into it. I hesitated. I was invisible, but I wouldn't be, just minutes from now. I was staring into a postcard, into the past, into a world I admired too much to ruin with my presence.

Children ran freely just beyond my gaze with dogs and chickens meandering between them amidst a whirlwind of smells, but the locals immediately stopped their movements when I broke the barrier from the forest path into the village square. I walked straight to the center of the square and paused. Time utterly stopped around me.

The children stopped playing, the animals seemed to have disappeared as my eyes slowly swept across the village panorama. Spinning completely around, everyone had paused their busy-work to look at what I imagine was the oddest sight they'd ever seen. Until I was told weeks later, I had no idea that I may have been the first white person some of those young children had ever seen.

I was cut out from a high school yearbook photo and clumsily glued into a picture of a far-off land I would have seen in one of those National Geographic magazines in the basement bathroom with the green, plush carpet. I didn't have the bushy white beard, and I looked absurd, but at that moment, I was the explorer.

My emotions were shifting back and forth like a pinball bouncing between jubilation and terror, tears welling up in my eyes ready to cascade down my cheeks from whichever emotion won out in the end.

Sweat dripped off my pink, blotchy face, salty stains streaking down my shirt, my skater shoes more horribly out of place than ever before.

'I can't even pull these off in Bangladesh.'

Out of the corner of my eye, I could see a figure approaching. Turning my head slightly, unsure if it was a friend or foe, I saw a local woman advancing towards me with what felt like a smile, but I could only judge from her eyes, as a veil was covering the rest of her face, but I could feel a warmth in her glance.

I remained frozen in the moment as she drew closer, thinking it best I simply not move at all lest I offend anyone who was watching. I had learned that this part of Bangladesh was strongly conservative Muslim, and many of the women would not even make eye contact with me or shake my hand, much less talk to me. At least that is what I'd read. But here she was, nearly in my face.

What she did next will remain a moment locked in my consciousness forever. I can still see and feel it as if it had happened an hour ago.

She confidently lifted her veil, revealing her warm face, raised her hand with a dusty towel, and wiped the beads of sweat off my bright red face. My cheeks burned and my eyes squinted. It felt like a religious initiation, standing closer now to this woman than I'd been to the gentlemen in the middle seat on the flight to Dhaka.

In that moment, thousands of miles from all the people closest to me, she became my mother, my father, and my family - attending to me like a lost child in her village, with the ease and comfort a grandmother would show to her loved ones. We didn't exchange a single word.

'God is love'.

Within moments, she stepped away, dusty sweat-soaked cloth in hand, the buzz of village life resuming as she retreated. The children were shouting, the chickens squawking, and the men reverting their gaze back to bagging vegetables, weighing out fresh slabs of meat, and organizing the dented tins of children's sweets on their wooden carts. I can still see her veil slowly slipping back across her face as she turned, fading back into th,e crowded square behind us. But I'll never forget her eyes.

"Jeff! You look lost, big guy!" A strong voice piercing through the unfamiliar village noises with a British accent shouted toward me. Turning around, I saw three Westerners fast approaching in the bed of a beat-up old truck, dust swirling behind them. Resembling a zebra, I couldn't quite tell if the truck was black with white paint or white with black paint? It was so chipped and fading that it was impossible to know. "How

the hell are ya, mate?" Jump in, we'll take you to the house."
Suddenly back again with many of the people I had volunteered
with in Phuket four years earlier, I felt like I was home. This
was family, these were the people adventurous enough to do the
crazy shit I'd done to get here. These were my people. I was still
processing what just happened as we bounced away over uneven
terrain into the forest to a three-story cinder block home that
felt like the Ritz.

During the time I spent in that village in Southern Bangladesh,
I saw many things, met many people, and again, had my
perspective on life challenged and nudged in different directions
daily. But what I remember most was standing in that village
square, a stranger wiping sweat from my brow, and walking
away without ever exchanging a single word. That was the power
of travel. That was the feeling I was incessantly chasing.

Placing myself in danger has never been my goal. It's the
connection I seek, and in this part of my trip, I needed to connect
with good humans again to restore my trust in the world after
my experience in Kuala Lumpur.

'Thank you Travel Gods. You came through yet again.'

I felt like I was sacrificing myself to the world in many of
the situations I ended up in, but I always held a deep down,
fervent belief that if I gave myself up to the world, the world
would protect and take care of me. I'd now traveled enough to
know carefree from careless, and while I always kept my eyes
open to danger, I often ventured a bit further than most into
the unknown, just to see what the world would hand me and
discover the lessons hiding in the dark.

There is no feeling like being completely alone, utterly lost,
and without any connection to anything you've ever known.
It's pure freedom when you find it. I was always amazed at how

much more fully I interacted and engaged with the world around me when I was stripped of my familiarities. Before departing Bangladesh, I used Skype for the first time in my life to call my parents back in Maryland.

"I was simply lost in an unending sea of humanity, Dad."

Know when to laugh, know when to cry, and know when to ask yourself why you are in each situation. And ask yourself how you should respond to each. Perhaps it is to seek shelter, retreat to comfort, or to help others in need. Sometimes, the best response is to just throw up your hands, put a smile on your face, and laugh boldly into the unknown before you.

Getting a peek at the dark side of the world that is out there in Malaysia followed immediately by the healing kindness of a stranger while lost in a village in Bangladesh, one thing was clear to me - I was collecting tales faster than I could process them.

But I wanted to *tell* stories too, more structured and meaning-ful narratives – not just random anecdotes. And while I wanted them to be passionate, and spark change, I also wanted them to be fueled with goodness and good intentions–to focus on the light rather than the dark.

7

Switch off the Bad News, Search for 'The Good News'

"When I was a boy and I would see scary things in the news, my
mother would say to me, 'Look for the helpers.
You will always find people who are helping."
- Mr. Rogers

A Warm Island Somewhere, 1999 (probably)

I don't remember where we were, but it was an island somewhere, warm and sticky, but the nights were breezy. Escaping
the long months of winter in Washington, D.C., we were sitting
out on a wooden dock at a restaurant table waiting for our meal
–my sister, my parents, and me. I like to think I ordered the local
seafood, but I probably went straight for the pizza or spaghetti.
I must have been about 14.

We were talking about the future that night around the dinner
table, more specifically, where my sister and I saw ourselves

in the coming years, and what we were curious about the most, what sparked our interests.

"I want to create a TV show called 'The Good News'" I said without much thought, but still shy to say it out loud because I didn't know exactly what I meant. My mother laughed—not a cruel laugh, but a loving laugh, like the idea tickled her in the best way possible. She loved the intention and pushed me further, as she always did, for all she ever wanted was for me to be happy, and she never missed an opportunity to prove it.

Passing a local artist who was painting miniature postcards one fall day, she could see a spark of curiosity in my eye. A conversation quickly followed, inquiring where he got his paint and pencils. A jumbled comment in high school while listening to rock music on the radio resulted in my unwrapping a VHS entitled "So You Wanna Be A DJ?" a few days later. The slight interest I expressed in animals during my early high school years resulted in an internship at the local animal hospital by the following month. My happiness was always her north star, and she'd do anything to lead me towards it, so she pushed further.

"What would 'The Good News' be about?" she asked kindly, like she'd planned the question before I finished getting the idea out of my head, thrilled to see a spark of initiative in my young mind.

I hijacked the dinner conversation with my rambling ideas that night, dreaming of creating a rival for the evening news, a daily broadcast dedicated to only highlighting the good that was going on in the world, only the stories that would make you smile and leave you feeling upbeat. I wanted to create a place to highlight the random acts of kindness across the globe, to show strangers helping each other and people accomplishing great things out of love, not ratings. Someone needed to celebrate these stories – led by the heart, the invisible threads that connect people and make us all human. I wanted to remove the negative feedback loop playing across all the nightly news channels I saw in the US. All the stories seemed to be fueled by stabbings, murders, jailhouse beatings, corporate fraud, home invasions, and tax evasions. If you watch enough of that, you start to go crazy, to forget that basic human decency even exists at all.

I wanted to create a TV show that would inspire the feeling those astronauts have described, looking down on our beautiful world from that tiny porthole in space.

'Aren't there any good stories to tell out there?'

But I didn't own a TV network, and I wasn't even old enough to drive yet. The start of a spark in my mind to chase stories, the same as I'd seen in those glossy National Geographic pages, was beginning to burn brighter and brighter. Because while I had almost paralyzing imposter syndrome and had zero confidence in any professional skill, finding a story and telling it to the world seemed straightforward enough. I just needed to get to those places and find the stories to tell. Then maybe I could find the best way to share them all later.

Cape Town, South Africa. May 2010

Before I could graduate from the Brooks Institute, I had an eight-week gap between classes and was searching for my next story to tell. With my sister studying abroad in South Africa that semester and one of my best childhood friends, David, living there, I was quick to take out another loan and bet on myself to sort it out later. Do you know how quickly a student can get a high-interest loan for $10,000 in the US? It's scary. Within days, my bank account had a few more zeroes in it, and within weeks I'd landed in Cape Town, South Africa, eager to spend time with family and friends and to find more stories to tell.

I was chasing a thread that was never far from my mind in recent months. It was a thread I'd started to pick at a couple of years earlier when I'd first come across the plight of leprosy in India, a story I knew would highlight a lot of good people – some Good News, if you will.

As I sat in a dark and quiet hotel room on the outskirts of Cape Town, jet lag waking me up far before the city around me was stirring, I dove down rabbit holes behind the dim glow of my laptop. I learned that leprosy was still infecting thousands of people a year – over 740,000 still living with the disease in 2020. While 95% of people are immune, some don't know for ten or even twenty years that they have it with repeated injuries, loss of sensation, and deep infections being their only clue at the end of a long dormancy. And yet over 200,000 new cases were still being reported each year in some 120 countries, including the USA.

'With modern medicine, how is this possible?'

The World Health Organization deemed leprosy eradicated globally at the end of 2000, reducing what little funding was left to just a trickle. But by defining eradication as only 1 in 10,000 people having the disease, it meant that India alone, a country with over 1.3 billion people, could have 130,000 new cases every single year without causing a blip on the radar. As far as the World Health Organization was concerned, this wasn't a problem. But I couldn't let it go.

'How is this story not being told?'

Surely this would be the type of compelling documentary that would put two young filmmakers on the map in the storytelling world, while shining a light on a critical human situation. These people had stories to tell, and I was determined to chase them after I graduated. In n all my research about this issue in South Africa that early morning, one name kept popping up.

' I need to find this guy named Lucky!'

But finding him proved to be a bit tricky. His name was 'Lucky' after all, and he was a field doctor working throughout large swaths of the South African countryside. I could only find bits and pieces about the work he was doing, but I knew he had a story to tell. In my research, I learned that South Africa was still suffering from new leprosy cases each year and that the Leprosy Mission, with whom he worked closely, was the NGO doing most of the work in the country. The head office had messaged me back before breakfast that morning, and within days, I was on my way to a remote area outside of Durban on the eastern cape of South Africa.

Waiting anxiously on a crumbling curb outside my hotel, I stood looking for a man I'd never met. He was just another middle-aged black man, driving in just another beaten-up white truck, down just another dusty African road. But I would be the one who was lucky to meet him, lucky to hear his story, and lucky to see the amazing work he was doing. With only my camera and tripod in hand, I stood awkwardly in that budget hotel parking lot, hoping he would recognize me, since I stood out much more than he did. Pulling over out of a swarm of traffic, right on cue, he reached across and opened his car door.

"Jeff? Welcome to Kwazulu Natal. I hope you like driving."

Lucky was kind, soft-spoken, and shy. He couldn't quite figure out why anyone would want to hear his story or see his work. We drove in silence down endless dirt roads through the South African province that day and for the rest of that week.

We made what small talk we could, Lucky slowly opening up and trusting me enough to hear his story. We visited a remote grass hut village just to allow him to change the bandages of one man who had no one else to care for him, a two-hour drive each way. We visited a single mother sent to the outskirts of her village, forced to raise her young children outside the view of the community, so that Lucky could change her bandages and give her counseling.

Ghastly ulcers, gaping festering wounds, near total loss of sensation in both hands and feet, and deadly infection were a constant concern. The stigma of leprosy was so strong that these people had all backs turned on them. But not by Lucky.

I only spent a few days with Lucky, the quiet, thoughtful doctor who was dedicating his life to comforting and caring for patients stretching for hundreds of kilometers throughout the entire province in Eastern South Africa. From the borders of Lesotho to Mozambique, Lucky opened my eyes to the plight and pervasive problem that leprosy was still causing in these communities and inspired me to try and tell a bigger story, on a global scale.

Lucky was the good news. I had my first story that felt like it truly mattered and needed to be told. I knew there were more Good News stories, and I was determined to find them, but I needed help to tell this story of leprosy first, and I knew exactly which Irish Pub to find it in.

8

STIGMA: Some Realities Die in the Darkness

"Be yourself; everyone else is already taken." -Oscar Wilde

Ventura, California, USA. October 2010

"What do you know about leprosy?" I said out of the blue to Ryan as we sat downing pints of Smithwick's at our favorite Irish pub on the corner of Main Street and Chestnut, ankles kicking the barstools below us.

Dargan's is a classic American-style Irish pub. Green clovers and Irish flags line the walls, illuminated Guinness signs hang in every direction, and Celtic limericks are nailed to the wall above the urinals. The menu is filled with buffalo chicken tenders, quesadillas, and bangers and mash - but I never saw anyone order them. A clock counting down the seconds to St. Patrick's Day sits above the exit.

"Uhh, what dude?" he responded with a chuckle, his long

surfer hair and chilled-out attitude floating in the air between us. "Like from the Bible?"

This was our local college hangout, the pub where everyone knew our names, and as some collection of our friend group was there more evenings than not, Ryan usually maintained a strict "do not talk about school" policy. But on this day, we'd just graduated, and there was no school left to talk about, so it was on to dreaming up new projects out in the real world.

"I've got a story for us to tell, but I can't do it without you."

Kathmandu, Nepal. November 2010

Ten weeks later, we were in Kathmandu, Nepal with a month-long filming schedule throughout India, Nepal, Cambodia, Thailand, and Vietnam ahead of us. We were way outside our comfort zone, and we'd pushed the envelope to a breaking point. Sure, we'd graduated with degrees in Visual Journalism, but this wasn't a classroom anymore. This was the real world now, and we owed it to the people we would find 'out there' to know how to tell their stories.

After following Lucky and seeing the struggle of the people he helped in South Africa, I knew the wider story needed to be told. Since that time, most people I have talked to about leprosy have been under the illusion that it had gone the way of the Black Plague – and around the same time, too.

Ryan and I had been drinking buddies for years after meeting at Brooks Institute, both pursuing our degrees and often bouncing between classes together, but this was the first time we'd actually worked on anything as a team. The ink was barely dry on our diplomas, but we were eager to prove we deserved them and set off to tell the story of leprosy. In our first attempt to make it in the production world, we threw some clothes and all the camera gear we owned into bursting backpacks and headed for the other side of the world to make a documentary.

But at this point, only days into the project, sitting in Kathmandu, we were already burning out, wondering if we'd bitten off more than we could chew. We'd seen and heard things in India that we were still trying to process, and we had all of Cambodia, Thailand, and Vietnam ahead. We were overwhelmed.

'Have we taken on too much? Do we have what it takes to tell such an important story?'

After nights of bouncing between cheap hotels and fighting jet lag, this was the best sleep we'd had since landing in India ten days prior. Emerging from thick woolen blankets into the chilly Himalayan morning air, we sat at a small table on Krishna's patio and shared breakfast together. Hot milky tea, local bread, honey, and butter with tangy yogurt and fresh-picked berries. "These people, they do not have anyone who fights for them." Krishna said as he took a sip from his steaming cup of chai, his cool morning breath blending with the steam in the air as it evaporated into the green hills behind him. Krishna was short with jet black hair and a thick mustache, tight collared shirt, kind bright eyes, and a towering personality with an infectious laugh never more than a few words away. "Growing up here, in this place, with my parents having the disease, we lived separately from the rest of my village," he said matter of factly, as he motioned to the winding road through a patchwork of simple brick and metal structures behind us dotting the hillsides below.

Krishna continued, "Many of those with leprosy in this village still live in horse stables, like livestock, you know?" Pushed to the edges of this village, itself already on the outskirts of Kathmandu.

Slowly putting our forks down, Ryan and I listened quietly to the story of Krishna's early childhood and how he had developed a passion, his life's mission, to help as many in his community as he could. Finally meeting in person at his foundation outside of the Ring Road in the Kathmandu Valley the evening before, after months of communicating via email, we'd greeted each other with huge, warm hugs like we'd known each other for years.

Krishna himself didn't have leprosy, part of the 95% naturally immune, but after seeing how his parents and community struggled, he had dedicated his life, just as Lucky had, to trying to comfort the afflicted, reverse the stigma, and develop and grow the small community where he was born. Developing it into something society wouldn't give it a chance to become wasn't proving to be easy, but Krishna was a different breed.

Krishna, along with his wife Leila, had built solar-powered ovens, they were making huts out of recycled glass bottles and producing organic dish soap from local plants and nuts. They organized a free health clinic and built a new kindergarten. They planted a biodynamic garden, served healthy food in a cafe, and gave jobs to those who were ostracized the most by society. Working tirelessly they brought jobs, skills, empowerment, and hope to hundreds in the Kathmandu Valley.

We were trying to find the Good News, no matter how hard some of the realities we were facing were proving to be, and we'd found it in this modest, determined visionary in the valley of Kathmandu.

Krishna took each breath with a calmness and a strength I'd rarely seen. He listened deeply, just as Mr. P had, each action rich with purpose and intent, his daily life overflowing with meaning from sunrise to sunset.

* * *

For years, I frantically clung to the feeling of being safely held inside a community I knew inside and out, one that knew me better than I knew myself. I've often wondered whether that cocoon of safety during my childhood is actually what helped me build the capacity to bounce from country to country chasing the opposite feeling in the years since: Being outside my comfort zone, surrounded by unknown elements, people, languages, cultures, and perspectives. And no matter how uncomfortable I've been, nearly in tears at certain points, there has always been a lesson to learn, a new level of wisdom to gain, and stacking these experiences has become an obsession.

Learn to welcome that which scares you, what makes you want to retreat, and take the road less traveled. Being a teenager, unsure of what will come next in your life and how you'll meet it, is the same feeling as stepping off a plane in a new country, unsure of how to engage with the unknown and what you'll find. Both feelings precede moments of great growth, experience, and opportunity, so welcome them.

But sometimes even I am slow to drink my own medicine, slow to take my own advice. High in a Himalayan valley, Ryan and I had found the Good News, but the next leg of our journey was only filled with bad news, and we were not one bit excited to welcome it, nearly too frustrated and exhausted to appreciate the beauty amidst it all.

9

Welcome Everything: Damn You Travel Gods!

*"Travel is fatal to prejudice, bigotry, and narrow-mindedness,
and many of our people need it sorely on these accounts."*
- Mark Twain

India/Nepal Border. November 2010

It wasn't so much the 620-mile (1,000 km) bus ride that bothered me. It was the realization that in the US this distance would take 10 hours to drive, but from Kathmandu, Nepal to New Delhi, India, it would take us 22. I've been on plenty of long bus rides and was quite used to them by this point, but I knew this one would exponentially age us both. "Dude, at least it saves us a night's hotel costs." Ryan quipped, his American enthusiasm shining a bit brighter than mine that afternoon. He could tell I was struggling, and like any good teammate, he was quick to take a positive approach. And I knew he was right.

Money was going fast and we were on a tight budget. Pulling out of the noisy and colorful Gongabu bus station in Kathmandu, we grabbed the last two empty seats, packed away our camera gear, and donned apprehensive smiles. Looking around, we realized we were the only ones on the bus not sporting a Nepali or Indian passport, and we were in for one hell of a local experience.

Not only would the bus ride last an entire day and night - we'd long given up on the hope of sleeping - but it was the fact that it was through terrifying mountain roads with no guard rails that made the journey especially harrowing. It felt like our bus was a pinball being violently bounced back and forth along the endless switchbacks, nearly fourteen hours of which were in total darkness because of the time of year.

The drivers can't fall asleep—I get how important that is, but there has got to be a better way to stay awake than ~~playing~~ blasting every single R. Kelly and Justin Bieber music video in existence, I shit you not. It was absolute torture. With each hairpin turn of the road, the poorly connected TV and buzzing speakers screamed with static, as if even they couldn't take it anymore. If that wasn't enough, the spinning red disco lights illuminating a small glass statue of Ganesha, the patron saint of travelers, made the setting all the more surreal.

"Haven't they ever heard of Redbull?" I yelled to Ryan. "Who let Justin Bieber make this much horrible music?!", he yelled back. We both tried to laugh but were closer to tears.

As miserable as the bus ride was, I was aware of how amusing the whole ordeal was as well. However, beyond the jokes and bearing the arduous journey, I was plagued with doubt and worry as well. Not about our safety that night, which was in the hands of the Travel Gods and Ganesha, but about what we were doing there in the first place. I was smart enough to know that Ryan was the real talent between the two of us. I knew it was my job to find the story, schedule the interviews, handle the logistics, and put him in the most picturesque spots we could find. I was happy just to be producing the project and running a couple "B" cameras as needed, constantly plagued with imposter syndrome and the all-consuming worry that we had no business being there. Jumping into the next adventure was my coping mechanism –it always had been, but there were higher stakes now. Putting my education and reputation on the line was one thing, but now I had roped someone else in as well. But just because we were miserable didn't automatically mean we were growing, or learning anything new, and it didn't mean I was any closer to finding my place in the world. There wasn't any easily identifiable lesson I could latch on to. We were just two miserable foreign travelers on a very long bus ride through some impossibly dark mountains a very long way from home.

'Will we even finish this documentary? And if we do, will it even make sense?'

We'd decided to take the overnight bus instead of paying an extra $47 to fly the hour and forty minutes between capital cities, a decision we would have given anything to rethink at that point. It was a decision, however, that we were lucky to be able to have in the first place, because in spite of the relatively small budget for this trip, a flight between cities was an option that most in the world simply don't have. It was a valuable perspective for two socially advantaged American kids to learn up close - even if we didn't like the music. Again, the Travel Gods arrived right on time with a mirror and forced us to view our privilege in it.

This was one of those low points of traveling, the worst of the worst, and when we finally arrived at the Indian border crossing of Birganj, our laughable mishaps turned from misery to downright hysterics. Stopping .6 miles (1km) from the border itself, the lumbering bus spat us and our gear out on the road as the dusty afternoon light filled with smoke and exhaust from the collection of vehicles lining up to cross into India.

With too much gear and equipment to carry by hand, we balanced our bodies and all our belongings on the back of a bicycle transport, and moving at the speed of pond water, pedaled towards the border atop the cart of the young boy who offered us a lift. Like a sequence out of a Wes Anderson movie, we couldn't help but find a sliver of humor at the sight of ourselves. Upon arriving at the border, it was no surprise that we had to bribe our way into the country as well - one final hurdle ending a harrowing 24-hour nightmare journey. And the bribe cost a lot more than the one I'd pay in Tajikistan some six years later.

During our journey, we felt like we'd stared certain death in the face, as we swerved around those cliffs, even thinking a few times about bailing out, and in the end, we'd been taken advantage of. A bribe appeared to be the only way out of this endless journey. With most of our remaining rupees crumpled up and handed over in frustration, we were stamped, processed, and back in India.

Early the next morning, Ryan and I found ourselves as tightly packed as sardines in what felt like the cattle car of a lumbering Indian Railways train. In a sea of Indian people, colors, smells, and sounds, we were on a train bound for, what we hoped, would be New Delhi. Accidentally purchasing the wrong tickets, we ended up without seats for the 12-hour train ride, we'd have to stand. All we could do at that point was to laugh and resign ourselves to the situation, and we weren't sure we were even heading in the right direction...

As often happens with travel, the world rewarded us for simply doing our best as we stood awkwardly griping both our camera bags and the faded blue metal window casings as the train lurched forward. As soon as the Travel Gods noted that we had given in, they leaped into action, and without being able to speak a word, a welcoming Indian family we'd barely noticed kindly beckoned for us to join them on their bench, offering us warm food and warm smiles – a mother and father seeing two lost and out of place children from the other side of the world, taking them under their wing in their own world

'God is love. Damn you, Travel Gods, you've done it again!'

We spoke without using words, only with facial expressions and eye contact, as they selflessly shared what little homemade food they'd prepared for their journey. Shortly after passing the ripped roti around our crowded circle, their small son crawled in my lap and fell asleep with the innocence only a child could show, an innocence I felt sincerely privileged and humbled to be able to honor. I couldn't help but smile. We couldn't have been more different, and yet something unspoken connected us all that night. The world rarely gives out such uncomfortable experiences without offering the antidote as well, however not often so close together in time. And while Ryan put on a brave face and sat through all the discomfort with me, I realized that not everyone relishes the uncomfortable travel experiences, nor enjoys them, as I had come to. What to one man may feel like an endurance challenge may feel like pointless suffering to another – and neither is wrong. Sometimes a travel lesson comes at the end of a hellish bus ride, but sometimes it is just a hellish bus ride. In this instance, it was a train ride that, thankfully, did finally sputter to a stop in New Delhi with enough time to get us on to our flight to Phnom Penh later that evening.

Traveling doesn't always mean going out into the world,

wildly grinning, saying yes to it all, and trusting every stranger you meet with the same trust you give your neighbor, but it doesn't mean closing yourself off from the world either. Traveling is all about being in the moment, aware of everything around you with heightened senses, and being present no matter what happens. This was now the balance I was trying to strike as I explored the world–jumping on every opportunity to have such experiences and putting myself in positions I was so certain my father had never been in, while trying to maintain an awareness that all experiences had lessons to teach, whether I'd understand them in the moment or a decade later.

One thing will always be certain. Whether at dorm room parties, in shopping malls, or on harrowing Nepali bus rides, horrible American pop music will track you down and haunt you wherever you are on earth.

10

Never Stop Searching for Yourself: What the Khmer Rouge Taught Me About Friendship

"Far and away, the best prize that life has to offer is the chance to work hard at work worth doing."
-Theodore Roosevelt

Redlands, California, 2003

Long before I left on that flight alone to Thailand, before I knew what a kilometer was, that some people called zucchini "courgette", and that Timbuktu was a real place (it's in Mali, Africa), I was a hefty college freshman with little self-confidence, trying my best to hang with the cool kids. I was clinging to anything I thought might resemble a direction in my life, and I grasped onto some pretty thin straws. I wore a puka shell necklace, recorded rap songs, even tried to be an oil painter, and while none of them felt right, they were all more comfortable than just being me, exposed and raw.

College life in the United States has a kind of aura around it, and for good reason. I didn't realize how the stereotypes of college dorm life and wild parties had made their way across the sea until I started traveling. So many times, often in a hostel or an airplane lounge, people would make comments like "Is it just like in the movies?" or "Do you really drink beer out of red cups?" In many ways, my college experience was straight out of those movies. I lived right into the stereotypes of the early 2000s, from the sideways hat to the fake diamond in my ear, frat parties, party houses, and "accidentally" taking the same Intro to Painting class three semesters in a row.

Going to college in the US is one thing, but doing it in California is quite another, playing into even more of those stereotypes seen in movies around the world. I was a lost soul during my first two years of college, but with enough fellow students in the same boat, I didn't stand out too much at the beginning. During my first week, my freshman counselor made a comment, half in jest, which I took way too seriously. "No one is expecting anything out of you your first semester, so just have fun and try everything." He certainly meant academically, but I took it as a free pass to indulge in all the fun and careless enjoyment of the US college social life, and I did so until well into my third year - and maybe, if I'm perfectly honest, right up until the day I found myself crying and alone on my 30th birthday on the other side of the world more than a decade a later.

I was always down to have fun, the first one to show up at a party, the last to leave. I was the go-to guy for fun, everyone could count on me for a good time hang, and I took it as a serious responsibility. I even wore the same thing for nearly an entire semester and turned into a cartoon character of myself, an alter ego one of the juniors named 'Wallace'. I loved being Wallace–Wallace was a lot of fun, and I can find about 500 college students from Southern California in the early 2000s who would agree with me. While my ADHD had kept me moving quickly from friend group to friend group, it also had me bouncing from class to class, rarely completing a single assignment and rarely taking classes that had any relationship to each other. One day I wanted to be a DJ, the next, make to artisanal mustards or work on a fishing boat in Alaska, and it showed in my transcripts–a jumbled mess of low credit classes that mapped out a Jackson Pollock painting more than a career path.

I was more lost than ever, and the laughter was starting to wear off. So on the day the university admissions office finally called and informed me that I could only get credit for taking that painting class once, for a total of three credits, I knew change was coming. Wallace had to go, and so did I.

I just didn't know what I wanted to do with my life as I didn't have the sense of direction so many others around me seemingly did. Most of the other students were partying hard on the weekends as an antidote to the pre-med or philosophy studying they were hitting hard during the week. I was just doing it to avoid having to face the fact that I was now 21 with no clear direction or game plan for what I wanted to do with my life and suffering from a massive dose of imposter syndrome. I was here, I'd made it to college. That was the goal, right? But when was my life going to pick me up and show me the way forward? And when would my mind finally slow down long enough for me to think clearly?

All that fun was actually just overcompensating and covering up the glaring reality that I had no direction in my life. I planned my weeks around the parties and the fun, only begrudgingly going to classes when I had absolutely nothing else to do. I got into all the music the other students were listening to, and the college bands many of my friends were in. I didn't have the dedication to learn any instruments myself, but I sure loved being absorbed in the excitement around them. It was like being a member of a lost tribe, but a tribe nonetheless, and when you're that age, being accepted is all that matters.

I've never been one of those people who can sing the lyrics to songs, quote famous musicians, or recite all the words when a classic comes on the radio–but two lines from one of my friends' bands stuck with me for years after leaving the excitement of campus life in the search for another tribe to join.

For years, those lyrics stayed in my head, randomly popping in months or years apart, but they were always there.

'*What you are to be, you now become. I won't fear what I don't understand.*'

Those 15 words became a mantra of sorts to me, two lines from the same song–a guiding light that started to direct a little bit of my hopeless wandering for the first time. Those words didn't push me into any particular direction, but in whatever direction I turned, I went there with a bit more intention and awareness that even if it was scary or uncertain, I wouldn't be afraid. I began to believe that whatever I found myself doing was helping me to become whoever I was meant to be, no matter how long that took.

Just a few months after I first encountered those lyrics for the first time, the Tsunami struck in Thailand. I would like to think that on some level, I felt *called* rather than just *driven* to chase it for a needed sense of purpose. My decision to go to Thailand led me to photography, to Brooks, to trying to tell stories with pictures, and beginning to feel a real passion for something in my life. The breadcrumbs had continued being strewn out before me, but dammit if some of them weren't crazy-hard to find or even recognize as breadcrumbs at all

'What you are to be, you now become. I won't fear what I don't understand.'

I kept coming back to those lyrics, and I continued to find others along the way who seemed to have found genuine meaning in their lives, as they boldly followed their own paths.

Little did I know that years later, I would meet two more of those memorable people deep within the Cambodian jungle.

Siem Reap, Cambodia. November 2010

The sunrise was at 6:09 that morning, but with all the camera gear, batteries, and backpacks to prep, we were up well before 4 am. Tucked into the back of a squeaky tuk-tuk, black and grey equipment bags piled up on our laps, Ryan and I sped down the dusty back roads of Siem Reap heading for the entrance gate to the Angkor Wat Temple Complex. A warm November air blanketed us in the darkness of night as we bounced along toward the glowing horizon of the rising sun. After the draining weeks we'd just been through, it was time to step away from leprosy for a couple hours to enjoy the silence of a sunrise over one of the most iconic structures on earth. It was time to breathe in, breathe out, and take a pause.

Often called the Eighth Wonder of the World, the great Angkor Wat was built by Khmer King Suryavarman II in the early 12th Century and covers a vast area of over 400 acres, the largest religious site on earth. With extensive Hindu and Buddhist history, this country-defining landmark is known the world over and is the pride of Cambodia, appearing on both its flag and currency. It even featured as the cover story for the May 1982 issue of National Geographic under the title "Temples of Angkor: Will They Survive?" Perhaps my chunky elementary school self had poured through its pages in the bathroom with the neon green shag carpet.

Ryan and I sat in silence, camera gear stacked so high on our laps we could barely see each other, as we both peered out of the tuk-tuk at the complex ruins beginning to surround us. The dark sky was showing hints of the day to come, and we were unsure if the air around us was filled with fog or smoke, as the cryptic scene ahead grew in mystery. Backpacks flung over already sweaty backs, we marched towards the vast moat ahead, ancient temple ruins dotting the horizon– imposing walls, arching doorways, and massive sandstone slabs of stone in every shape and size surrounding us as we trudged down well-worn pathways.

Entering the 900-year-old Angkor Wat Complex through the ancient western gate, the stunning temple expanse came into view, with the faint outline of its tallest towers slowly separating from the night sky behind. We walked in silence, a rare chance to soak it all in. While most visitors clammer ahead towards the main temple to claim the best spots to watch the sunrise, Ryan and I found ourselves fading to the side, content to move away from the growing number of tourists, choosing instead to perch ourselves high on an adjacent tower structure that had a welcome ledge and a wide view of the wonder before us.

The midnight blues of the Cambodian sky slowly filled with wisps of dark lavender as the full profile of the massive temple came into focus before our eyes. Resembling a delicate sandcastle, each increase in morning light revealed more and more intricate carvings on every exterior. The horizon dotted with towering palm trees and brightly unfurled fronds came alive before us.

As we sat in silence the firmament transmuted into every shade of orange imaginable. The fields and ponds were filled with rich amber, the thick mud of the earth became a warm red, and the outlines of the temple, a muted rust. The skies above exploded with shades of saffron and salmon, and it felt like the whole world was bathing in warm light. In the distance, we saw two humble figures approaching us down a winding footpath. Wrapped in flowing ginger-colored robes, chalky sandals, and shaven heads, both monks raised their gaze towards us with a warm smile - the only eyes, it seemed, not gazing towards the temple ruins and rising sun.

'Are we in their spot? Is this their temple we sat on? Have we disrespected the Gods?

Hoping we hadn't started our day by offending a pair of Buddhist monks, we sat in silence as they approached. Perching themselves on the ledge next to us, the four of us sat motionless for a few seconds that felt like hours.

'Are you allowed to talk to monks?'

The silence continued in a curious standoff.

"How are you?" one said through a growing smile and thick accent. "Great!" We happily responded, any hint of awkwardness instantly dissolving into the morning air.

As we sat together watching the sunrise envelop the ancient jungle around us, we shared a heartfelt and meaningful connection with these monks. Greeting us with warmth and genuine connection, they showed interest in who we were, why we were there, and in experiencing a little piece of their daily life with us. Eager to practice their English and understand our story, they allowed us to we pepper them with questions about theirs. Strangers no longer, we connected over the simple things in life while experiencing a daily wonder I opt to sleep through most days - the rising of our sun.

Lucky, Krishna, kind monks - all strangers one minute, inspiring human connections the next. I'd gone into each interaction fearing the unknown and came out the other side changed. Each one of them, champions of the Good News of the world, if you will, was confident in their beliefs, steadfast in their direction, and had captured the meaning of their own lives. Wherever I was willing to leave my comfort zone, the world continually revealed to me the basic goodness in the people I encountered.

'What you are to be, you now become.'

It was time to make the motto I kept chasing a little more permanent in my life. But how that ended up happening, I never saw coming.

Phnom Penh, Cambodia. November 2010

The rain just would not stop, it was a downright biblical monsoon rain - and it happened every day this time of year. Ryan and I had sat for nearly two full days in our dirt-cheap cramped and humid hotel room in Phnom Penh, a sputtering air conditioning unit rattling too loudly in the window to keep it on all night, waiting for the rain to stop. Moving on to the bustling Cambodian capital city after our time filming in Angkor Wat, we were happy to get soaked as long as it meant leaving this drab, cheap hotel room overlooking the outskirts of the bustling city.

We decided we couldn't spend another minute sitting there

and decided to head out on an adventure to see what Cambodia had in store for us. We cleaned our lenses, wrapped up all our gear, covered our cameras in plastic bags, and threw on our backpacks. Making our way to the curb in front of the hotel we flagged down the first bright yellow, chrome-plated tuk-tuk that passed, quickly cramming in our backpacks, equipment, and ourselves. "We'd like to visit the Killing Fields", I told the round-faced driver.

The Killing Fields, Pol Pot, and the Khmer Rouge are all a part of Cambodian history that is simply unavoidable when talking about the story of this culture, especially when it comes to the effects of an ongoing public health issue. We were there to document leprosy, after all. We had so much to learn, and we were about to get a lesson about Cambodia and its people we'd never forget.

To be honest, neither of us felt inclined to have much of a conversation with the driver, both sitting with eyes glazed over, staring at the passing fields and huts, heavy rain soaking our arms, happy to at last be out of the hotel room and on the move. Our driver, however, was pleased to have two young travelers in his tuk-tuk and wished to take the opportunity to practice his English and build a connection with us. We had a pleasant conversation for the first few minutes, talking about the endless rain, of course, and slowly made our way through the twists and turns of Phnom Penh towards the outer limits of the city. The concrete jungle of Phnom Penh dissipated behind us as we continued the 9-mile (15km) journey to The Killing Fields of Choeung EK.

"My name is Evan," he said as he turned around. It is quite common in Southeast Asian countries for the younger generation to take on Western-sounding nicknames. As the conversation continued, we realized the similarities between us and quickly warmed to each other. He and I were even born in the same year - 1984. I thought this guy must have been at least 10 years older, and after hearing about his life, we understood why, but that wouldn't be until hours later.

You have to work hard to find someone in Cambodia who doesn't have an intimate connection to the devastation the Khmer Rouge left behind during their reign of terror in the country. Between 1975-79, the fighting between Cambodia and the occupying Vietnamese communist army ravaged this country, not coming to a final end until 1989. In the end, Pol Pot's genocide killed between 1.5-2 million Cambodians, 25% of the entire population, and you can still see it on every street corner in the country, the deep violence experienced by so many of a single generation worn silently on the faces of so many locals.

In the 1990s, I was growing up a careless and carefree child, oblivious to the outside world around me, let alone across oceans. My only visions of the world outside of the United States were in the colorful and exotic images of those National Geographic magazines beckoning me to explore the wonders of the world. What I didn't know was that what lay between those pages was sometimes dark, violent, and senseless beyond my comprehension.

While I was learning to memorize the months of the year, Evan was asking his mother why her brother had no legs and why he didn't have grandparents. I couldn't help but feel the first-world privilege dripping off me again as I sat there listening to him speak, which made me uncomfortable in my own skin, feeling deeply ashamed I did not know more about this country's history.

As soon as we finally splashed our way into the flooded muddy parking lot of the Killing Fields, the rain picked up again and absolutely unleashed on us, but we didn't mind anymore, happy to spend the extra time waiting in conversation with our new Cambodian friend. Hidden under the flimsy protection of the thin plastic that covered his little yellow tuk-tuk, we awaited every word that came out of his mouth, feeling increasing shock and horror from the stories he was telling us so matter-of-factly.

The Killing Fields are literal fields on the outskirts of the Cambodian capital city, marked by sunken, dirt holes, where thousands of bodies of slaughtered Cambodians were once discovered. Exiting the tuk-tuk, Ryan and I grabbed our gear in somber silence, both out of respect for the place in which we found ourselves as well as in response to the feeling of knowing what had happened here. We didn't intend to, but we ended up walking in separate directions, both making our way through this haunting landscape in our own way, at our own pace.

Now simply marked by small brown, wooden hand-painted signs, with the number of bodies discovered in each, those sunken dirt holes stand as silent shadows of the horrors of history—what the worst of humanity is capable of. 800 children in this one, 450 women in the next, and on and on and on as far as you can walk for as long as you can handle it. In total, 8,895 bodies were discovered here after the fall of the Khmer Rouge regime. Most of these victims were political prisoners hauled to this former orchard from the Tuol Sleng (S21) prison in Phnom Penh, a former high school and one of the most brutal and feared of Pol Pot's prisons.

Looking over the pockmarked terrain, I could see Ryan standing motionless, surveying the scene in front of him, tripod slung over his shoulder, eyes almost at his feet. The burden of the history presented before us weighed on his mind in real time as raindrops the size of marbles pelted down on his stoic profile.

Navigating the dirt holes that lay before me, now half filled with monsoon rain and alive with the last remaining raindrops falling into the muddy brown waters, the reality of what these fields had witnessed was unavoidable, unfathomable. Being in such a devastatingly tragic place elicited a deeply human response in me as the thought of what had taken place there engulfed my mind, merging with dizzying unbeckoned replays of my privileged childhood - more fortunate than I had ever realized to have had one that was devoid of terror, genocide and the never-ending stench of extinguished human life and potential.

At the center of the Killing Fields stands a huge monument "Choeung EK", a towering obelisk made of more than 5,000 human skulls, silent and screaming through its presence so that humanity can never forget what happened here. Whether you've read every book on history or only learn about the Killing Fields when you arrive in Cambodia, you won't leave the same person as when you arrived. The Killing Fields offers equal opportunity impact whether you want it or not.

We filmed the clips we needed for the documentary mostly in silence, unsure how the frames we captured here would begin to tell the story of what this country had witnessed. Climbing back in the tuk-tuk, we struggled to convey to Evan our understanding of the gravity of what happened to his people. We let the sounds of the rain drown out the further conversation we would have had, remaining lost in our own thoughts instead.

After some time had passed, asked Evan if he would allow us to interview him and record his incredible story. We had no idea how it would fit into our documentary, but we both felt deeply that it deserved to be told, to be remembered, to be recorded. "Of course," he said, "But only if we become friends first." He asked us if we had any plans and if we'd like to see where he lived. "Let's go!" we chimed in unison.

Ryan and I were gradually recognizing the beautiful opportunity the world had given to us - the opportunity to forget about work, forget about our filming schedule, about getting the shots on the shot list, and connecting instead with the very people who were more a part to our human story than we'd ever be. When we needed it most, the world had just orchestrated another encounter with a stranger in a country as different from ours as could possibly be, one of the most precious gifts travel can give.

Chatting with Evan as he drove back toward the outskirts of the city, we heard about his family, his childhood, and his story We heard about where he went to school and about his family members who had been killed or maimed or vanished. We were both stunned at the friendly and upbeat attitude he possessed after going through all that he described. But, of course, we are all products of our environment, and this was his. He'd known nothing else, just like my Dad being raised in the American Mormon Utah of the 1950s. Evan wasn't ignoring or brushing off his past, because he had decided to embrace life and live it to the fullest, while giving his history the respect it deserved. From the bright banana yellow plastic seat of his squeaky tuk-tuk winding through the streets of Phnom Penh, in the pelting monsoon rains with two strangers, on the way to his home village, he was giving us a master class in history, perspective, and what it means to be human.

The loud sputtering engine was drowning out some of our

exchange, so he asked if we wanted to meet his friends and family as well. Ryan and I didn't need half a second to answer that question. We were 100% up for whatever Evan chose to reveal to us. Winding through an endless ocean of motorbikes and crosswalks, we entered a neighborhood far from the tourist center. Pulling into a small gravel driveway next to a concrete building with nothing more than a few windows, our small little yellow tuk-tuk came to a stop just as the sun started to go down across the hazy horizon. As spiraling smoke slowly circled from the chimney, we were only illuminated by the dull broken glow of a solitary flickering street lamp hovering overhead.

Stepping into the small cafe, we were clearly out of place—two foreigners abroad in an otherwise local hangout. The tables were plastic, the chairs too, Angkor beer logos splashed across them all. Smoke from both cigarettes and a flaming BBQ mixed in the air, Cambodian instrumental music was playing far too loud, crackling out of speakers with a loose wire, but no one seemed to care. The scene was perfect. At the far end of the room, three tables had been pushed together to hold the dozen local men sitting around them who motioned for us to join - reeling us toward them like a lost ship at sea to a lighthouse in the distance—friendly strangers eager to connect.

Beers were poured and repoured, strange plates of vegetables and peanuts appeared on the table out of nowhere, platters of unknown meats arrived by the dozen, and competing smells overpowered our noses. Introduced to each man one by one, Ryan and I learned that they were all tuk-tuk drivers like Evan, and all had a common background. They had come together to share their stories with us, two strangers from another world who had shown interest in hearing about their lives.

'I will not fear what I don't understand.'

116

Only one or two of them spoke enough English to communicate with us, but over the course of many hours that evening, we sat together laughing, telling stories, and sharing our lives. We arm wrestled, had chopstick peanut eating contests, devoured pints of watered-down local beer, and laughed. One guy was named John Rambo, another was Elvis.

But it was one particular man's story that stuck with me the most.

His Western name was "Part", a random word to us, a Western name that hardly stood out among his friends. Part was a bit older than most of the drivers assembled that night and quite clearly had first-hand experience with the horrors of the Khmer Rouge. He only had one leg, and in Cambodia, chances are better than not that this was either from direct fighting or from stepping on a landmine, which, we soon learned, is what had happened in his case. Part had been more reserved than the others during our rowdy conversation, with few words uttered during the meal, but he listened eagerly and was always smiling warmly when we made eye contact. He was shy, but his eyes clearly had a story behind them.

At only 12 years old, the fighting was growing closer to his village, and as the only male left in his home, he made the impossible decision to leave his female family members and join the resistance on the front lines in the wooded area near his home. While I was busy at 12 years old watching Allen Iverson's rookie season in the NBA, hearing The Macarena on repeat, and trying to sneak into the theater to see the new Tom Cruise movie *"Mission Impossible"*, Part was trying to keep his remaining family members alive before he hit puberty.

Part said he fought for years, unequipped, unskilled, and untrained—with little support and zero compensation. He lost his leg trying to protect his family and it is something that he is, and should be, fiercely proud of to this day.

Sitting there in those plastic chairs sharing stories around the table in a smoke-filled roadside hangout on the outskirts of Phnom Penh, those lyrics again popped into my head.

'What you are to be, you now become. I will not fear what I do not understand.'

At that moment, faced again with the huge impact strangers can have on your journey, I made a decision. Lucky, Krishna, monks, volunteers, strangers in a far-off village - they had shown me the light in the world, and I wanted to remember them for it. Eager to cement the value of chasing the unknown and the rich gifts it can offer, I made up my mind.

With the help of our new friend Evan, I was able to hear my signature lyrics spoken in Khmer, the local language, and I asked Part if he would hand write them for me on a piece of scratch paper I pulled from my backpack. "I want to remember your story forever," I told him. His hands were shaking. He didn't know how to write well, but with painstaking precision, sitting together as friends, he wrote out my two increasingly important life mottos in Khmer. Just as Evan had requested, we had heard their life stories, but only after we had become friends.

The evening never seemed to end, suspended in smiles and laughter until the wee hours of the morning. The day had started with Ryan and I staring at unending monsoon rains from a stale hotel room, and it was ending with more life lessons about history, culture, war, friendship, and community than we could even begin to process. Stumbling back into Evan's silver and yellow tuk-tuk, he handed the keys to Ryan to drive us back to our hotel. "Look, you're driving a tuk-tuk in Cambodia!" Evan screamed over blaring Cambodian pop music while all three of us laughed like we'd been best friends since childhood.

I've gotten many tattoos on my travels, from Athens to Tbilisi, to Los Angeles to Thailand, but my first, and favorite, will always be Part's handwriting across my chest in his beautiful Khmer prose - two mottos of my life staring back at me every morning in the mirror. They continue to remind me of those I met along the way and how they have helped me to understand the world and my role in it—to know that what I am to be, I am now becoming and to never fear whatever I don't understand.

I hadn't found home yet, and still didn't know where I belonged, but I continued to follow those who had and to pick up breadcrumbs to illuminate my treasure map along the way. They'll always be a "Part" of me.

But no matter how much I wished otherwise, I couldn't escape my own life forever, by setting across the globe to chase yet another story that belonged to someone else. Before long, I found myself back in Los Angeles faced with the monumental task of editing terabytes of footage into a coherent story —and still no clue how to turn any of it into a career.

11

Belonging: Long Live the Red, White, and... Bleh?

"Home isn't where you're from, it's where you find light when all grows dark."
– Pierce Brown

Los Angeles, California, USA, Winter 2012

"This is your home now, but it won't be forever, Mima would quip with a smile, hands a blur with pancake mix and bacon grease as she whipped up breakfast for me in the small 1950s beach house where I'd spent my summers growing up. My grandmother was a maniac in the best sense of the word. She often told my mother that without religion holding her together, she'd be topless on the back of a Harley-Davidson. If it was religion that was keeping her from doing that, I was all for it.

But California was my home now, as she so emphatically stated. Ironically, by the time I moved to the same small, cozy, beach town to go to Brooks, she'd already called it home for nearly fifty years, and now that I'd graduated, I suspect she felt justified in taking on some parenting responsibilities herself. She'd made the same move to California as a teen too, jumping on a train from Utah to the shining lights of Los Angeles, arriving overwhelmed at Union Station in the 1940s and never turning back. She wanted the same for me as well, to take a leap and never look back, but she could tell that I was scared, too.

I was too immature to absorb much parenting or life advice from anyone - even after graduating and well into my 20s. What if I could "make it" in LA? Shouldn't I stick it out to see? What if my big break was just around the corner? Maybe I'd meet someone who would connect me to National Geographic? Or the Discovery Channel?

I knew how cool it seemed to friends back in D.C. that I was living in Los Angeles, CA, and that I'd just finished going around the world to "shoot a movie". I never went out of my way to correct any misconceptions of what I did, happy to let my legend proceed me, because I still didn't have anything better to correct them with. I was safe from rejection when I was in school, but as soon as I graduated from Brooks and was released into the wild and unforgiving creative scene in Los Angeles, I shrank back into my shell. Ryan and I had finished STIGMA, and it had played in some film festivals and even won some awards - but it certainly hadn't sparked any next steps for either of us. Too proud to leave the city, too intimidated to put myself in a position to fail and risk the anthill of clout I felt like I had, I just stagnated.

I'd graduated with the "Outstanding Achievement Award", which, in the small confines of that school, felt like winning an Oscar as I stood up in a bright red suit on stage, accepting the award at graduation, but when I stepped into real life in Los

Angeles, that award felt more like a participation medal you'd give a 6-year-old with a pat on the back – something you would put in a macaroni frame and stick on your fridge door with a brightly colored magnet rather than a badge of honor that I could use to win my way into interviews.

Echo Park, a neighborhood that was on the fringes of L.A. and home to the cheapest rent when I'd moved there after graduation, was becoming too popular now, the hipsters pouring in and tripling the price of a latte overnight, bringing oat milk with them. I didn't recognize myself in the changing city, didn't see a place for me, and felt like a fraud. Desperate for work, I freelanced, I applied to jobs I'd never get, I stood outside a Target and harassed people to sign petitions for $1 a signature. I had seven interviews for one job, a junior print producer at a publication company, a job for which I was far too overqualified. I started on a Monday and was fired before lunch on Wednesday, my check for $68 arriving in the mail a couple of weeks later. "It's just not a good fit." a pair of HR reps muttered as they slid a white document across a large glass conference table for me to sign.

'How can anyone get ahead here?'

I had accepted that long hours were just part of what came next for me, accepted that I'd ride the wave until I burned out like I saw so many friends do - white knuckle any job no matter how miserable, because that's what you had to do to live in the City of Angels. And you know what? I was still jealous of those friends, because they were part of a machine. No matter how miserable they might be, they were part of *something*, while I was, once again, sitting outside looking in, with the confidence of a deflated circus balloon.

A starry-eyed hopeful in a sea of starry-eyed hopefuls, many of whom were silently screaming with the same crippling imposter syndrome I had, I felt so deeply isolated. I worked so hard, and spent so much time, money, and energy on getting my degree so I could be a visual storyteller - but I couldn't get anyone to pay me for anything, let alone to tell their story with pictures. And now I was facing the thought of shredding an image and life in LA that I had spent nearly a decade working to build.

But the difference between myself and those around me was they were presumably able to organize their thoughts, make sound decisions, and plan out their next logical steps. Whether or not the long hours, endless demands, or corporate dysfunction ate away at them, they had tools I did not have to combat these things or had somehow mastered how to use their minds to their advantage, which never failed to baffle me.

I thought I was on top of the world when I graduated, but two years later, I was ground down, had lost all hope, and had no idea where to turn next. That $10,000 loan I'd taken out before flying to South Africa to meet Lucky was nearly down to double digits, because the cost of living in LA was monstrous without a job. Despite the happy face and go-lucky attitude, I was running out of options, no longer able to convince myself there was a path ahead for me in California.

"Hey man, great to see you - you're doing awesome with the National Geographic photography!" an old high school acquaintance clamored excitely as we made small talk over a humming crowd at a friend's gallery opening one evening. "Oh, thanks, man." I said quickly - too thrown and proud to correct him at the moment. "Wait," I said a split second later "I don't work for National Geographic, hopefully, one day though." He'd seen the photos I'd posted from those trips to India or

Bangladesh, some clips posted from STIGMA, and assumed it was a career rather than a glorified, self-funded field trip. The small talk ended, and the moment turned stale, he went to refill his drink. I stood awkwardly alone, exposed.

'Maybe he's right – time to chase that dream. It's the only way out of LA. I just don't belong here anymore.'

The truth was that that was my dream job, the one I had always dreamed of and hoped the world would serve me up on a silver platter. The other, more confronting truth was that I didn't have the confidence to truly pursue it, and while all I wanted was to be off traveling the world, being paid to capture stunning moments of people, culture, nature, and rituals throughout far-flung civilizations, I never had the guts to do what would be necessary to make it happen. I was too paralyzed by the idea of having a photo editor pay me for work, and I wasn't confident enough to capture images and submit myself. I was too timid to put myself to the test and too proud to buckle down and do the inner work needed to get there.

So here I was at 28, my entire career ahead of me, giving up on making it in LA and thinking of packing up all my belongings – fleeing reality for the other side of the world again, this time with a girlfriend who, while on a completely different journey, saw an escape to Thailand as a distraction from the work ahead of her as well. "It's just too saturated with people in the industry here, man." I'd say when friends asked why I was leaving. I knew it was an answer few could argue with, and the conversations wouldn't need to go much further - but it wasn't the truth, either. The hollow feeling that came every time a job application went unanswered, awkward coffee meetings that didn't lead anywhere, and 15-hour unpaid camera gigs for the chance at an IMDB credit was all-consuming. It was time to pack it up, and I only knew one place to go – the first place I'd run away to and found any meaning.

'*Back to Thailand. That should buy me some time.*'

A complete cop-out, returning to Thailand was far less grand than I made it out to be on social media. I knew the adventure and wanderlust that it would exude would mask my utter lack of direction or meaning under the surface, but I also knew that few would be able to see through it. Once again, I was giving myself to the world and hoping, praying, that any direction at all would emerge once the plane landed, but of course that's not how life usually works, and deep down I knew it, too.

Within days, my room was packed up, cheap IKEA furniture distributed to my remaining roommates, and my dusty travel trophies removed one by one from the shelves and stuffed in stacked boxes. Once proud to display them as shiny talismans from my treasure hunt for meaning, placing them side by side in beat-up boxes ready for storage was a sobering reminder that I had yet to find any.

* * *

If you have ever been to Long Beach, CA, sailing down a winding maze of twisting freeway lanes and off-ramps, you may have driven past my things, my stuff, the proof I exist in this world. Sure, I travel with a laptop and a couple of extra t-shirts, but my stuff, my physical memories are stored behind a small, metal door in a storage unit in Long Beach, California between an auto body shop and a gardening center.

Days before moving to Thailand for the second time, in early

2013, I rented the smallest storage unit available and placed the few remaining possessions I had inside - but it wasn't filled with old clothes and furniture. Postcards and snowglobes never did it for me - I always wanted to bring back more unique things when I traveled, which meant this storage unit was filled with some pretty odd things - odd things that all held immense value to me and no one else. An intact bottle of wine I'd found in the Tsunami wreckage almost a decade earlier, boxes of my grandfather's antique cameras, lots of foreign money, and mysterious masks. Currency from Bolivia to Botswana, Egypt to Ecuador, and everywhere in between, useless one hundred trillion dollar notes from Zimbabwe next to out-of-commission Soviet Union bills. I love imagining the things they've seen, the hands they've passed through, the web of people, and the stories they connect, all stuffed in an old cigar box. I've collected metal masks and wooden ones, painted and carved, stone and tin, each with their own backstory, sitting together in beat-up cardboard boxes, wrapped in old t-shirts, eyes forever open, staring into the darkness behind that small metal door in that tiny storage unit in Long Beach – until I return one day. Compulsively collecting these trinkets from around the globe, I thought merely possessing them would bring me the clarity and direction I was so desperate to find.

A decade earlier, I'd left college after the tsunami in Thailand to escape having to find a direction in my studies. Once again, I was escaping to Thailand, trying to flee the inevitable fact that my career seemed to have no direction, and I wasn't willing to face the discomfort required to push it further. And for my girlfriend, I represented someone who would help her conquer the unknown, navigate the anxiety of international travel, and distract her from her own journey until she was ready to face it.

No matter how many times I moved, uprooting my life, leaving behind scores of close friends, and starting fresh with nothing, I was always in search of two things. I was in search of a partner, a companion, someone with whom to share my adventurous search so I didn't feel so insane doing it alone. And I was looking for belonging, always thinking I'd find both at the end of the next runway – a kindly stewardess coming on the loudspeaker when the wheels squeaked down – Ding! "Welcome home, you are now free to move about your life. Enjoy – you're crushing it!"

Instead, the announcement was closer to – Ding! "Welcome to the middle of nowhere, you don't know anyone here and have no idea why you boarded this plane. Good luck figuring it all out, you idiot!"

That is exactly how I felt as the wheels skidded to a stop at the Phuket International Airport in March 2013, an awkward excitement masking the deafening reality that we had no plan and no goal. We'd escaped LA. Now what?

Tel Aviv, Israel. March 2014

In the Spring of 2014, I found myself in the lowest place on earth, not emotionally (that was still a few months away), but physically. An old friend from Brooks lived in the city and had offered his apartment while he was out of town for a few weeks, and I'd jumped at the chance to visit a new country. It was only March, but the sun was relentlessly beating down on my neck as I walked the muddy shores of the Dead Sea, some sixty miles southeast of Tel Aviv.

I wasn't hoping for some deep clarity or insight to come to me, but the sounds of horrible techno music a few hundred yards away on the beach didn't enhance the mood. For better or worse, that music was mostly drowned out by the burning sensation on the soft skin of my feet as I crossed the hot mud, baking in the scorching Israeli heat on the banks of this surreal landscape. Where I had come for some relaxation and a cultural experience, others were just coming to enjoy a rowdy afternoon in the sun with friends.

Naomi wasn't your average 22-year-old. We both went to the Waldorf school together when we were children growing up outside Washington, D.C. We didn't cross paths too much then, only knowing each other because our community was so small. Our families' kids spread out across many of the lower-class grades together. Her father, Rob, a mentor of mine for years, had always been a stoic male figure in our small school community, happy to pass down what wisdom he could whenever given the chance, regardless of the years between conversations.

So when I landed in Tel Aviv a few days earlier, it was only natural to reach out to Naomi, like finding a long-lost sibling on the other side of the world. I didn't know the first thing about Israel, only the trauma and pain the region had dealt with for the last 65 years since the Israeli War of Independence in the late 1940s. But Naomi, herself Jewish, had felt the call to join the Israeli army a few years prior and had uprooted her entire life to be here - one of the few female snipers in her division, I'd been told.

I was in awe of how seamlessly she fit into the culture there –dusty army fatigues rolled up as she drove us the sixty miles from Tel Aviv to the Dead Sea, effortlessly speaking Hebrew at every military checkpoint we passed, dirt particles bouncing through the hot air in her truck as we bumped down endless desert roads through ever more desolate scenes.

We swam in the Dead Sea all afternoon, or floated rather - swimming is impossible since the salt content is eight times higher than any ocean in the world - leaving us magically buoyant on the shining surface some 2,000 feet (61m) below sea level, at the lowest point on earth.

I didn't even hear the music blasting from the SUV parked down the beach after a while. My mind somehow blocked out the thumping of the bass and replaced it with the awe I felt just floating on the surface of the moon, bathing in the silky smooth ancient minerals covering my body - chloride, bromide, magnesium, and potassium.

The crystal clear, blue waters contrasted so sharply with the jagged, white-crusted red rock formations around the edges of the sea - a crater in the middle of the earth from a different millennium.

Naomi had found her home, her belonging - or at least the place that spoke to the depths of her soul louder than anywhere else in the world had to that point. I wanted that, to find a place and a culture I couldn't imagine not having in my life. I instantly recognized it in her, and it was beautiful. Even if this was just a passing phase, just a chapter of her story, she was living it boldly, passionately, and with no regrets.

Back in Tel Aviv that night, we sat on cheap plastic stools eating crispy, hot falafel, and creamy homemade hummus in the warm Israeli evening breeze. I went to sleep feeling invigorated, thrilled to see how an old friend had found her sense of home in this great, big, confusing world. I left Israel further impassioned to find mine. I just had to keep searching for it, continue stacking those breadcrumbs of experiences my Dad never had that I was nevertheless certain would land me at the finish line.

Phuket, Thailand, Spring 2014

A few months after arriving in Thailand for the second time, my girlfriend and I had enough remote video editing work to pay the bills but barely enough to save for more than a fun night out on Bangla Road, the debaucherous tourist heartbeat of the island. One humid evening, sweat sticking my thighs to a cheap plastic office chair, I was Skyping with my parents back in Maryland when they first brought up they'd bought a small house in Cuenca, Ecuador. It was a city I'd never heard of and a country I only knew because of a 5th-grade report I'd done on the Galapagos Islands. For years, Ecuador represented for me, not the rebirth of my parents, but the very real end to my "home" as I knew it - in the most literal and physical sense of the word.

It was the first conversation of many which would, over the next couple of months, end with them quite quickly selling the house in which I grew up in in Silver Spring, MD, and packing up all my belongings into storage units. Emptying the only home I'd ever known, they loaded all their stuff into a shipping container sailing to South America, which would arrive a couple months after they did.

How could I blame them? I'd taken my entire life overseas many times at this point, more often than not to a time zone which made picking up the phone for a quick call difficult without prior planning.

They'd mentioned Cuenca a few times before, and I knew they had traveled there d together, but there is still a shock when you hear that your childhood home is going to be sold, especially when you'll never get to step foot in it again. I was more than 9,000 miles away and couldn't afford the cost to fly back just to take one last look at my bedroom, or a second to smell the smell of *home* one step inside the front door, just one last time.

But they were following their path, chasing their dream, following their breadcrumbs, and finding their new version of home far off in an unknown land high in the Andes. They were searching for their 'belonging', too. They were on the same journey I was on, of course, in a different part of the same circle.

Who says the quest to find your home only happens once and must be done by the time you start a family? To some, finding home is a physical location, to others, it is an emotional state. To me, - and to my parents, I'd learned - it seemed to be both. And it seemed to take a lot of jet lag and airline miles to find it.

When you start traveling, it's a bit like taking the red pill over the blue one. As soon as you step on that first plane, alone, and head out into the world, there is no turning back. No matter how hard you try, you'll always know there is more to explore, a pull at the back of your mind like a child tugging at your pant leg, refusing to let you forget they are there. You've seen the other side, caught a glimpse of what is out there, and it takes hold of you.

Some people can live with this feeling, knowing the world is always out there, appreciate their travel experiences for what they are, and integrate them into their daily lives. For others, the pull is much stronger, like a beckoning call, whenever life gets tough, to jump on the next plane to nowhere in particular - just one more hit. I've answered that call for years.

* * *

Realizing that home, and belonging, are not only physical places but also feelings, is one of the most powerful lessons about life that travel has taught me. While few get the opportunity, as adults, to revisit their childhood home, untouched since they grew up, it doesn't mean that things that evoke the same feelings or emotions can't be found, or created, around the world, if you decide you are going to create them.

Go out into the world. Find that feeling of home, and chase the smells, sounds, and faces that make you feel comfortable. They may not be found inside the four walls of the home in which you grew up, or even in the city or country where you spent your childhood, for that matter, but follow each road ahead, and see where it leads you. They say 'all roads lead to Rome' and while a few I followed indeed had, no matter how many roads I went down, none seemed to be heading back to America, the place I always thought would be home at the end of my road, the place to which I always thought I'd return.

However, before I could find home, wherever it may be, surrounded by the comfortable and familiar, I had to get more uncomfortable, over and over again. Sometimes it was overcoming a fear, confronting a lack of confidence, or feeling exposed to the world, but before anything else, I needed to feel at home in my own body.

And for me, I found all of the above at the base of a waterfall, high in the jungles of Southeast Asia.

12

Get Comfortable Being Uncomfortable: Never Regret a Swim

"Twenty years from now you will be more disappointed by the things you didn't do than by the ones you did do. So throw off the bowlines. Sail away from the safe harbor. Catch the trade winds in your sails. Explore. Dream. Discover." - Mark Twain

Phuket, Thailand. September 2013

Moving from Los Angeles, CA to Phuket, Thailand with a girlfriend I knew I'd never marry, with problems I knew wouldn't get solved by importing them to the other side of the world, didn't feel like a forward step, but it was a step nonetheless. I wasn't strong enough to end the relationship, and if I'm being honest, my rose-tinted glasses were wearing rose-tinted glasses - always holding out a sliver of hope things would improve. And when you're looking through the world with rose-tinted glasses, reg flags just look like...flags.

Nearly ten years earlier, when I'd lived in Thailand for the first time, I had felt more alive than ever. I felt important, like what I was doing mattered – and like it was an acceptable thing to be doing at that age. Now, nearing 30, it felt too predictable, played out, and repetitive. While my girlfriend may have had her own problems she was trying to escape from, I had mine too. Doing it together only distracted me from them for a bit, but it felt like buying a new TV with a high-interest credit card. We'd be fine for a little and then get bitten in the ass down the road.

As long as I kept running, moving on to the next adventure before the ink had dried on the passport stamp of the last, the only thing the world expected of me was to sort basic elements of survival – to find shelter, food, and water. But if I stopped, even for a minute, I'd be forced to think about retirement, a 401k, dental visits, and blood glucose.

'A problem for another day, dude!'

A couple of months after we settled in Karon Beach on the southwest side of Phuket island, one of my best friends, David, and his girlfriend came to visit – two familiar faces in a new world we were eager to show them. We found ourselves winding our way through lush green, unknown jungle roads, the noises of the sputtered engines of our twin motorbikes trailing behind us as we searched for the Bang Pae Waterfall in the remote Pak Lok region in the north of the island.

Phuket doesn't have many waterfalls, and while Bang Pae is its largest, it's not all that impressive, even during the summer season when there are steady rains, but the 20-minute hike through the sticky Thai jungle is worth it. Bright-colored tropical plants dot the trail, accompanied by the slow and constant drone of the rescued gibbons that are housed in the same forest, and the endless buzz of exotic, and unnerving-looking, insects. Something for the senses at every turn.

As we walked up the thin, muddy path between scattered rocks, vines brushing our ankles and elbows, I was certain that each touch was something looking to eat me. Thailand has over 200 types of snakes, including what the locals call "boomslang", a flying tree snake which can launch itself over 100 feet (30 m) to escape a predator and can grow up to 5 feet (1.5 m) in length. It is considered "mildly venomous" which gave me no comfort.

'How can something be mildly venomous?!'

A high-pitched scream pierced through the drone of insects, accompanied by flailing arms and rustling branches as my girlfriend frantically tried to escape the innocent strap of her backpack, grazing her neck the wrong way.

Following the eerie calls of the gibbons that filled the trees around us, we emerged into a clearing at the base of a true jungle waterfall, the last few turns navigated by following its muffled roar. I hadn't even thought to bring a bathing suit with me, although I knew we were going to a waterfall, on an island, in 100+ degree humid September heat. That's how little I wanted to go swimming. "Jeff, c'mon man, you'll never regret a swim!" David said with a spark in his eye, a mop of disheveled sandy brown hair atop his head, already stripped down to his boxers. His challenge was at least half genuine, knowing full well that he was prodding me out of my comfort zone for both his delight and my personal development.

'I knew this would happen.'

"My Mom always tells me that, and it's never been wrong," he said, stepping his feet in the water, refusing to accept I wouldn't join him. He knew I was uncomfortable but wouldn't let up. The fact our girlfriends were there to witness the exchange only added humor to my humiliation. His intent wasn't malice, but I struggled to find the amusement in any of it.

I was never the first to jump in the pool at a summer birthday party, never the first to suggest a trip to the beach or the lake on a weekend. It's not because I don't love to swim, I've just never loved my own body enough to be quick to show it off. I started adding on the weight in high school at about 15 or 16, and my self-confidence plummeting as fast as the weight ballooned. 230lb, 240lb, 265lb. By the time I graduated from the Waldorf School at 18, I was "Big Jeff" to many, and as I went off to college a few months later, this had only increased, quickly becoming part of my identity and something I tried to own faster than anyone could place the label on me.

I tried to hide the vulnerability by wearing it like armor.

I'd tell myself I came off as someone girls could feel safe and protected around and someone guys wouldn't want to mess with. The higher the scale, the larger the shield I wielded. In reality, I was just another overweight American teen, well on my way to prediabetes, joint problems, and heart disease if I didn't act soon. In a 2021 survey, a shocking 44% of American college students described themselves as overweight or obese. Nearly 8.4 million students were feeling the same discomfort in their bodies as I was, no matter how individual the struggle felt to me. But having rail-thin, darkly tanned locals staring at me now like a misplaced snowman high in the Thai jungle, made me all the more self-conscious.

So, as our girlfriends stood to the edge and watched, feeling torn between retreating to what was comfortable or trying to be cool and join in, I reluctantly stripped down to my boxers too, porcelain white love handles bouncing atop a tight elastic band, displaying them proudly to the world.

Perched on the nearby rocks, the local Thai families had a

137

good laugh as the two of us *farangs* (what the Thais call western foreigners), pasty as the clouds and standing in our boxers, slowly waded into the surprisingly cold waters at the base of that 50 foot (15 m) waterfall tucked into the Thai jungle. The water was freezing, the shallow pools barely deep enough to cover our snowflake white kneecaps as we chuckled and our girlfriends watched in amusement from the nearby slate gray boulders dotting the water's edge. David was laughing at the sight of us, I was nervously giggling at what creatures may be lurking in the dark water we were wading into - too uncomfortable to stand there exposed, too uncomfortable to get into the water either. Based on the exotic screaming insects in the jungle surrounding us, I wanted nothing to do with whatever amphibious vermin were now surrounding our lower bodies.

But I didn't regret that swim, and haven't regretted one since, no matter how hard it was for me to strip down and get into the water that day. There is something about connecting with nature in such a primal way that is impossible to regret. In the decade since our adventure swimming in the Thai jungle, I have thought of David and that quote many, many times. Not only have I never once regretted a swim since then, but that experience has encouraged me to swim at times when a sane person may have decided otherwise. When I am faced with the chance to swim, even if I'm not convinced or it's not convenient, more times than not, I will strip down and take the plunge.

'You never regret a swim!'

Sometimes it is the most random-seeming piece of advice that can lodge itself in your brain and come back to the forefront of your mind over and over, finding any excuse to be relevant in your life when you need it most - and for me, that is some-times taking any chance I can to enjoy a swim, no matter the destination, season, or wardrobe.

We all have those points of vulnerability, and I hope to continue to uncover and expose new ones as I travel, but this was a big one, and one that stuck in my mind and continued to come back time and again after I realized it, providing me with countless great memories along the road after I decided to embrace the feeling and never regret a swim.

Travel is filled with encounters with strangers from different backgrounds, cultures, stories, upbringings, and perspectives – and many of them will share their own pearls of wisdom, their own one-line bits of life advice, an eclectic mix of valuable tools and guidance they've picked up from their own life journeys. Some will ring true to you, others will fall flat, and some may not even make a shred of sense at all. But listen to them all, especially the ones that make you uncomfortable.

* * *

Returning to the white sand of Karon Beach later that afternoon, the four of us laid out our towels on the hot sandy beach, and sweaty from the hike and long motorbike ride back, headed for the cool waters of the Andaman Sea. After our morning swim in the jungle, this one was a breeze. By that point, I was too hot to be self-conscious, but it came with a difficult conversation too.

Slowly floating away from our girlfriends, the chatter between David and me dipped as we enjoyed the calm of the salty bobbing waves against the warm afternoon wind. "Hey man, don't take this the wrong way." David began after a reflective pause. I already knew where he was going. After 25 years of friendship, it didn't need to be said to be understood, but it was still important that he said it out loud. "I don't think she's the one for..."

"I know." Without looking up, I cut him off before he could finish, the salt of the seawater stinging my blotchy red neck.

No amount of Pad Thai and sunscreen could cover the fact that I was running from my life, running from my problems, and had selfishly expanded that to include a partner doing the same. And while it made us both feel better on the surface, our relationship had an expiration date that neither of us wanted to talk about - but David did. And as all good friends do, he needed to tell me that he was watching, hoping for something better and supporting me to make the difficult next step. It wouldn't be easy, and it took a few months, but I'd had my confirmation from a close friend who was brave enough to say the quiet part out loud, confirming my own internal dialogue.

And so a year later, I found myself stripped down to much less than my boxers - this time emotionally, the lowest place I'd ever gone and the most alone I'd ever been, and it all happened only a couple miles from Karon Beach where David and I had our chat in the ocean on that hot afternoon.

No amount of swimming could save me now. I just had to try and stay afloat.

13

Embrace the Struggle: Chicken, Mustard, and a Bowl Full of Tears

"Growing up is never easy. You hold on to things that were. You wonder what's to come. But that night, I think we knew it was time to let go of what had been and look ahead to what would be. Other days. New days. Days to come. The thing is, we didn't have to hate each other for getting older. We just had to forgive ourselves... for growing up." –The Wonder Years

Phuket, Thailand. August 2014

Waking up on my 30th birthday, I felt more alone than ever, surrounded by stillness in a tiny 540 square foot (50 sqm) apartment in Phuket, Thailand. I was single, unemployed, overweight, had no friends or family within thousands of miles, and the path ahead for my life was pitch black, without the faintest light guiding me where to go next.

It wasn't the fact that my girlfriend and I had broken up and she'd moved back to Los Angeles a few weeks earlier that had left me so numb. (That relationship had ended months earlier, and we'd both finally admitted it was time to move on after living like stale roommates for too long .) It was because, for the first time in my life, I truly felt like I had nothing, and I had nowhere to run. The relationship had left me exhausted, questioning my self-worth, taking on problems that weren't mine, and absorbing them slowly over time. And I'd gotten used to an extremely cheap cost of living. I couldn't have even afforded to make it back to LA if a job was waiting for me at the end of the runway when I landed.

Thai apartments like mine were tiny, yet efficient. For $150/month, you can't really complain. Wifi and water bills combined for just $6/month. My motorbike parked outside was another $15/month, and it took me a week to go through a $2 tank of gas. My living costs were practically nothing, but I also *had* practically nothing.

The bed was behind a sliding glass door so the air conditioning needed to cool it was minimal, only inches separating the walls and surrounding bed frame. I could open the sliding window from the bed with my foot and the condensation that dripped down each morning created endless pathways of dancing droplets I stared at, lost for hours as the humidity outside met the cool chill of the sputtering AC I couldn't sleep without. There was a tiny kitchen with a tiny hotplate and a tiny table with a chair too tiny for me to sit on. The bathroom contained a sink, toilet, and shower that were all practically on top of each other - no shower complete without thoroughly soaking all three. And the walls were paper thin.

The small group of friends I'd made while living in Thailand the last year were mostly teachers at the international school and had all either moved away to assignments in other countries, like Peru or Singapore, or were gone for the summer, off traveling around Southeast Asia before the next school year started. I didn't have a job because I was previously editing tutorial videos through a contract my ex had, which she took back to the US with her. I didn't have a home because I was renting this tiny apartment month-to-month, and I had no idea what I was going to do next. And then, on this particular day, I turned thirty.

I started to cry. I cried a lot. I cried about being single. I cried about being alone. I cried about being overweight. I cried about having no drive, no discipline, no motivation. I cried about having no job, and I cried about having no money. I cried about having no home and being so far from the homes I'd always known, which no longer existed. I cried about Washington losing every single football game, (but that wasn't anything new - I'd been crying about that for as long as I could remember).

And I cried because all I was eating was a bowl of chicken and mustard on my birthday - my *thirtieth* birthday.

'Aren't I supposed to have it all figured out by now!?'

My main interactions for weeks had been reserved for the giggling teen clerks at the 7-11 and the waitress at the corner restaurant who would start preparing my cashew nut chicken and egg rolls before I could even sit down. I'd known for years I was an introverted extrovert, gaining value from social interactions and appearing comfortable around strangers but quickly becoming exhausted by them as well. This, however, was far too lonely for comfort.

Most days, I took my egg rolls home and ate them on my bed - often a double order - steaming droplets of condensation pooling in glistening beads atop the cheap crumpled blanket beside me. There are only so many glitchy episodes of *Friday Night Lights* you can stream before you lose your mind. I sat and endlessly watched fictional characters live out the most manufactured American Dream imaginable on my tiny laptop screen and wanted nothing more than to jump to a parallel universe where I was playing high school football in Texas with them – to rewind a decade and get a second chance to live my 20s over again in hopes that I could find a way out of this compulsive traveling Groundhog Day in which I had created my life.

Racing from sun up until sun down, my thoughts were no longer my own, just a stew of self-doubt, worry, anxiety, and despair. My ADHD had ADHD, as every possible scenario for my life ahead played out in my mind like the intricate veins of a leaf or the infinite ways to connect lines between the stars. Keenly aware that misery didn't equal growth unless I played an active part in the search, I was too exhausted to look for any meaning and too depressed to care.

With zero stimulus, interactions, or responsibilities, I couldn't have put my poor hyperactive mind into a more depraved situation if I tried. It had only one option – to absolutely spiral like a thousand lightning bugs caught in a thousand jars.

'Will I end up living in Thailand alone forever? Should I just accept my fate and become a beach bum? It's too late man, you're 30, and life's best opportunities are behind you now.'

So I felt particularly despondent waking up on my birthday that morning, like I was watching myself from across the room. Everything was moving like quicksand – slow motion and lethargic. I sat in that discomfort every day, welcomed the emptiness, the hollow feeling I couldn't shake between the sunrise and the sunset, and greeted it again the next morning.

However, on this morning, to my surprise, I found myself grabbing my keys, shuffling into my faded flip-flops, and walking to the staircase at the end of the hallway.

For weeks, I had been consumed with an increasingly troublesome inner dialogue, when I woke up each morning, that I was dying of AIDS. But on this morning, my birthday, I was finally going to find out, unable to make it through another day without knowing. My body on autopilot and my mind at a fever pitch, I headed for the Phuket International Hospital to confirm my suspicions, my only companion being the hot air flapping through the helmet straps against my neck as I sped towards my fate.

As I rode, my mind played out the rest of my life without my consent as I whizzed down the crowded Thai streets in a sea of brightly colored motorbikes, each one unaware of the utter insanity with which I was consumed. I'd tell my parents, my sister, and close friends the news, they'd be shocked but would be there for me as they'd always been. There'd be pity and a sense of loss, a collective sadness for what could have been, and that would be how my story ended.

'At least I went out into the world and tried to gather all the experiences I could.'

Pacing around the waiting room, I furiously swiped on my phone and tapped my feet for hours as I waited for the results of a full STD panel, the quickest $11 I've spent in my entire life. I couldn't help but think how long I'd have lived with this uncertainty in the US – the fear of astronomical medical bills a giant barrier to dissolving my hypochondria. I may have just lived with it forever, as the worry slowly ate away at my insides. In my final years living in LA, I never had health insurance at all, each day just crossing my fingers that I wouldn't be financially ruined by an accident of some sort, the stress gnawing at the back of my mind. I could barely afford to take care of my day-to-day needs, let alone my overall health. Oh, the irony.

Each ticking second on the clock pounded in my head as the minutes turned to years sitting in that waiting room. It had been a good ride, and I had no regrets. I wished I'd been able to get married, become a dad, and experience a family of my own, but not everyone gets it all, and I was making my peace with the reality I was facing.

"Mr. Johns?", the voice bounced off the sides of my head. I sprang up out of a fog like I'd been startled in the night and followed a young Thai doctor in a lab coat two sizes too big into his dimly lit office. His desk was piled high with stacks of patient files, papers, and x-rays sticking out at every angle, a plastic orchid and a computer older than I was - the huge rounded monitor humming from within - perched atop the chaos.

"Let's see here - you came in for a full blood panel. Your results are in, let me just..." he said to himself as he stared into the monitor and swiveled the attached mouse in his hand. "Ooof..." he said with a sigh, a pause, and a deep breath.

'I knew it!'

I screamed to myself in my head - his pause confirming all my thoughts.

'I'm not crazy after all. Ok, this is fine.'

The next seconds took years off my life. My heart was pounding, I couldn't feel my legs, and my fingertips were sweating.

'Have I manifested this?'

"Slow system," he said, glancing up at me. "You're all good, everything looks fine. Nothing of concern at all."

'I'm going to liiiiiiiiiive!'

The feeling rushed back into my limbs, the urge to spring to my feet and do my best Hulk Hogan impression was only held back by the thinnest of strings.

Handing me a stack of papers with various test results, he told me to have a good day and ushered me out, no idea of the internal dialogues boxing between the walls of my brain.

Dazed and jubilant, I approached the bright white light of the sliding doors and was met with the comforting embrace of the hot Thai air as they parted. Flipping my keys in my hand, I popped open the seat to my motorbike, stuffed the papers in the small compartment, strapped on my old plastic helmet, and couldn't stop the grin on my face, stretching from ear to ear. Throwing my heavy frame across my trusty bike, I sped off toward that tiny apartment and let out a piercing victory scream from the depths of my soul. I had cheated death, defeated the final boss, and lived to see another day - the first day of my thirties.

But, of course, I didn't have HIV, no I wasn't dying, and yes I would live long enough to see the next chapter of my life. I had been alone, emotionally, spiritually, mentally, and physically, in that tiny apartment, for sixty-eight days. The possibility that I had contracted HIV was literally zero point zero – it was impossible. But logic took a back seat during those dark weeks, my soul churning through uncontrolled emotions and my worst fears while I could only watch from a distance and keep my head above water as my mind slowly turned illogical fears into very real feeling concerns.

My body was on autopilot, my brain too focused on my newly-found gift of living to eternity to determine where I was driving, I sped right by my little apartment. To my surprise, I found myself heading to a tucked-away section of one of my favorite beaches in Phuket – Karon Beach, a familiar place I'd enjoyed so many good times at over the years. I'd lived in Phuket twice, once at twenty and now at thirty, but this visit to the beach was more meaningful than all the others combined.

Flipping the kickstand with my tattered flip-flop, I grabbed two large Chang beers and a bottle of orange juice to celebrate entering my fourth decade of life. Strolling to a quiet spot on the hot, white sand, I sat alone. Staring out across the blinding blue waters, colorful torn umbrellas dotting the bleached sand, it felt like there was nothing left for me there, like Thailand was telling me it was okay to move on, permitting me to continue my pursuit of love, liberty, and happiness somewhere else. My American Dream was still out there, but it wasn't in Thailand.

Phuket would always be here for me, along with the warm culture and people who had taken me in whenever I needed them over the years, but Thailand was pushing me out. This wasn't the place my search would end, and this wasn't the place my life would end. There was more to discover on my treasure map.

As I sat sipping cheap beer and warm orange juice, I realized it was time to self-start, that if I didn't stand up right then and start moving towards something else, something better, something at all, I could be sitting on that beach for hours, or days, and not a soul would come and rescue me. As the sputtering engine of my motorbike trailed up the jungle-soaked hills behind me, I finally admitted to myself that the story of my life abroad, the images and posts read by friends, family, and those I'd not talked to in ages was far more glamorous and impressive than the life I was actually living. I needed to get in touch with myself again and come back into my own body instead of living in my head. And somewhere, 12,000 miles

(19,000km) away on the other side of the planet, my mother must have sensed it too.

She always tells me to take off my shoes, remove my socks, and place my feet on the ground when I need to feel connected to myself again. So as I parked my motorbike outside my tiny apartment on that hot August day, all I could hear were her encouraging words in my head, pushing me to ground myself. Stepping into the small patch of grass between the concrete parking lot and a row of thick bushes I'd ignored dozens of times, I flicked my flip-flops to the side and just stood in the grass, toes curled around the blades like they were the neon green, shag carpet in my grandparents' basement bathroom – and I closed my eyes.

I could have been there for two minutes or two hours, but I didn't care how silly I looked. I felt people pass but still didn't open them. I felt naked to the world on my 30th birthday, stripped of all the conversation starters you'd pull out at a cocktail party - no job, no home, no friends, no relationship – and no medical problems. What did I care if some friendly Thai women passed me and giggled as they jumped on their motorbikes and sped away? My feet were in the grass, my mom would have been happy, and I was trying to remain grounded in the midst of the most tumultuous time of my life.

Walking back into the little apartment, I felt like I was re-treating into my pillow fort, the other residents of the building having no idea the turmoil I'd been dealing with inside, with only the thin walls separating our unique human experiences.

The utter solitude that I felt within those walls wasn't filled with terror, but rather, uncertainty. Like the lost feeling students have between their senior year of high school and starting their freshman year of college, torn between wanting to remain in high school forever but desperate for college to begin - floating in the ether between two of life's biggest chapters. But this wasn't high school, and I wasn't going off to college. I had work to do.

I applied to jobs on fishing boats in Alaska, jobs back at the Waldorf School in Maryland, internships in the Amazon, and even a job as a warehouse worker in Saudi Arabia. I was reaching into every corner of the globe for a straw to grasp, but nothing was reaching back. So when, a few weeks later, I heard an email ding in my inbox one morning with a job offer from Dubai, it felt like a life raft being thrown overboard to a drowning sailor. I had reread that job description every day for weeks, waiting to hear back, though still unsure of what a Chief Editor was and only hoping I was up to whatever the role entailed. Sixty-eight days I'd sat there, floating through life without so much as a hope to grasp on to. And now, finally, there was another breadcrumb to follow, this time in a part of the world almost completely unknown to me.

I was free, and I was starting over, but this time I wasn't running *from* my life, but *towards* it. For years, I had traveled compulsively, often against my best interest, hopelessly addicted to being on the move, and while I was about to do it again, this time it felt different.

'Wow, my next life chapter is in the Middle East... wait, is Dubai a city or a country?'

* * *

Focusing on the positives about the last two months was hard, but I made it my mission from that day forward. I gradually realized the opportunity I had been given, one in which I was so wrapped up, that initially, I couldn't get far enough away to see it. An opportunity at age thirty to press the pause button on my life while alone and single. Moving to a new city and starting a new job was a golden opportunity ahead. I could start fresh with a new group of friends and commit to making new habits. I could replace parts of my personality I didn't like with ones I did, shed traits that no longer served me. Whether I managed to or not, I had the opportunity to start over completely, and that was excitement enough to keep me going.

Remembering those sixty-eight days, languishing away in that tiny apartment on the fourth floor, tucked aside the thick, Thai jungle, I emerged energized, excited, and ready to boldly jump into my thirties - whatever they might hold. I'd processed my situation, felt every second of it, every worry and concern, and was ready to start fresh.

Sadly, life doesn't often allow you to press the pause button and gift you the time to slowly unravel your life and put it back together again. It would be years after leaving Phuket before I started to meditate, but looking back on those sixty-eight days alone, it was in many ways my introduction to mindfulness. That tiny apartment wasn't a prison, it was a gift.

Carry-on and backpack tossed sloppily into a waiting tuk-tuk, I closed the door to that little apartment, took one last look at that tiny bed surrounded by a glass box of emotion, and headed for the airport, as the cool Thai evening breeze washed away the last bits of uncertainty I had about the next stop in my journey.

A new chapter of my life was waiting, I was following the next breadcrumb on my treasure map. This time to the desert, the Arabian Gulf, and a culture about which I knew absolutely nothing.

I was off to seek my salvation, and had no idea just how soon I'd meet her.

14

Take the Leap: We'll Fall in Love or Never Speak Again

"If happiness is the goal – and it should be, then adventure should be the top priority."
- Richard Branson"

Dubai, United Arab Emirates. September 2014

A huge clock sat on the wall at the arrivals hall in Terminal 1, and the luggage belts were lined with palm trees. I'll never forget the sight, every bit the stereotype of the shiny oasis in the desert I had imagined. It was just past two in the morning, and arriving on Ukraine International Airlines from Kiev, I was finally in Dubai, my new home. The first sentence in my life's next chapter was being written with each step, and I convinced myself that I was ready to meet whatever lay ahead.

Here I was, stepping into the Middle East, one of the most culturally rich, misunderstood, and dynamic places on earth, while starting a new job and a fresh life that I had spent so many weeks envisioning. I couldn't have been filled with more butterflies as I walked down the tree-lined terminal into the arrivals hall - with just $837 left in my bank account. In Thailand, this was enough for nearly 4 months' rent, living expenses, and all the Singha I could drink. In Dubai, it would hardly cover a rowdy night out with friends, if I wasn't careful.

I was traveling light, a beat-up camera backpack sagging on my shoulder, and a cheap roller bag I'd grabbed at a Target years earlier, which had shockingly lasted me through years on the road and dozens of countries. My philosophy was that if I couldn't fit it below the seat in front of me or in the overhead bin, I didn't really need it. I walked confidently into the massive Arrivals hall like I belonged and had been there a dozen times before, but internally, I was anxious beyond belief.

'Is this a mistake? Don't they arrest you here for saying the wrong thing? What if I look at a woman directly, will I be whisked away to some backroom and tortured?'

My eyes darted from side to side, taking it all in, but only focusing on my forward movement. The hall was sparsely dotted with the black abayas and white kanduras I had only seen in movies, usually involving bad guys. The abaya, jet black silk robes from head to toe worn by the women, adorned by the hijab covering their hair, an oval revealing only their faces, elicited all the mystery I had imagined. The men wore the kandura, flowing and sparkling white from neck to ankles - neither the black nor white showing a single wrinkle or stain – pristine, untouched, perfect in their appearance, like competing chess pieces circling around me, guessing my next move.

Moving through the cavernous open hall, I located the taxi exit and made my way toward the unknown city beyond the glass doors – cloaked in the deep darkness of an early September night. A literally breathtaking hot wind engulfed me as I exited as I was met with the oppressive heat for which the region is so well known. Daytime temps in September often eclipse 100F/38C. I had never felt heat like this before, especially not in the middle of the night, and I was unprepared for its totality. I thought that all my time in Thailand had prepared me for heat and humidity, but this was different. It was thicker, motionless, and as heavy as a soaking wet blanket.

Sliding into the first taxi I saw, I felt numb, the dull tones of Middle Eastern music and static on the radio nearly lost under the hum of the engine. I gazed out the window at the utterly foreign and complete unknown of the city in front of me.

'Is this home? Have I arrived? Will I get married, raise children, retire, maybe die here?'

At this point anything was possible, there were no strings attached.

We sped down Sheikh Zayed Road, the longest road in the UAE and the major highway piercing the city from north to south. Extending over 310 miles (500 km) from Abu Dhabi in the south to the Emirate of Ras Al Khaimah in the north, it runs parallel to the Persian Gulf coastline. The main artery and lifeblood of the glowing metropolis, we passed the Dubai World Trade Center building, the first skyscraper built in the city in 1979, a rectangular version of the famed Capitol Records building I knew so well from Los Angeles. We passed all 69 floors of the Al Yaqoub Tower, inspired by Big Ben in London and just one of an endless collection of some of the world's most unique architectural masterpieces dotting the iconic skyline.

And we passed the famed Burj Khalifa, the tallest building on earth, peaking at 2,717 feet (828 m), it was impossible to ignore the striking similarities to descriptions of The Tower of Babel from the Book of Genesis. Each panel of curved glass seemed to reflect a different light in the neon landscape surrounding it with concentric levels weaving into the heavens, my face pressed against the hot taxi window to catch a peak at the blinking tip of this stunning man-made structure as we glided by.

I was already giving myself to this city, embracing the journey that lay before me, unsure of whom or what I would be met with but intent on opening myself to the experiences, challenges, and growth this next chapter would bring. But I was also nervous, nails bitten down to the stubs again, unsure of the bed I'd sleep in that night, what I would face when I awoke, and just how intense and overstimulating the next few weeks - hell, the next few years – of my life would be. And I was exhausted. I'd been awake for nearly 24 hours, too much adrenaline pulsing through my blood to rest my mind for even a second. I'd chased this feeling of total unknown over and over around the world, and no matter how many times I found myself experiencing it, the excitement and nervous energy my body released never diminished - one of my life's true defining sensations.

Making my way up to the temporary furnished apartment arranged by my new boss, I passed out on a bare mattress. A short few hours later, I was greeted with the realization that it was Sunday morning, which in Dubai, meant... Monday morning. Time to go to work. Hired as Chief Editor of a newly founded city guide WebTV startup, I was tasked with creating cutting-edge, viral, and inspirational video content about Dubai - a city and a culture I knew absolutely nothing about.

'How am I going to do this?'

I was in over my head, I felt sick to my stomach. I didn't have a fighting chance of success. For weeks I had been obsessed with researching Dubai, social groups, things to do, and places to see, but I had thought little of what I would do on my first day in the office. I thought I'd gotten the job because of my top-notch credentials after careful vetting and an extended search by the Managing Editor. I would later come to realize I was just a Western face on a US passport with a college degree that sort of fit the job description. White privilege was alive and well on the other side of the world.

* * *

A couple of weeks into the job, high on the 18th floor of a sand-soaked high rise in a sea of towering dust-covered office buildings emerging from an otherwise barren and windswept desert landscape, my heart pounded as the elevator doors opened.

'*Is this really what I want?*'

Two weeks earlier I'd been sitting on the white sandy beaches of Thailand listening to the soft sounds of waves lapping at my feet. Now I was hot and uncomfortable in a city where I didn't know a soul, dress shirt one size too small tugging at my love handles, doubting any abilities or skills I had that would have helped me succeed. I'd traded in a tiny, silent, apartment with zero expectations or responsibilities for a high-paced, results-driven position with zero guidelines or directions on how to succeed. I spent hours during the first weeks scribbling notes and charts on the large glass walls in an attempt to appear as if I had a plan, as if I were in A Beautiful Mind. Sadly, it was more of a blank mind.

The Jumeirah Lake Towers area is at the southern end of Dubai where dozens of high-rise towers had been built seemingly overnight in adjoining clusters with a man-made pond filled with algae-green water winding between them. The office interior was bare concrete, sparsely decorated with a handful of desks, a small conference room behind glass walls in the corner lined with glass windows looking down the eighteen stories to the shimmering construction-filled Dubai Marina skyline below. It was beautiful – in a post-apocalyptic kind of way.

'Am I too late?'

Had I arrived in Dubai just in time to ride the coattails of the city of the future into the next great civilization or had I arrived in a city beyond her glory years? Was I a king surveying his new Kingdom or a peasant stumbling on the ruins of one? Would this ornate experiment in capitalism and man-made ingenuity soon be swallowed back into the sands from which she had emerged?

"Hello?" a friendly woman's voice chimed from behind me, snapping me out of my frozen stare.

The sand from Phuket was still clinging to the bottom of my shoes, quickly being replaced by the dust of the Emirates as she waltzed into the office with a huge smile and a confidence that was impossible to ignore. Her hair was up, somehow both messy and expertly pinned down, strands of dark chestnut hair framing the warmth of her impossibly cute grin - and she was excited to be there. When I turned and saw her walk in, black silk pants, a white floral print blouse, gold earrings, watch, and necklace, I thought she was a successful sales rep from another office. Perhaps she was coming for a coffee, maybe a CEO of a popular startup next door, or a possible new client. But she carried with her something different too, something that was disarming, innocent, and light.

I recognized in her the same attitude I carried into every new chapter. - Somewhere along the way, she'd taken a leap too, without knowing where it would take her. I somehow knew that She had followed a breadcrumb of her own, and she'd landed here, in this unremarkable office building in a sea of sand on the very morning I was feeling unsure that I was in the right place anymore. She wore a smile that said "Bring it on!" and she smelled like a Mediterranean flower market - fresh, exotic, and naturally authentic.

This was Anne, and I couldn't look away no matter how awkward my stares made me appear.

"I'd love a coffee." she said happily in an unusual accent that sounded British but with something else behind it, "but can someone help me use this machine?" I was quick to jump up, half surprised I'd done so instantly, too curious to know who this beautiful woman was and happy to use any excuse to interact with her a bit. This was out of my comfort zone, but my body was moving faster than my mind could keep up.

I quickly threw the first pod I saw into the machine and pressed a random button hoping coffee would come out in some form. I didn't drink coffee and had never used a machine like this before. Sure enough, espresso started dripping out and before she could turn around I'd splattered coffee grounds all over my dusty brown shoes and pushed the mess under the counter. I handed her a coffee and she turned to leave. Where she was effortlessly classy, I was effortlessly clunky. I was mesmerized.

Much to my surprise, it became clear that Anne was French, and as she was extending her hand to open the glass door of our meeting room, I was quick to spit out "Ah cool, yeah I've been to Paris." Did I think it would somehow impress a French woman that I was so well-traveled that I'd even visited the second most visited city on earth? "Cool, I hate Paris," she responded instantly with a slight grin as she turned to close the door behind her.

'Ohh, feisty!'

Apparently, Paris isn't the only city in France - I needed to focus to stay afloat.

Anne was from the South of France, I'd eventually learn, a small town next to St. Tropez, a quaint and charming little village of only 12,000 nestled on the lapping turquoise waters of the Cote d'Azur in Provence.

'St. Tropez? Isn't that the place where supermodels are from or something?'

Not only was she beautiful, I was also learning that she was smart and witty, and I would need to sprint to try and keep up with her. She'd studied business in Nice, lived abroad for a couple of semesters in the Netherlands, and had just finished her master's degree in Strategic Marketing here in Dubai. She hadn't spoken a word of English three years prior when she left France, learning only through immersion from British roommates and American TV shows.

'Holy hell!'

This woman was everything an American boy could dream up and then some.

As with any great adventure, when you've opened yourself to all possibilities, anything can happen. Minutes before she walked in that first morning, I'd been staring out the window at the sea of glass and steel before me. Now my mind was swirling with ideas, playing out every scenario farther than I'd like to admit.

'Could Anne be the main character of my next life chapter?'

Anne was the third or fourth that day to interview for the

open position on the team, but she was the last, interviewing on a Wednesday, offered the job on Thursday, and starting the following Sunday. What I found out later was that this was actually her first job, having just barely completed her Master's degree days prior, with her parents flying in for the graduation ceremony yet to take place.

Over our first drink, an accidental work meeting that turned into a date, I nervously gulped a pint of Tiger beer as she effortlessly sipped a crisp glass of white wine. Sitting just inside the shadows of the blazing sun outside, I told her I had moved to Dubai from Phuket, Thailand, where I had lived for the last year and had broken up with my girlfriend a few months earlier. "We should go there one day." she said, half joking. "Pinky swear?" I said, extending my finger, serious as a heart attack - with a bold confidence that shocked me. She didn't hesitate to grab it and look me right in the eyes. "Swear."

'Wait, is she serious?!'

In the coming months, Anne and I were inseparable. Our flirtatious office emails turned quickly into text messages and on to dinners, dates, and drinks - all the drinks. What started as an innocent, fun, and secretive office romance - the first stranger I had met in Dubai - became an exciting, intense, and adventurous thread we both had to follow. Sneaking around the backs of our co-workers and spending every evening together after work, we'd meet up at restaurants and lounges just a stone's throw from our office but we felt invincible. We'd take separate taxis to work for months before we were found out by our co-workers, astonished they hadn't figured it out earlier, but too enthralled with our little tryst to care.

Neither of us seemed to have any control over our relationship. It was simply happening to us both, and we were along for the ride. A once-in-a-lifetime collision of two people who had leapt into this world to see what would happen. We both said yes. Yes to each other and yes to every adventure suggested - like we were pushing to see when the other would yell "Stop! I've had enough, you're insane!"

Bill Murray famously said "If you have someone you think is the one, take them and travel around the world. Buy a plane ticket for the two of you to travel all over the world, to places that are hard to reach and hard to get out of. And when you land at JFK and you're still in love with that person, get married."

There was only one way to find out if we fit that bill.

Bangkok, Thailand, December, 2014

The whole trip had been planned in a panic, but it was happening.

Anne had flown back to France to spend Christmas with her family. I had flown to Madrid to meet mine, a city that meant little to us other than the cheapest midpoint between Dubai, Boston, and Ecuador where we all converged. But now, Anne was waiting for me in Bangkok, her first time in Asia, and we had four days to explore, if I could just get there in time. She was holding up her half of the pinky swear, and I was literally chasing after her and couldn't keep up.

It was 4:15 am and I was standing alone at the Jet Airways check-in counter in Dubai, having arrived late from Madrid, demanding they reopen the plane and let me board my next flight. "You don't understand, my girlfriend is in Bangkok waiting for me for New Year's Eve. I MUST be on this plane." I panted, out of breath, sweating, and frustrated beyond belief that it was looking like I was about to miss a flight for the first time ever.

'Wait, did I just call her my girlfriend?'

Witnessing an absolute miracle, after pleading, begging, and refusing to back down, they finally agreed to update and re-print the passenger manifest - which absolutely never happens - called the pilot to hold the plane, and begrudgingly cracked open the jetway, allowing me to sneak on before the 5 am flight to Mumbai before heading on to Bangkok. The Travel Gods gave me this one. I knew I'd have to pay them back in the future - a bargain I was happy to make, because I was on my way.

As I stepped out of the cab and into the blinding morning heat in the bustling Sukhumvit neighborhood, Anne's excited wave from a balcony high above made my heart absolutely jump with joy.

'Adventure time - I cannot believe she is actually here!'

Time to put this short-lived relationship to the test and see if Bill Murray was on to something.

We started the day with Thai food for breakfast, duck curry, pad Thai, and fresh summer spring rolls with ground ginger, lemongrass, sweet onion, and turmeric. So far so good. Anne wasn't phased a bit. Weaving through the sea of motorbikes used by 87% of the Thai population, the most in the world, we made our way to the banks of the mighty Chao Phraya River. Catching a local water taxi, we headed up river, visiting the iconic temples of Wat Pho, home to a massive reclining Buddha statue 49 feet (15m) high and 105 feet (46m) long, and Wat Arun, The Temple of Dawn, built in the 17th century, and one of the largest in Thailand. Sitting high atop the terrifyingly steep steps ornately covered in colorful misshapen glass tiles, Anne was soaking it in fully, smiling, filled with energy. For the most part, she followed my lead that day, but she was often the one bounding ahead as a warm afternoon glow spread over the mega metropolis that felt like a playground built just for us.

Thailand would always be part of our story now, that much was written, but we were yet to find out how long our chapter would last. I knew from the moment Anne and I met that there was something special between us, but seeing her eat a scorpion on the streets of Bangkok that night with a grin on her face, washed down with a glistening tower of Chang beer, sealed the deal. I was hooked.

Waking up three days later in a new year, on an island 430 miles (700 km) to the south of Bangkok, the bed covered in body paint, heads pounding louder than the music the night before, that pinky promise had been paid in full. My mind raced thinking through the night before. We'd finished cocktails served in plastic buckets on the beach. Anne cruised through the limbo with a flaming pole above her with ease, and I'd watched her jump in a boxing ring, throw on a mouth guard and mitts, and box a Russian woman twice her size.

'Who is this woman?!'

Whatever test I thought we were putting our blossoming relationship through no longer existed. We were just getting started. This thing was for real. If we'd flown back through JFK, I would have proposed on the tarmac.

What started as a pinky promise between two flirting strangers, daring to see how the other would react just weeks earlier, had turned into an adventurous love affair. Both of us leaping out into the world at the same time, only holding on to each other, we had all the nervous and excited energy of a couple of teenagers on prom night.

Now we just needed a place to channel it.

TAKE THE LEAP: WE'LL FALL IN LOVE OR NEVER SPEAK AGAIN

15

Follow the Spark: What Doesn't Suck?

*"So, come with me, where dreams are born,
and time is never planned."*
- J.M. Barrie

Dubai, United Arab Emirates. March 2015

Friday brunch in Dubai is like a religion, and if you really want to let loose for an afternoon, maybe the most fun you can have with $100 and your pants on. Weekends are Friday and Saturday in most of the Muslim world, and around 11 am on any Friday of the year, we would start to feel a buzz and excitement ripple throughout the expat community in Dubai. I can feel it now, just thinking about it – that feeling before spontaneous day drinking with friends when anything can happen.

The UAE has a modest population of just over 10 million people, but a staggering 88% of them are expats—less than 12% are local Emiratis. While a substantial percentage of the expats are migrant laborers, most from India, Bangladesh, and Sri Lanka, of the Western population, Brits make up the largest share - and the bars, restaurants, and sports clubs are catered towards them.

It's fancy dress for everyone–summer dresses and Sunday slacks. The same excitement as before a friend's wedding with a whole day of celebrating ahead, but on weekly repeat. In anticipation, the girls, most single and looking to let loose, laugh together as they exchange dresses and make-up. The guys, sitting around making jokes, animated and charged, create a hive of excitement. Anne was dressed to the nines this particular Friday, with detailed make-up, pinned-back hair, and dark red lipstick. I was dressed in oversized basketball shorts and the same H&M black dress shirt I'd worn two days in a row at work. I was well out of my league. "Good day to get dressed up a bit, innit?" a friend of Anne's chirped my way. I was too unfamiliar with her dry British humor to be offended at the obvious dig at my wardrobe.

Everyone in Dubai is making a tax-free salary with more disposable income than they've probably ever had, and most have never had more fun. All seem oblivious to, or ignore the contrasting lives of the tens of thousands of less fortunate expats around them who are serving their every need. The taxi drivers, the construction workers, and the wait staff experience the city of Dubai very differently. I attempted to ignore this as well.

'That's just how things are done here, right? Part of the culture?'

By midday on that Friday, all the elevators in all the towers across town were stuffed with a collage of pastel shirts and competing designer fragrances fighting in our nostrils. Spilling out of a swarm of taxis around the city, expats line up at one of over sixty 5-star hotels, second only to London, for the fantastical brunches waiting inside. A sea of British millennial slang fills the air "Oi mate, she's well fit! We're getting proper battered today, lads!"

Any hotel worth its weight offers a blowout brunch on Fridays in Dubai, and with so many high-end hotels in the city, the competition creates some truly unique and bizarre offerings. How about an 80s-themed sushi brunch? A pool party brunch? There is a 12-hour brunch, an overnight brunch, and a midnight brunch. And then there is '*Saffron*', the timeless gold standard and truly over-the-top brunch in Dubai. At over $150 per person, located in the iconic Atlantis The Palm hotel, diners have three hours to live out their wildest gastronomical Willy Wonka fantasies.

Every brunch is a boisterous mix of unlimited alcohol - wheel barrels of cider, kegs of beers from around the world, random carts serving everything from mojitos to bloody marys, and servers waltzing around with shots lined up on trays as long as your arm. The most gourmet foods you've ever seen assembled in one place - fresh lobster, salmon, and caviar, a taco station, a burger bar, and a sushi corner. An Asian section, endless marinated meats, fine cheeses, and decadent desserts - oh, the desserts. How many chocolate fountains are enough?

'*Who are those people on stilts? Where did that mariachi band come from?*'

* * *

By the Spring of 2015, Anne and I had still only known each

other a few months, even though it already felt like a lifetime. Once again, we'd met at our favorite booth just after work on a Tuesday, hidden in the back corner of UBK, a wannabe British-style pub in the heart of one of Dubai's busiest expat communities, Jumeirah Lake Towers.

Soaring clusters of skyscrapers from A-Z circled above our heads with the still pond water stagnant between them, we were hiding in the shadow of the office building where we worked but were a world away.

We were a bit antsy to do something different. After all, there were only so many times poor Anne could try and teach me how to count one through ten in French. She was a determined and patient teacher, but I was an inattentive and much too excited student. "Bonjour. Ca va? Je m'appelle Jeff" I was nervous to whisper, so odd to hear another language fumbling out of my mouth. It felt like we were in our own little clubhouse back there, and we were. The friendly waiters knew our names and knew to keep the drinks coming as long as we were laughing - which was yet to stop.

We'd had a fun-filled couple of months, but was she getting bored with me? Surely she couldn't possibly be *that* into me, right? I was so head over heels for her that I worried she could tell and would back off. But I noticed something in her that gave me hope—something I instantly recognized. She had a level of focus that reminded me of Mr. P and his intimidating eyebrows. She was truly listening to me, engaged and present in every interaction. And when we were together, everything slowed down and blurred into nothingness and everythingness. I felt calm. Desperately trying to keep her attention and wanting her to stay interested in spending time together, I decided to take another step and was eager to gauge her response.

I embraced traveling and experiencing the unknown by taking a leap and trusting the world to keep me safe. And it appeared that she was doing the same with me –accepting both me and my stories of adventure and taking the leap to join me in our trial by fire in Bangkok a couple of months earlier. We were both clearly interested to continue building whatever we seemed to be putting together so quickly. I was eager not to mess this up, because for someone to trust me enough to show them the world was an absolute gift, another beautiful opportunity the Travel Gods had given me. Sure, we could take another trip, and I knew we would, but maybe we could do something together that would keep us even more connected.

"But what *doesn't* suck though?" I asked, just to see how she'd respond. People often voice their negative opinions ten times before they say something positive–100-1 if you've ever glanced at comments on YouTube. But here was a chance just to focus on the good - the Good News. "What about a travel blog that just shows places and experiences that don't suck?" We laughed, but we also thought it was a great idea–the first spark of a project that would define our relationship for years to come.

Sitting there in that hidden back booth, we realized that for the same cost as a few of those Friday Dubai brunches, we could travel to some pretty amazing destinations together. Just a short flight from Dubai, but truly a world away, were cities I'd only ever dreamed of visiting - Cairo, Khartoum, Beirut, and Bombay. During a 48-hour weekend, without taking any time off work, we could start small, hoping to recapture that electric feeling we'd had in Bangkok and to see how long it would last. If we planned it right, we could easily spend weekends in India, Egypt, Istanbul, or Nairobi. So we got to work.

We searched for flights leaving on a Thursday night that

returned on a Sunday morning, hours before we had to be back at work. "We should film our trips." Anne said, moving her phone out of the way as two fresh pints slid onto our table one night. Two weeks later, we were in Sri Lanka, a few weeks after that, Zanzibar. "You have all this video and photo experience –teach me how to do it." Two months later we filmed our first "48 Hours in…" adventure video guide in Beirut, and then we couldn't stop. We made a Facebook page and a YouTube channel and cobbled together a basic website. It wasn't a TV show, but with a couple of beat-up old iPhones, basic video editing skills, and a thirst for more adventure, we were determined to find stories to tell.

'This is amazing! Where should we go next?'

But at this point, on this particular Tuesday night, with Anne having waltzed into my life and changed it for the better, I realized that after living in the largest cement city on earth for the last 7 months, I was missing nature terribly. I was longing for a different kind of adventure - to see some greenery.

For my first few months in the Gulf, I'd ignored the quiet voice in the back of my head that continued to tell me how much I missed the trees, the flickering light bouncing between their leaves reflecting across the sidewalks, the smell of those virgin leaves washing over my face, and the muting silence of city noises being filtered, like oxygen, through their branches. It turns out I had deeply absorbed what little nature was available growing up in Maryland, and I was aching for it again. Something needed to change, and while I wasn't ready to move from the UAE, I needed a quick fix.

I needed a hit of pure nature, and for the first time, I had a partner to find it with.

16

Feel Insignificant: Capitalism is no match for Nature

"The problem with driving around Iceland is that you're basically confronted by a new soul-enriching, breath-taking, life-affirming natural sight every five goddamn minutes. It's totally exhausting." - Stephen Markley

Silver Spring, Maryland isn't a big city by any means, but as part of the greater Washington, D.C. metro area, it is far from a village or country town either. The outline of D.C. is unique—a diamond shape with the winding Potomac River eroding the southwest corner as it flows towards the mighty Chesapeake Bay. Silver Spring, MD sits just atop the diamond, like a lopsided crown above the nation's capital.

While Silver Spring's 82,000 residents make up just a fraction of the six million in the greater Washington, D.C. area, all the towns blend into a hive of frantic activity and extended city life.

The empty fields are few and far between and the quiet parks stand out as rare havens in an otherwise sprawling urban chaos. Rarer yet are back-to-back minutes without a siren blaring somewhere in the distance.

When I was growing up, any day I managed to see an animal other than a house pet or squirrel sprinting between trees collecting acorns was a treat. Chickens and cows were as far from my mind as giraffes and elephants. Maryland is pretty darn flat too, and while I don't remember when I saw my first mountain, the desire to see more of them is something that has motivated me ever since. I was always just too lazy to climb them. There is an excitement in winding up an unknown mountain road, warm sunlight dancing across your face as it sprinkles through the dense green blanket surrounding you - the idea that anything could lay on the snaking road ahead, competing natural smells of stems and soil rushing in as the windows open.

So after growing up with what felt like an absence of natural wilderness, when I moved to Dubai in 2014, I thought I'd be able to quite easily blend into city life. I'd be unaffected by the absence of trees and fields, be able to focus on making money, growing my savings account for the first time, and emerge with a little financial stability. This was a fresh start, I thought. New relationships, new city, new job, new life. Just focus straight ahead to get ahead.

But as it turned out, that magical feeling of wanting to immerse myself in wilderness and greenery was a bit stronger than I'd thought.

And now, if she'd take the leap, I had Anne to go chase it with.

Reykjavik, Iceland. June 2016

Iceland had always been on my bucket list to explore, but I didn't know if Anne felt the same way. To her growing up, it was just one of many countries a short flight away, so it didn't seem as exotic to her as it did to me. But it was another adventure, and she needed zero convincing. "Yes! Let's do it." So, when we landed in desolate and wild Reykjavik on a bright blue summer day, we were both as giddy as children on Christmas morning. The land of Vikings in the midnight sun had called us to witness it, maybe the initial inspiration stemming from those glossy National Geographic pages in the bathroom with the neon green shag carpet that had been brewing in my mind for decades. The February 1987 issue had a huge section on Iceland after all. "Iceland: Life Under the Glaciers" - a striking cover image of a wild-haired Icelandic girl looking straight at the camera.

We only had four days to explore all we could, and throwing our small backpacks in the trunk of a rental car, we immediately headed for the hills, trying our best to get lost among the endless twists and turns of volcanic stone and swaying Nordic grasses in front of us. Within minutes of leaving the airport behind us, we were in pure nature - everything I had been craving. Something felt deeply magical to both of us in this land. Nature felt closer here, and I felt more connected to Mother Earth than I'd been for a long time. The people, customs, and history of Iceland remain more closely aligned with the earth than anywhere else I have been.

Iceland only has one major highway, the Ring Road, which encircles the entire island in a massive 828-mile (1,322 km) loop, so we could feel comfortable heading out with no direction.

'*How lost can we really get?*'

There was a feeling in Iceland that awakened a deep and primal excitement - like stomach butterflies when you visit your grandparents, but on steroids. It filled us both with maniacal laughter as we found our way down the Ring Road, unsure of what magnificent natural wonder would greet us around the next curve.

Tossing and turning in bed that night, I just couldn't sleep. Something felt out of place. We'd spent the day hiking down trails, around waterfalls, and up mountains, and I should have been exhausted, but the warm light pouring in the window was calling to me. While it was well past 3 am, the sun shone brightly outside covering Reykjavik with a warm glow. Turning over, I quietly got out of bed, slipped on my shoes, and wandered out into the silent streets of this charming capital city. There is no way to describe the feeling of walking around a city center in full sunlight in the middle of the night, other than a dystopian dream. It truly all felt fake. The stoplights were blinking yellow, the storefronts closed and still. The roads were empty, the air was calm, and the light was inviting, as if the sun was saying "It's just you and me kid."

Walking down the yellow line dotting the main street in the city, I made my way to the outskirts of town without seeing one soul and found myself walking through the lush grasses of Arnarholl, a small hillside park at the eastern end of Reykjavik's Old Harbour. This infamous hill was the spot where Danish vagabond Jorgen Jorgensen had declared himself King of Iceland in the early 1800s and had a fort built for himself armed only with his drunken men and a collection of canons. Standing on this modest hill, I paused to soak in the unique scene in front of me. An entire city bathed in sunlight without a single person enjoying it but me.

Our days in Iceland all blurred together, as the sun never fully sets between May and August—no darkness to separate the memories into days of the week. Following the winding roads through vibrant lupine fields exploding with purple and contrasting with the tapestry of greens and browns behind, we made our way to the Snaefellsnes Peninsula on the west of the island.

Snaefellsjokull, a 7,000-year-old volcano and the famed home of Jules Verne's 1864 classic *The Journey to the Center of the Earth*, stands ice-covered and unassuming across the horizon. After donning warm woolen hats and headlamps, our boots crunched along the thick gravel as we entered Songhellir, the most famous of the Icelandic "singing caves". Traversing the gaping cracks in the earth's volcanic crust in every direction, we followed a local guide into the darkness below, each step filled with both excitement and a tingle of fear at the back of our necks, while some of our senses enhanced and others contracted. Said to have once been home to Barour Snaefellsnes, the half-man/half-troll who used to live in the cave and was the protector of the Snaefellsnes Peninsula, we quickly stepped away from the world of science and logic into the realm of mysticism and lore.

Pausing after a lengthy descent into the earth's crust, we were told to reach up and flick off our headlamps, and we were met with complete and blinding darkness. This was a black so thick and encompassing that we couldn't help but laugh, having one of our most basic senses utterly wiped out in an instant. But our laughter quickly turned to complete silence as our guide began singing "Sofðu unga ástin mína", a dark Icelandic lullaby. "Sleep, my little love. The rain is weeping..." the song starts, "There is much that darkness knows... Sleep well, sleep tight;" it continued. Standing there in that absolute darkness, we were completely cloaked in native narratives and nothingness. "Hardship will teach you soon, while the day turns into night, that people love, lose, cry, and mourn."

Lingering in that haunting silence for several long minutes, we desperately clung to a moment too magical to release

We climbed mountains, hiked to waterfalls, soaked in the midnight sun, swam in the Blue Lagoon, went birdwatching, sailing, and off-road karting - all filled with a joy for the natural world we hadn't realized had been muted for so long. It was soul-nourishing on the most basic human level. We even stopped to pick up hitchhikers, figuring if there was anywhere we'd trust strangers in our car, it had to be along the magical roads of Iceland, where anyone needing a ride was sure to be experiencing the same feelings of natural wonder that we were. Dropping them at their destination, Anne and I high-fived that we'd done a good deed and didn't get murdered for it—perhaps a bit of Good News along their journey.

After visiting Iceland that summer, something changed in both of us - in only four days. We just couldn't keep it to ourselves. It was a treasure too raw and immense to not at least try to share with those closest to us. Before we left Iceland that summer, we'd already begun to plot a return during the winter months to see the island's twin personality, the other half of her natural beauty. A love affair that began with the midnight sun surely grows stronger when you meet the northern lights, right? It must.

Reykjavik, Iceland. December 2016

The midnight sun was long gone, replaced by 18 hours a day of pure darkness, the few remaining hours awash only with the warm glow of a sun struggling to lift its tired head over the horizon. Light glistened on the surface of the barren ice-covered landscape in an eerie and beautiful warmth - an endless golden hour–any photographer's dream.

I had fallen in love with photography because of its potential to capture a moment, to freeze it in time. In Iceland, I was instead chasing a *feeling* with my camera, as if the sun was escaping behind the vast landscape it nourished with both secrets and answers I longed to know. Furious clicks of my camera shutter were the only tools I possessed to attempt their capture.

Traveling again by car with no clear goal or destination, we got lost in national parks, explored nearly extinct glaciers, traversed intense black-sand beaches, and ran through freshly fallen snow towards infinity - endless nature in front of us, like we were chasing the shadow of the sun before it slipped back to sleep.

Standing in Thingvellir National Park early one morning, the faintest blue light fighting to be seen in the sky, we tugged on wetsuits in 14F (-10C) air to brave the two-degree arctic waters. Naturally filtered for generations, the only place on earth possible to dive between tectonic plates, we slowly lowered ourselves into the crystal clear waters of Silfra, the clearest I've ever seen, and silently floated above one of the earth's greatest rivets, separating the North American and Eurasian tectonic plates after they had been split open during a great earthquake in 1789. "You'll never regret a swim!" I reminded Anne, as we came up for a breath of air. Neither of us regretted that swim either, although Anne has never looked so cold. Seeing her willingly float in near-freezing waters with me in the middle of winter was one of the many times I fell in love with her.

"If you forget why the world is magical, you go to Iceland and you go to Iceland now." I excitedly proclaimed, a huge smile spilling across my heavily bearded face, the excitement palpable in my delivery as we wrapped up filming our "48 Hours in Iceland: Winter" video.

My younger sister, Julia, had taken an overnight flight from Boston to Reykjavik just after Anne and I had arrived ourselves. My parents, flying from their home in Ecuador via Florida had made their way through three continents as we all found each other together in a small family home on the outskirts of this arctic city center. "Now what?" their faces all seemed to say to us. "We've heard so much about Iceland! Now we're here - where is the magic?" Thrown off by the time change, the lack of sun, and the resulting blanket of darkness, we understood. "Just wait," we said, unsure of the enchantment the landscape would conjure for us in the coming days.

I checked every weather site available, apps indicating cosmic activity and solar activity, anything to increase our chances of seeing the Northern Lights as a family before our time in Iceland came to a close. This was a bucket list item for all of us - none of us having ever seen the magical galactic glitter in the heavens above. But all the swirling rivers of greenish-blue lights in the sky would be invisible to us if it was cloudy.

We were in Iceland together for 10 nights, and the first nine were cloudy and overcast, far too much to hope to see anything behind the cloud cover. But we had one last chance to capture a sight of the midnight rainbows we'd heard so much about – the lights and colors I had first seen on that basement floor in the bathroom with the neon green, plush carpet.

"Let's all jump in the car right now and drive out to Thingvellir." I said with enthusiasm, hoping for complete buy-in. It was 8 pm on New Year's Eve and it had already been dark for nearly five hours. "Come on, this is our last chance to see the lights, and the apps say there may be some activity tonight," I said with increasing excitement - met with nothing but "Bleh". We were in a cozy house, in warm clothes, holding hot drinks in our hands. Heading out into the frozen Icelandic winter darkness was a tough sell. I wouldn't let it go though, slowly warming everyone up to the idea and distributing coats, hats, gloves, starting the car, and offering to drive.

A few minutes later, fully bundled up from head to toe, from snow boots to thick gloves, we were piled into the rental car, ice crunching beneath the tires, as we left the dim city lights of Reykjavik behind and headed into the vast and complete darkness that is Thingvellir National Park in what felt like the dead of night. My parents especially, never ones to let me down, bundled up to their eyes in layers of ice wear and thermals, were shivering but cheery - hopeful that nature could cash the check my enthusiasm had written. For happy residents high up in the Andes mountains above the equator, anything other than constant mild spring temps was a shock.

Not knowing exactly where to go - since all you have to do is look up - I veered off onto a small dirt farming road after the blinking city lights had vanished behind us, and slowly pulled the car over to the side and parked, total silence cloaking us as we came to a stop. Excited to see what would happen, we all bravely cracked open our doors, zipped up, and left the warm blanket of the car heater behind. Standing outside in silence, we started gazing into the night sky, unsure of what we were expecting to see. Ten minutes passed, then thirty, and after forty-five minutes, we started dipping back into the car, one by one, for a quick heat bath. I was growing increasingly resigned to the fact that tonight was not our night.

'Not on this trip Travel Gods, but I'll be back.'

After looking up for what seemed like hours without taking my eyes off the endless black, dotted with pin-pointed stars, I

181

started to see something faint, a wisp of what looked like a cloud, half certain that my mind was playing tricks on me. "Guys! Come out, I think I see something!", I cheered with childish excitement. Clustered in front of our rental car in the middle of nowhere, on a random farm in an Icelandic National Park, the five of us stood in complete awe of the natural world as that wisp of cloud turned into increasingly colorful moving patterns across the sky, growing in size, movement, and color. Time froze, and we posed in stillness and reverence as the sky came to life in front of our eyes –as if we were witnessing a royal ceremony put on just for us.

I've never experienced a more collective hush. My one hand clasped in Anne's, the other arm around my sister, my Mom and Dad huddled in silence next to us - this was a truly magical moment and an incredible way to finish the last hours of 2016 together. "See! Aren't you glad you didn't stay home?" I thought to myself, but the moment was too beautiful to ruin with a wisecrack. We were here, together, and that is all that mattered.

Staring up at the sky as the magnificent Northern Lights continued their ethereal dance across the heavens, nature's fluorescent laundry blowing in the winds of the cosmos, I deeply felt my place on the planet and felt the push I needed to start taking my life in my own hands.

The irony of standing in the National Park where, in 930 AD, the world's first parliament was established, wasn't lost on me. If the Vikings thought this was the place to start to organize their laws and lives, it was certainly a good enough place for me to start organizing mine, too.

* * *

After visiting Iceland that summer and winter, our entire approach to traveling changed. We became obsessed with getting off the beaten track and more into nature, getting lost in countries many have never heard of, in forests no one knows, running away from the noises of busy city life in search of the silence, and calm that undisturbed nature provides. Being able to search out and uncover that silence, standing in nature together and breathing in the moment has connected nearly every destination we've explored. The earth has a hum, nature has a voice, and if you're still enough to find it, you'll realize that it's the same song being sung in every corner of the globe.

At the time Anne and I arrived in Iceland, I felt quite well-traveled, having wandered through dozens of countries and cultures around the world, but the feeling this little arctic island gave me was different than anything I had ever experienced. It's ironic to feel more connected to the world around you and all the people in it when there isn't another soul as far as the eye can see. I wasn't able to grasp my place in the world surrounded by swerving humanity in endless hours of LA traffic. I didn't realize the role I played in society by walking through the pulsing waves of humans clogging the streets of Delhi, and I didn't understand that we're all connected by sitting in a 12-hour economy seat from Istanbul to Tokyo, stuffed in a metal tube piercing the skies, with 300 other souls beside me.

I felt my place in the world for the first time standing in the silence of untouched Nordic tundra which hasn't changed in millennia. Iceland made us feel small. Iceland made us feel inferior, meaningless, just a speck of dust on a giant rock, hurtling through space and spinning over 1,000 miles an hour. It was a stunning wake-up call.

Time and time again, as I looked out over the ancient landscapes, Iceland reminded me just how little I mattered, and, strangely, that gave me an overwhelming feeling of empowerment. When you're reminded how small you are, how small a physical space you actually take up on this amazing planet, you realize there is nothing out there that's going to help you, that you've got to do it all yourself. This earth owes you nothing, it owes *me* nothing, and standing there in the unforgiving natural beauty of Iceland, I realized I needed to take myself in hand. I wasn't the center of the universe—I was merely a spec in it.

I felt exposed in Iceland as if it was just the earth and me looking at each other in a mirror, and the reflection looking back at me wasn't my authentic self – it wasn't the best version of me. All 285 pounds (129kg) of me was desperate for a change, and this time not of landscape or culture but of resolve and discipline to sculpt out who I really was. I needed to become the best I could be for Anne as well as myself. If I wanted any fighting shot at spending the best years of my life with this stunningly adventurous and beautiful woman who had walked into my life, I needed to level up. I needed to harness the power of my mind to my benefit, rather than my detriment, and I needed to do it fast. Ironically, just spending more time in nature was already helping my mind, calming me with fresh air, which is a key tool in reducing ADHD. If the medicine for a calmed mind was more nature, I'd happily take more of what the doctor ordered.

What I only realized now is that when Anne and I met, high up on the 18th floor of that dusty office, overlooking a sea of dirty skyscrapers nearby, we both saw a tiny spark in the other, some deep, nearly hidden but unavoidable glimmer of what may be if we both decided to explore it further. We were two magnets at different points of our lives whose backgrounds couldn't have been more different, but whose destinies led us to that same office. There was something between us from the moment we met that we both understood.

I'd thought for years that I was searching the world for my ultimate travel partner, my co-pilot, my trusty sidekick to adventure with - that I had myself all figured out and just needed to find the same in a partner. But what I was really looking for—what we all are looking for—is someone who inspires in you the confidence that you can become the best version of yourself, and the belief that you can do the same for them. What Anne and I saw in each other was dressed up in fun nights out, spontaneous trips around the world, and carefree adventures, but deep down, it was the mutual, unspoken understanding that maybe, just maybe, we were well-matched to go through this adventure called life. "Better together." Anne often said with a smile.

After all, every human wants just three things. We all want to be happy, healthy, and loved, and I believe that we go through life trying to find the person, or people, who will help us get the most of all three. After water, food, and shelter are taken care of, what is life without health, love, and happiness? I didn't want to find out, and I saw in Anne the opportunity to fill my life with more of all three than I'd ever had before.

Feel small in the world, feel meaningless, experience your place on this planet deeply, and then use that to drive your ambitions forward and accomplish great things. Even if only for yourself, do it anyway, because if you take care of yourself, you are better equipped to take care of others, and the world around you will follow.

We still love a good Friday brunch, though, don't get me wrong, and on this day, after this particular boat party brunch a few months after that first trip to Iceland, I made the decision to ask Anne if she wanted to spend the rest of her life with me, wherever it took us.

I just had to plan how to ask her, and where.

17

Trust the Locals: Mahmoud, Terrorists, and a Proposal

"There are no strangers here; only friends you haven't met yet."
- William Butler Yeats

Dubai, United Arab Emirates. October 2016

Over 80% of the world's population lives within an eight-hour flight of Dubai with one-third of them living a four-hour flight or closer. This means that the United Arab Emirates is an amazing place from which to travel in nearly any direction. With India three hours one way and Egypt four hours the other, both the Great Pyramids at Giza and visiting the Taj Mahal in Agra were on our list before we moved out of the region. If we held back from a couple more brunches, we could buy flights to both.

Boat parties on a Friday in Dubai are something of a favorite pastime for Anne and me. Brunches, but on the sea—what could be better? A January day in Dubai can feel like a July afternoon in Los Angeles with average temperatures around 75F (24C), music pumping away, BBQ wafting, ice crunching, and conversations with friends turning into laughter for hours on end.

By the time we made it back to land on that particular afternoon, we were all in a pretty goofy mood, to say the least. With no intention of putting a stop to the fun, we headed to Barasti, an absolute institution in Dubai, one of the busiest beach bars on earth.

With a little liquid courage at my back, I decided that this was the perfect time to shoot a quick Whatsapp to Anne's mother, Karin, who was back in France with Anne's Dad enjoying what I'd like to imagine was a perfectly relaxed and calm Friday afternoon on the French Riviera, as it was only 3:48 pm when she got my message.

"Can we Skype sometime soon? I want to ask you and Christian something pretty important." I sent it off thinking we'd arrange a time in the coming weeks for a little chat. As with most of the friendly messages we had sent each other over the last year, this one had ended with a couple of emojis as well. Within three minutes, Karin responded, "Of course –if you want in 30 minutes when Christian is finished with his painting lesson." Three minutes after that, I was out of Barasti and in the back of a cab, heading to our apartment to ask Anne's parents if I had their blessing to ask their daughter if she would marry me.

I was far more nervous than I thought I would be, but speaking with them over a slightly lagging video call, they graciously agreed to give me their blessing, and that of course, it would up to Anne. I felt it was the polite and correct thing to do to make my intentions known to both of them before I approached Anne. This wasn't a surprise to Anne. She knew exactly why I was leaving her and all our friends that evening. It was the end of October, and I'd promised her I'd propose before the end of the year. We had weekend trips planned to both India and Egypt in the coming weeks, so I went into full-on planning mode after I hung up from that Skype call. I think her parents thought I'd propose that night, but they'd have to wait a few weeks.

Because of the Prophet Muhammad's birthday and the UAE celebrating their 45th National Day, we had two back-to-back three-day weekends leading up to the end of the year - which was just what we needed to be able to check both Egypt and India off our travel list. But just as we were planning our chaotic weekends away on one side of the world, an entirely different chaos was coming to a boil back home in Washington, D.C.

"I am coming over tonight to watch you watch the election results." a text rang out in a group chat Anne and I had with some British friends. On the night of November 8, 2016, we all sat transfixed on the TV screen in our JLT apartment long into the early morning hours as Donald Trump's victory became more and more apparent. When I first landed in Phuket over a decade earlier, I often brushed off light-hearted jokes about George W. Bush, but America wasn't a laughing stock then. Some remaining post-9/11 sympathy remained around the world. Now, sitting in the dark of our apartment in Dubai, Anne and our friends snoring peacefully in a puddle around me, the America I had grown up with looked more like a caricature of itself. Our entire political system echoed a bad Saturday Night Live skit so cringy that my friends couldn't resist watching me see it crumble in real-time.

As I had done so often before when life got uncomfortable, I only knew one solution - a plane ticket and a backpack. But this night left a lingering question in my head.

'What is happening to America? Where is the America I grew up with?'

Proposing to Anne meant signing up for an international marriage, a lifetime of families scattered on different continents. But if we were ever going to leave Dubai, where would we go next? Where would home be? Anne wasn't interested in going back to France, as the language barrier would be a huge hurdle for me, and now the US was losing the shine I thought it would never lack. Marrying Anne meant the very real possibility that life as I know it, as I had envisioned it, may not end up with a white picket fence and a +1 country code.

However, that was a problem for another day. First, she had to say yes.

Agra, India. December 2016

As quickly as the stars aligned (a literal prognosticator in the UAE) and the holiday dates were confirmed by the moon-sighting committee, we had our backpacks stuffed and flights booked. We'd attempt to visit the Golden Triangle in India – Delhi, Agra, and Jaipur – for one weekend, and then pop over to Cairo to explore the Great Pyramids the next, working the short week in Dubai between the two adventures.

The Taj Mahal was too cliche of a place to propose, I thought, and I was right. I saw two other guys on bended knee amidst the morning smog that covered the famous landmark when we visited there early on the morning we landed. We finished a whirlwind weekend in India, ate curry and naan until we were sick to our stomachs, explored all the temples we could, went to a nightclub in Delhi, hung out with some elephants, and got car sick, almost missed our return flight back to Dubai – all the classics. But my mind was on Egypt for much of that time, and on the young Egyptian man I'd been communicating with about our upcoming trip.

Mahmoud is one of those people who comes into your life with nothing but good intentions, a clear heart, and a positivity that almost seems too good to be true. I'd come across his name and Whatsapp on a travel message board and sent him a message late one night a few weeks earlier. And now, here I was, messaging this stranger in Egypt, to help plan how I was going to propose to Anne, one of the most important moments of our lives. He was gracious, excited, perfectly understanding what I wanted to do, and we were about to meet him.

"Jeff and Anne?" The friendly voice escaped the crowded terminal bustling with travelers, taxi drivers, and waiting family. As soon as we cleared immigration in Cairo's busy Arrivals hall the next weekend, there he was waiting for us - his warm smile greeting us like we were long-lost family. His driver, Islam, was waiting in a sputtering white car outside. We were quickly on our way down the busy morning rush hour streets of Cairo heading to his own neighborhood to grab us the most authentic Egyptian breakfast possible - a meal we still talk about regularly.

It is an argument that has been fought for thousands of years, but if you ask us who makes the best falafel in the world, we'll always say Egypt because of this breakfast. The Lebanese, Jordanians, and Israelis would be quick to argue, but there is something about that Egyptian ta'meya, as they call their falafel, that is just different. Maybe it is the fava beans they use instead of chickpeas, maybe the garlic, maybe the leek, the cumin, the coriander, but whatever it is, it is pure magic.

As Islam made his way through the bustling Cairo streets headed towards the Great Pyramid complex that morning, we happily sat in the back seat munching away on our falafel and pita. One of the first things Mahmoud told us that morning was how Egypt was making a comeback, how the recent years had slowly seen the economy improve, the security getting tighter, and the tourists were finally starting to return. He told us all about the history of the Pyramids, the story of the entire Pyramid complex, and all the folklore surrounding them, and he told us he could even read hieroglyphics himself. Mahmoud spoke impeccable English, was a wealth of information, and one of the most passionate people we'd ever met.

Making our way through the checkpoints and ticket lines leading to the Pyramid gates, we almost couldn't believe we were standing there, but my heart was racing for another reason altogether. I was clutching my backpack a little bit tighter that morning, an engagement ring tucked in a small box sitting in a hidden zipper pocket. It felt like it was glowing red-hot on my back, and everyone could see it, knowing my intentions and waiting for me to make my move.

The entrance into the Great Pyramid of Khufu, the largest of the three in the Giza complex, is almost hidden, and you'd only know it by the handful of tourists dotting the large limestone blocks leading up to it. Standing at the base of the 450-foot (139 m) giant of a structure–the largest structure on earth for more than 3,800 years–we felt almost invisible, our eyes unprepared to process what we were seeing. Our hands were not quite sure what they were touching as we glided our fingers along the massive square blocks, many as smooth as silk, their perfect geometric shapes and construction utterly baffling –an edifice that has been standing in the same place since it was built in 2580 BC, some 4,500 years ago with. A history so mind-bendingly vast, that Cleopatra was born closer to the invention of the iPhone than she was to the building of these Pyramids.

Everything about these structures is mind-blowing and doesn't make a shred of sense. Khufu's pyramid has a base of over 570,000 square feet (5300 sq m) - almost the size of ten American football fields. The construction of the pyramid used a whopping 2.3 million stone blocks, which range in weight from two to thirty tons. The math here simply doesn't make sense, an average of 800 tons needing to be placed each day during its construction. That's twelve stones an hour, one every five minutes, every hour of every day for twenty years. And the stones themselves? They came from over 500 miles away. The entire base of the pyramid is on a completely flat plane, only off by .8 inches (2cm) some 4,500 years later. The four sides of the massive structure are perfectly aligned to North, East, South, and West. It is simply stunning, and one of the greatest mysteries on our entire planet.

"How is this possible, Mahmoud?" I was quick to voice. "I don't know, man. Aliens." he said with a smile. Mahmoud studies history, is an avid believer and researcher in his culture, history, the ancient scripts, and language, and even *he* doesn't begin to grasp how any of this was possible.

We climbed deep inside the Great Pyramid that day, up the pitch-black narrow staircase leading to its hollow core - hunched over and cramped inside its cavernous veins. We explored the remaining temples of the Giza complex, drove to the ancient site of Memphis, and saw the massive statues of Ramses II as well. We visited the ancient city of Saqqara, a necropolis site that is home to the oldest pyramid in history, the stair Pyramid of Djoser, built during the 3rd dynasty around 2600 BCE.

As we turned away from the crumbling structure, Mahmoud

motioned for us to follow him away from the main towering pillars that mark this site, through the winding stone pathways that have stood in the same place for thousands of years, battered and beaten smooth by seemingly endless monsoon seasons. Greeting a smiling local man with intense eyes and a bright white cloth covering his head, we entered a small doorway that led further into unmarked and unimpressive ruins – or so it seemed from the outside. Once inside, what we were met with were vivid and detailed hieroglyphics, the most colorful and impressive we could have imagined, telling entire sagas of the ancient Egyptian people across the walls and ceiling of these inner chambers. We were left utterly speechless as we walked back out into the blinding December Cairo sun.

"Egypt sure has a brilliant and beautiful heritage. Jeff, what does America have to offer?" Anne said to me as a joke as we walked across the windswept path back to meet Islam, who was patiently waiting for us. "Apple pie and hot dogs!" It was difficult for us to find a country and culture as young as U.S. when we traveled, but finding one older than Egypt was even harder.

As the afternoon sun started to make its way towards the sandy horizon, Mahmoud knew exactly what to do; he'd helped me hatch this plan after all. Driving through the small neighborhood tucked behind the shadow of the Great Sphinx, two horses were waiting for Anne and me. They took us slowly through the winding neighborhood streets for what seemed like hours. It wasn't as romantic as I'd imagined. Kids were playing and screaming in the streets, dogs were barking, trash fires were burning and, more than once, unpleasant smells filled the air, but we kept on going. I knew it would be worth it. Anne wasn't quite so sure.

Finally, turning down a dead-end street, the horse's hooves now in loose sand, we made our way into the desert sand dunes just as the bright orange sun was spilling its last rays of afternoon light across this ancient desert. Mahmoud stood back, and we got off our horses, walked a few meters into the dunes, and I worked up the courage to drop to one knee to ask Anne if she'd marry me. I pulled out a Bluetooth speaker and threw on a playlist of our favorite songs. She knew what was going on, but let me play it out. As we shared a tear of joy and nervous giggles on one of the most memorable days of our lives, we watched the December sun set behind the desert before us, the three Great Pyramids mere black triangles dotting the otherwise barren landscape, just as they have done every night for almost 4,000 years.

Mahmoud had done a lot for us that day, but we wouldn't fully realize it until we got back to our hotel that night - flowers, champagne, and a bed covered with rose petals were waiting for us. However, what else was waiting for us was wifi, which we hadn't had since we landed that morning, and the messages were quite distressing. "Please tell me you are ok!" one said. "Are you guys safe?" said the next.

Completely unbeknownst to us, only hours after we'd been waiting in the security checkpoint line to get into the Pyramids, a terrorist cell calling themselves Hasm, a faction of the Muslim Brotherhood, had detonated a bomb in one of the metal trash cans lining the road backed up with cars waiting to enter that very same security checkpoint. The blast killed six Egyptian police officers while they had been patiently checking the IDs of arriving visitors and their accompanying vehicles for anything unsafe, just as they had done for us hours earlier.

Mahmoud had known, the second this happened, of course,

his phone vibrating with notifications and safety alerts, but he hadn't shown us a single sign. Determined to keep this information from us, he had deftly whisked us further into the ruins of the Great Pyramid Complex and away from danger. Messaging Islam to meet us at another exit, we drove outside of the busy Giza area to the ancient city of Memphis, leaving us none the wiser, continuing to pepper us with facts and excitement about the remaining ruins we'd visit that day. He knew this was a special day for us and how much it would mean for our entire lives, and he, a proud and patriotic Egyptian, wasn't going to let terrorists spoil that for us.

Anne and I spent that evening excitedly sharing the news with family and friends with the silhouette of the Great Pyramids in the sweeping vista out our window, stale imported champagne filling our tummies. The next morning, Mahmoud again came to greet us, warm and friendly as always, excited to show us the famous Egyptian Museum, home to over 136,000 ancient artifacts, as well as to Khan El-Khalili, the largest souq on earth. But then my phone buzzed with a new alert from CNN.

"Breaking News: Blast at Cairo Cathedral kills at least 25."

As Sunday morning parishioners were sitting in church, mostly women and children, 26 pounds (12 kg) of TNT worn in a suicide vest violently exploded in the chapel of St. Marks Orthodox Cathedral in Cairo's busy Abbasia district, killing 29 and injuring 46. The bomber was just 22 years old. ISIS would later claim responsibility for the attack.

Mahmoud was heartbroken - his beloved Egypt was exploding around him, and there was nothing he could do about it. Before I could even ask him how he shielded us from the news just the day before, it had happened again. This broke our hearts, too, but I knew there was no way I could allow us to go about our visits to the souq and museum that morning as if nothing had happened. I'd just Anne asked if she'd spend the rest of her life with me just twelve hours earlier, and I intended for that to extend a bit longer than a weekend in Cairo.

Mahmoud understood but asked if we could trust him to take us somewhere else. He canceled our visits to the museum and souq but had another idea. Driving through the endless Cairo traffic that morning, I'd be lying if I said I wasn't completely on edge, making eye contact with each passing driver, hyper-aware while at stoplights and stop signs, jumping at every passing car horn. Islam pulled over as we made our way down a busy street and Mahmoud got out of the car, leaving us unaware as to what was happening. A few minutes later he reemerged with a small cardboard box and placed it in the trunk, signaling for Islam to continue driving.

Soon we were out of the dust of Cairo's central traffic and making our way up the sycamore-lined neighborhood streets, the houses spaced further and further apart. Islam pulled into what appeared to be an empty dirt lot, and Mahmoud motioned for us to get out of the car. We were still on edge, eyes darting in every direction.

Following him to the edge of the empty dusty lot, his plan slowly revealed itself as we saw the great heights that we'd climbed, the sprawling Cairo metropolis gradually coming into view and extending as far as the eye could see across the horizon. The Great Pyramids were now just small dots in an otherwise endless sea of brown, sandy buildings, and highways. The edge of the cliff on which we were standing was lined with simple Arabic-style cushions and sun-worn woven rugs. Taking a seat, Mahmoud faded into the background, and Anne and I took in the view, soaking in as much as we could from the last few hours of our engagement weekend adventure to Cairo.

Out of the corner of my eye, I could see Mahmoud and Islam approaching, both singing a traditional Egyptian song, their hands gently covering the homemade chocolate cake Mahmoud had stopped to pick up on our way out of Cairo –the small cardboard box we'd given no thought to.

I've rarely smiled as much as I did in that moment: two strangers in a foreign land, committed to leaving a warm and welcoming impression on us as we celebrated our engagement weekend, and fiercely determined that we'd remember the fresh fruit that adorned the chocolate cake, the sweet mint tea, and the billowing shisha pipe next to us far more than the cowardly terrorists who had attacked their beloved homeland that weekend.

We sat together for a long time on that ridge, overlooking the Cairo outskirts. Islam, Mahmoud, Anne, and I are connected for life now, having shared one of the most unforgettable adventures of our lives, and for all the right reasons.

* * *

Traveling can be scary, but taking the chance to let a passionate local show you their country can completely change a travel experience, especially when it ends up being one of the most important trips of your life. I'm glad I trusted Mahmoud, and deeply grateful that people like him exist. People like Mahmoud and Islam are the Good News as well, just like Lucky in South Africa and Krishna in Nepal – and they are everywhere you look, in every country.

Nine months after our memorable weekend in Cairo, Anne and I were married in Ste. Maxime, the charming coastal town she grew up in in the South of France. Surrounded by family, friends, and open vineyards, we celebrated long into the night - our French and American halves fully integrated, cultures combining in a jubilant mix of friendly chatter and rosé. Lavender and laughter filled the air. Naomi couldn't make it, but her parents had, and Rob turned to Anne and me in a lull between the songs. "Did you know that Alice and I got engaged in Cairo, too?" he asked with a smile. "We were in a dark and smoky bar in Cairo. It was the 1970s, and we were on our own trip around the world. Alice was fed up that I didn't have the balls to ask her, so she proposed to me!"

Travel connects people, and our personal stories crisscross continents and generations. Rob and Alice got engaged in Cairo some 40 years before Anne and I did, and who knows, maybe we even passed by that same smoky bar. No doubt it's gone largely unchanged since then.

Hearing Rob and Alice's story made me wonder why I hadn't heard more adventurous world travel stories from other Americans, especially older generations. Aside from parents who went to Vietnam, grandparents in WWII, and older siblings spending a semester abroad in London or Paris, I never remember hearing stories growing up from Americans heading out into the world to explore, let alone for more than a week-long vacation at a 5-star resort.

'Why don't Americans travel more?'

18

Take the Road Less Traveled: Why Americans Don't

"Life begins at the end of your comfort zone."
- Neale Donald Walsch

Amman, Jordan. October 2017

"If we leave work right at 5 p.m., we should be able to make the flight, no problem - only backpacks though. No checked bags." I texted Anne. It was a typical Thursday in Dubai - the last day of the working week in the Muslim world - and we had a 7:35 p.m. flight on Royal Jordanian direct to Amman, to spend just forty-eight hours exploring all we could of the bustling capital city, the ancient site of Petra and the magic of the Dead Sea.

We'd done over a dozen 48-hour adventure travel video guides for *What Doesn't Suck?* by this point, having traveled to places we knew people didn't know much about, maybe had on their bucket list, or simply didn't think of as a place for a fun weekend getaway– places like Beirut, Tajikistan, Istanbul, and Serbia. But after having gotten married just a few weeks earlier, we'd decided it was time to start thinking of our next chapter, our life beyond Dubai and what came next. However, our time in the Middle East wouldn't be complete without seeing the ancient site of Petra - and we had just one weekend to do it.

Flying east from Dubai over Qatar, Bahrain, and much of Saudi Arabia, by the time we landed in Amman it was nearly midnight. 27,300 - that's how many Starbucks locations there are in the world, but no matter how remote they are, seeing those green letters will always feel like a safe space to me when I travel - covered in a warm blanket of capitalism, if only for a second.

While I may feel nostalgic when I see Starbucks, I've rarely ever drunk their coffee. However, on this occasion, we were trying to sprint to Petra and arrive before dawn, the first people into the ancient ruins well before the sun came up, so I really couldn't say no to a Pumpkin Spice Latte before we started the four-hour drive south.

Picking up the rental car went more smoothly than expected, even though as the bottom of our Renault Duster bounced over the speed bump exiting the airport, it felt like it may fall off, we were on our way and had miles to go before we slept. The roads were well paved and semi-lit all the way down Desert Highway 15 to Petra, 143 miles (231 km) south along the Israeli border. It was just the two of us, the darkness of the desert, and the open road ahead.

Feeling like a sell-out as we headed down the road, always aware that I stick out like a sore thumb when I travel, my Starbucks in one hand, iPhone in the other, 80s pop music filling our ears as we passed traditional Bedouin neighborhoods, the stereotypical western tourist exemplified to the max, I thought about why Americans don't travel more.

'Surely other Americans fall in love abroad? Many must not return home to the US. Why do I rarely meet any?"

Only 55% of Americans use all of their holiday allowance each year, leaving a jaw-dropping 600 million unused vacation days on the table annually - and many only get 10 days to begin with. That's over 1.6 million years of vacation that Americans opt willingly not to take each year. The European mind simply cannot comprehend this fact – and neither could mine.

There are several reasons most Americans rarely travel outside of the US, however, sad as it may be. Only having a handful of vacation days in the first place isn't a great start, but 44% of Americans don't even have a passport to begin with, unable to leave the confines of the USA even if they wanted to. Having white sandy beaches, beautiful mountains, red rock deserts, and vibrant cities all within their own country helps to ensure that many or most Americans, spend what few holiday days they do have inside rather than out of the country. If you only had two days and could fly 90 minutes to a beach in Florida or take a 9-hour flight with a 6-hour time change and spend five times the price to do the same in Croatia, you'd make the same choice, too - I get it. But this is also why Americans have the stereotype of not knowing much of anything that goes on in the outside world. We're raised with a notoriously red, white, and blue-centered vision of the world through our education, movies, and pop culture. I grew up thinking quite literally that the USA was the center of the universe.

'Where are all the students studying abroad? Retirees? Do they know what they are missing? The opportunities out there?'

Driving through the pitch-black night between Amman and Petra, white kilometer markers whizzing by Anne's window, I thought of the perspective these differences in culture had given me – and more importantly, the perspective I gained about my own country and culture, observing it from afar. But I could also not help but slightly envy the blissfully unaware who had never traveled and don't live their lives torn between a million different places. I never meant to take the red pill when I first started exploring, and some days, if I'm being honest, the idea of taking the blue pill and leaving the exhausting feeling of knowing the entire world exists out there feels comforting in some way.

I embody every stereotype of the big, grinning, clueless tourist – unendingly upbeat and enthusiastic about it all – like a golden retriever puppy at a neighborhood BBQ. Everything is exciting and new, the naivety more endearing than offensive, or so I like to believe.

I've been that happy puppy for years as I've traveled the world, constantly excited, often with little clue about what was around me but trying to learn as I go along. I've embraced knowing little about the world until I was there, on the ground, exploring first hand.

And I've owned as many guidebooks as I have tuxedos – zero. I want to discover a place first, then read about it second, and Petra would be no different. As the pumpkin spice began to exit my bloodstream, we were almost there, one of our great adventures awaiting us when the sun rose.

It wasn't until nearly 4 a.m. that we pulled into a small dirt parking lot just outside the gates of Petra with only 90 minutes to sleep before waking up so we could be the first in this ancient city. We reclined the seats as much as we could, tucked sweatshirts under our heads, grinned at each other, and tried to get a little shuteye, turning off the car and cracking the windows just enough to let in the cool night breeze and the subtle sounds of the old-world village we had found ourselves in.

Anne and I were utterly alone that morning, freshly married and exploring one of the most mysterious ancient sites in the world. Hand in hand, we walked deeper into the ruins with the excitement of young children on the last day of school, knowing we would find a gift in the form of an unforgettable morning of exploring together but unsure exactly how it would unfold - the best start to any day on the road.

Walking into Petra is like walking on the face of the moon. Called "The Rose City" the alien rock formations, pockmarked with mysterious orbital gaps, strange and towering formations high above our heads, came into focus as we wound our way into the unknown, the light barely enough to see the shadows around the next bend. The ¾ mile (1.2km) gorge called "the Siq" is the result of tectonic plates ripping apart ever so slightly, with towering walls 600 feet (180m) tall and sections as narrow as 10 feet (3 m) in width. The cavernous winding pathways to the antique city were the perfect preamble to such a mysterious place and only acted to heighten our wonder as we eagerly peered around every corner, feet kicking up sand, hands gliding along the smooth stone edges of the wavelike stone walls that followed us more closely the deeper we ventured until the earth cracked open before us, and we caught the first glimpses of a picture we'd seen a thousand times.

The Treasury, the iconic site often featured in National Geographic, the cover story of the December 1998 issue, and The Monastery, scattered ancient columns and vast floor plans of long forgotten neighborhoods, dot this incredible landscape, and we managed to see them all without encountering a soul.

If you've ever been to Petra, you know the magic it holds, and how the sight beyond each turn can differ drastically. Founded by an ancient civilization over 7000 years ago, the Nabataens might have settled this site as early as the 4th Century BC. Nomadic Arabs who took advantage of the emerging incense trade routes, the Nabataens focused their wealth on building Petra as a major regional trading hub. The Treasury, "Al-Khazeh" in Arabic, is believed to be the mausoleum of the Nabataean king Aretas IV, constructed at the height of the empire when the city was home to over 20,000 inhabitants. A UNESCO World Heritage Site since 1985, it was named one of the New Seven Wonders of the World in 2007 and described as "one of the most precious cultural properties of man's cultural heritage."

Leaving the mystery of the Treasury behind us - the only site we'd known about in Petra - we followed the dusty winding path as it opened into a vast basin surrounded by rust-colored cliffs. Giant stone columns covered the landscape and, meandering through this vast open living museum, we made our way to yet another winding path which quickly vanished up a steep incline, boulders the size of SUVs sprinkled heavily in front of us. Quickly out of breath and panting heavily, the shadows retreating into the crevasses around us as the all-seeing sun enveloped the scenes around us, we turned a corner, and that's when we saw her.

Sitting on a small rock in some of the only remaining morning shade sat Rosa, bright colored scarf around her head, warm and welcoming smile on her face, almost as if she'd been expecting us - because of course she had been. We just so happened to be the first to cross her path that morning, and much earlier than she had expected anyone. She sat with a couple of her friends - a collection of Jordanian women - who beckoned us to sit, take off our backpacks, catch our breath, and drink a cup of mint tea with them. They insisted. They each had a stand where they sold handmade local items of different sorts. Small tables adorned with scarves, hats, postcards, carvings, and paintings lay scattered up the path in front of us, each hidden behind protective sheets, their little shops not yet open and ready for business.

Welcomed by their warm embrace, we joined them on the shaded rocks, sipped their tea, and shared stories about each other's journeys. Rosa had been working and living in Petra for decades, her friends as well, and loved welcoming travelers from around the world and sharing her infectious Jordanian hospitality with them. Overcoming our language barrier, I shared that Anne and I were just married and had dreamed of exploring Petra together for years. Quick to spring to her feet, she bounced up the path to her small stall, reached behind a sheet, and brought out a beautiful cream-colored handmade shawl, presenting it as a wedding gift to Anne and me.

"Congratulations to you both." she said smiling, "Now get going. You still have a long walk ahead." It was both an apt description of the walk we had ahead that morning as well as a poignant metaphor for our road ahead as a newly married couple. We thanked Rosa, dusted the sand off our shorts, threw on our packs, and carried on up the steep path, looking back to smile and wave at the kindness behind us.

After continuing around the rocky formations for what felt like miles - endless twists and turns as we climbed higher and higher - we finally emerged at The Monastery, the top of Petra and an absolutely astonishing site. Towering above us, carved into the massive side of a foreboding rock face, was the most ornate and imposing structure yet - truly something from another world.

Imagine a government building with dusty rose-colored stone columns, peaks, and doorways completely carved into a solid piece of rock hundreds of feet tall in the middle of nowhere. It was 100% Harrison Ford, literally, as it was featured in *Indiana Jones and the Last Crusade*.

We were alone - the first visitors to make it to this point that day. Our only company was a smiling old man who made us strong Jordanian coffee from a shaded shack, and his dog, the ever-friendly trusty companion any traveler knows well. We sat mostly in silence, both in awe of what our eyes were seeing but also painfully aware of how little we knew about Petra, about Jordan, and about the people who had lived here and built these magnificent things.

Six hours and 11 miles (18 km) later, we walked back down the Siq, the same meandering pathway now awash with light. Once mysterious, dark, and quiet, the path was now clogged with endless tourists smelling of sunblock, dust and sweat filling the air, replacing the magic that filled it just hours earlier with the undeniable presence of tourism, the hot desert sun revealing all, filling the shadows that had earlier remained so elusive.

Sitting high up on a rooftop bar that evening in Amman, drinking a local amber ale and eating falafel, we marveled at our day, how much we'd seen, and how exhausted we were. We'd never heard of the Nabataean people, had no idea the marvels hidden in the rocks of Petra, and had once again been gifted the reminder that strangers can often turn to friends no matter where you travel. On that day, the journey truly was the destination.

* * *

I've learned a lot while traveling, a lot about the world around me and even more about myself. I've learned that I love being an excited golden retriever puppy when I step off an airplane in an unknown place, and I always will. It's an American enthusiasm I will never lose, no matter where I live.

Traveling down that dark road in Jordan, I was reminded of the perspective I bring with me everywhere I go, not only from my unique childhood but from my American heritage and the view of the world it has embedded in me. I was taught that America was not only the center of the world but the best the world could ever get, the height of human achievement and happiness – First Place, Number One. And when I first headed out into the world, I was confident that those sentiments would be validated and confirmed back to me with each country I visited.

It has taken me years to understand that not everyone sees America as the bullseye heart of the globe, and even longer for me to come to terms with the fact that it is all a matter of perspective, and that things can change over time.

Traveling can be scary – I know – especially when you go into the unknown where the sights, smells, language, money, food, and people are all different, but that's also what makes it so damn magical, and so worth it. Surrender to the unknown, step into the shadows, feel that extra sense of excitement, and see what you find.

If you can find someone to do it with, you've captured lightning in a bottle.

I had taken that step, of course, committed to Anne, and there was no turning back now. But it wasn't until I was standing in the unforgiving sun of the Sahara Desert a few months later that I was reminded just how long I'd been away from home. And how, finally, with a little discipline, I had found some tricks to finally gain a little control over my hyperactive mind, one step at a time.

19

Pause to Reflect: Sudan Has More Pyramids Than Egypt

"As soon as I saw you, I knew an adventure was about to happen."
– Winnie the Pooh

Dublin International Airport, Ireland. January 2014

The sun was just setting behind the large glass windows of Terminal 1 as I stood waiting to board a cheap Ryanair flight from Dublin, Ireland to London Gatwick in England. A kind stewardess had announced the boarding of my section long ago, but I was pacing the busy hall on the phone with my younger sister who needed to talk as I eyed the rapidly decreasing line of passengers disappearing down the jet bridge. Faced with big life decisions, to stay in Boston where she'd been going to school or to return back to the Washington, D.C area where we'd grown up, she was racked with anxiety, and the life choices before her felt crippling.

"Do I stay in Boston, find an apartment and build a community?" she stumbled through. "Or, like, just go back to D.C. and try to find a job there? Mom and Dad aren't even there anymore." I felt her confusion, her worry she'd make the wrong decision, one that would impact the rest of her life. "There is no right answer, Julia," I said. "They are all the right answer. Whatever decision you make, that is the one you were supposed to make. The experiences, friends, relationships and lessons you learn will always be a part of your story, and you'll never be able to remember your life without them in it, whatever they are."

Shuffling awkwardly in circles around the shiny tile airport floor, I felt proud of myself. *'Huh, that actually sounds like pretty good advice.'*

I hoped someone walking by had heard it and agreed as they continued on their journey. "Whatever choice you make, you've already made it. It's already happened, it was always meant to happen. So enjoy it - take the leap!" I said as I abruptly brought the conversation to a close, the gate attendant making the final boarding call from the loudspeaker while waving me over.

Dubai, United Arab Emirates. March 2018

"Want to go to Sudan with me?" the text read, buzzing on the office conference table as I wrapped up a weekly production meeting. My chair quickly spun as the conversation ended, three more messages from Anne dinging in my pocket before I could get to my desk high above the sand swirling below in desolate Dubai Studio City. "Apparently Sudan has more pyramids than Egypt?!" The texts kept coming before I could fire off a response. It was the start of another adventure. Anne had turned into just as compulsive a traveler as I was. We had found our drug.

Anne and I had both moved on from that first job where we met the morning of her interview a couple of years earlier, but here I was, still staring down at a sea of sand, steel, and dust on the outskirts of Dubai.

This is how many of our weekend trips would start. One of us would receive the monthly or seasonal airfare deals from one of the budget airlines in the Gulf region, and we'd immediately start plotting our next escape - usually to the country we'd heard the least about - and Sudan fit perfectly. However, Sudan proved to take a bit more planning, since it is a less commonly visited destination. After a few visits to the consulate in Dubai, a lot of paperwork, visa applications, and passport photos, Anne and some good friends with a similar adventurous spirit had their visas sorted. As Trump had recently labeled Sudan 'State Sponsors of Terrorism' (This label was removed on Dec 20, 2020.), I had to go through an extra layer of red tape and was emailed a copy of my visa and told it would be waiting for me at the immigration office in Khartoum when we landed.

'I'm taking the leap and trusting you here, Travel Gods!'

Our weekend adventures usually meant odd flight times to maximize our time in each country, which always left us exhausted and out of it when we returned. Sudan was no different. Our flight left Dubai at 2:40 am early on a Friday morning, landing in Khartoum just a couple hours before the morning prayer calls filled the streets. To my surprise, the immigration offices actually had my visa waiting for me as we were processed in - the Travel Gods had come through again. The four of us, blurry-eyed and confused, rolled through the nearly empty streets of the dusty East African city in hopes of getting a few hours of sleep before our true adventures kicked off the next morning.

Some people read guidebooks from spine to spine, print out blog posts, and bookmark travel articles online, meticulously planning each minute of every trip. Anne and I prefer to just show up and then decide what to do once we land, but in a country like Sudan this was simply not possible. The only way we could be granted a visa was via a sponsoring tour company. Sudan sees very few tourists, barely surpassing 800,000 international arrivals in 2018. Between 1994 and 2004 the total number each year averaged only 45,000. For this reason, we had few choices of where to stay and hired one of the small handful of tour companies who could help us get to the lost pyramids of Meroe - the real reason we'd picked this oft-neglected country.

The first twenty-four hours of our trip were spent exploring the vastness of Khartoum. Its sprawling brown buildings spread before us for miles, the mighty Blue Nile floating west from Ethiopia meeting the Brown Nile flowing in from Uganda before they merge and continue their path towards Egypt and out into the Mediterranean Sea. Their meeting point is a clash of colors, deep blue blending with silt-filled water before mixing together to continue their unique journey north - 4,258 miles (6,900 km) to the northern tip of Africa.

We visited the Sudan National Museum, a treasure trove of historical artifacts, mummies, hieroglyphics, carvings, and art dating back millennia. We visited local churches, markets, and military ruins. Once ruled by Egypt, we learned that Sudan was invaded by Turkey in 1820 and ruled by the Turks for nearly ninety years after - which all came as news to us.

'Did I miss this in school? Was I ever taught about Sudan?'

There is nothing more exciting than researching the place you are in, interest sparked by a massive monument you come across but know nothing about, seeing letters from an unfamiliar alphabet, or witnessing a custom you've always attributed to another country or culture. We'd read about the whirling dervishes of Sudan when we landed but still weren't sure what to expect. Spilling out of our dilapidated, trusty van as the clunky sliding door slammed behind us, we were there. Well outside of the city center, we dodged the bustling traffic of Farooq Road and followed the locals into the city's largest cemetery.

"Are we even allowed to enter?"

Every Friday, Sufi Muslims across the city of Khartoum, across Sudan even, make their way to this sprawling urban cemetery and walk through the endless rows of burial mounds to the Sheikh Hamad-el Nil Tomb, located in the center of the cemetery - and then they start to chant.

We navigated the maze that was before us, conscious to follow previously laid footsteps and not wander over the top of grave sites, decades old or freshly laid. We could see a large crowd gathered in the distance, the true size of the assemblage growing larger as we proceeded. The city noises of motorbike engines and honking horns diminished in our wake and were replaced with the amplifying sounds of the rhythmic chanting just beginning.

The crowd, easily in the hundreds, had formed a large circle around wild-eyed priests and devotees, each wearing ornate and colorful patchwork garments adorned in beads, fur, animal bones, or colored glass - each different, each unique. With someone continuously beating on a large drum, the chanting slowly conformed to a steady monotonous tone. Someone else circles the perimeter of the mass we've become a part of, blowing incense into the faces of those watching. It's primal, ancient, eerie, and mystical.

As if compelled by the unknown surrounding us, more fanatic

devotees began to twirl, some slowly, others in a more frantic pace, each chanting in their own speed and style, some eyes closed, some wide open, the bright whites of their eyes fixed wildly on something unseen by the rest of us, contrasted starkly by their rich, dark skin. Although few foreigners were around the circle, a couple of older German men were nevertheless taking photos, looking like washed-up versions of Indiana Jones, long lost on some National Geographic expedition from the past. And then there were the four of us, two Brits, an American, and a Frenchie, quietly observing - our eyes as wide as the men wildly dancing in front of us.

"Welcome to Sudan!" a friendly voice said behind us. Turning, giant smiles and inquisitive eyes of the friendly locals greeted our gaze, mostly young men who were excited to see us experiencing a bit of their local culture, as out of place as a peanut butter and jelly sandwich on Mars. They were eager to ask us what we knew about Sudan and to tell us more. As the rich orange sun started to slide behind endless rows of brown buildings outlining the cemetery, we made our way back to the busy road, the air filled with a cloud of fine dust illuminating the warm glow across the city. Just before we exited the cemetery, a group of older men beckoned me toward them to take a picture together. Placing one of their colorful hats on my head, carved wooden cane in my hand, we smiled in unison, snapped a photo and all laughed together. There were few words exchanged, only smiles and the unspoken connection we had made. We were humans, interacting with other humans in a far-off land, eager to show the other we only meant well. No phones, no screens, no transactions, no expectations.

Driving back across the bridge where the Blue and White Nile mixed, we were soon back to our dust-filled hotel and in our dust-filled rooms, eager to get some sleep before we started the grueling 250-mile (400 km) drive north into the vast Sahara Desert early the next morning.

As the early dawn light began to fill the streets the next morning, large drums of water were roped down to a jeep with more miles on it than I could fly in a lifetime, and we left the busy traffic of Khartoum behind and headed straight for Djebel Barkal. An ancient holy mountain, Djebel Barkal stands just outside the ancient cities of Karima and Napata, the once thriving capital of the 11th-century Nubian Empire of Kush. Bouncing along sand-swept roads that extend for as far as the eye can see, coming to a hazy point at the horizon, we realized just how truly massive the Sahara Desert is, how small we really were, and how much had come before us.

Surrounded by nothing but arid, desolate dunes in every direction, marked by the handful of smaller pyramids that line its base, Djebel Barkal appeared as an otherwise lonely structure, a mountain left behind when the others departed thousands of years before. A towering object in an otherwise barren landscape, I knew I had to climb it.

Early the following morning, the scorching sun already hotter than I had hoped, I set out from the quiet protection of our peaceful lodge in the mountain's great shadow and trekked across the blanket of sand at my feet towards its shifting base.

Covered in so much loose sand and rocks, no well-worn path existed; my only route up a unique path each climber must decide on their own. Jumping from boulder to boulder up the steep face, it felt as though the whole mountain could collapse at any time, the ground moving with every step, dissolving back into the ancient sands from which they had once sprung. Making my way to the summit, with chalky palms and out of breath,

I peeled back the t-shirt covering my head and soaked in the truly unique scene before me. Karima, the ancient town we found ourselves in, was decidedly smaller than I imagined - the handful of remaining structures clustered together in an endless sea of sand. All that sat below me were three small pyramids, our modest camp, and an outpost connecting a thin power line struggling to break free through the windy scorched air.

With sand in every direction but one, I approached the edge of Djebel Barkal as the mighty Nile revealed herself below. The immense greenery that sprouted along her fervent banks, had provided sustenance and life to millions of people for thousands of years as she wound her way north to Egypt. The dividing line between the brown, dry sand and the lush, green river banks could not be more contrasted or spectacular. Nowhere else on earth had I seen such a clear and distinct line between the living, the thriving, and the vibrant and the dead and the past, ancient and discarded.

Djebel Barkal held secrets too. Caves filled with hieroglyphics - precise, bold, untouched, as colorful as the day they were carved over 3,000 years ago. Every cave where we stopped along our journey did too, as did the ruins, tombs, pyramids, and ancient structures that seemed to appear in every direction we drove. There was endless treasure to discover in this otherwise empty, still, and largely forgotten part of the world, one that was once the very center of human civilization.

Making our way to Meroe some 120 miles (200km) to the East, the famed pyramids we'd come so far to explore awaited our arrival as the sun began to dip towards the horizon, long shadows extending rapidly across the landscape like doors creaking closed down a vast hallway.

Approaching the site of Meroe, words cannot explain how

simply out of place these ancient structures look, like a handful of children's marbles carelessly tossed onto the carpet of time. Some pyramids are crumbling back into the earth, some look as though they were built just yesterday, all impossibly lost in a sea of rippling dunes in every direction. Remnants of a thriving Kush dynasty before its collapse during the Bronze Age, these pyramids represent the rule over huge sections of what is now Sudan and Egypt, for some 500 years. Endless layers of sand covering endless layers of human history, struggles, victory, and defeat are now reduced to only a whisper for those listening carefully.

As our fingers gently glided along the stone edges of the massive slabs of rock forming these pyramids, we all had the same thought.

'What else is out there in the world I know nothing about?'

Walking through the ruins as the sun finally dipped behind the sandy horizon, I received a notification on my watch, "Five years an expat!" it flashed, digital characters dancing on my wrist, snapping me back to the present. Feeling lost in the middle of nowhere, I marked five years since I threw my belongings in that small storage unit above the 405 Freeway outside of Los Angeles between an auto body shop and a gardening center and boarded a plane, again to Thailand and again in search of adventure, myself, and my place in the world.

It marked five years since I'd again started running both to and from my life, hiding from the world while getting lost in it, looking for meaning and purpose by trying not to think about either. I found a bit of both standing there that evening in the flowing sands of the Sahara Desert. Anne standing next to me, our good friends lost in the ancient ruins with us as well, our home just a short flight away, all things I could never have imagined I'd find when I stepped on that plane leaving Los Angeles five years earlier. Yet there we were, there I was. It was all real.

Settling into wind-beaten nearby tents, straight out of the pages of National Geographic, with thick cream-colored canvas tarps bolted to the sand by thick twin and wooden spikes, we welcomed the cool evening breeze and bid farewell to the blazing hot March sun until it returned in the morning. It felt like we were on a proper expedition in one of the most remote corners of the world, with just a couple of friends, a friendly Sudanese local to show us around, and nothing but silky sand and silence as far as the eye could see.

There is a silence that one finds when you're in the presence of something as old as these pyramids, the same silence you get when you stare into a Van Gogh in a museum, examining each tiny brush stroke as the murmurs and shuffling feet behind you dissolve.

That night, Anne and I sat outside and gazed at the horizon in silence, hand in hand, both stunned at where this particular adventure had taken us - and then we looked up at a sight that took our breath away. Sparkling above us in the pitch black sky as the warm breeze brushed our faces, hundreds of miles from any form of light pollution, we could make out the Milky Way in her immense intergalactic brilliance. Like the Northern Lights in Iceland, this celestial sighting bathed us in a hushed reverence like a tingling blanket from above. "The things we do, love," she whispered as I held her hand a little tighter.

* * *

We often talk about our expedition to Sudan as the place where we went the furthest outside most people's comfort zone. It's a place few would think to go, where few would think to explore on their own or to use holiday time to visit. Such a missed opportunity.

But Anne and I have missed a lot too since we moved away from the countries we once called home, over ten years ago now for us both. We've missed weddings, graduations, birthdays, and the funerals of four of our grandparents. We've missed long dinners with family, chance encounters with childhood friends at the supermarket, and visits to the dentist who has known us since before we had teeth—but we've gained a lot, too.

We've celebrated weddings with friends and family in ten countries, made friends in corners of the world we didn't know we had friends yet to make, and had experiences - like sitting under the Milky Way in the middle of the Sudanese Sahara Desert - that we know would make those grandparents smile from ear to ear. We know they'd be happy to see us out exploring the world, turning strangers into friends, and gathering stories, wisdom, and experiences to share with generations to come.

Whatever decisions you make, always take time to pause and reflect, tracking back the breadcrumbs that led you to where you are on your journey, and try to understand them. Because, after all, the decisions have already been made, you've already lived them, and you'll never be able to remember your life without them, just like my sister Julia deciding to stay in Boston - it was always Boston.

For Anne and me, this meant taking our next step, too, and finding the next breadcrumb on our now combined journey. Where to, we didn't know. We just knew we had to take it, and the more time went on, the more sure we became that it wouldn't be in The Middle East.

But now we had each other, and we'd take the next step together wherever that might be.

20

Know What to Chase: Not All That Glitters is Gold, Even if It Comes Out of an ATM

"There are people who have money, and there are people who are rich."
- Coco Chanel

Dubai, United Arab Emirates. February 2018

"Madinat?" Anne said, as we both dropped our work badges in the bowl by the door and quickly threw on a fresh shirt. Another Thursday night, another work week completed, the need to release the stress again as predictable as the Earth circling the Sun. The tension of our respective jobs had been building month after month, especially mine, and the need to be distracted with expensive cocktails grew with it, especially on this night.

Waving at an idling dusty taxi in our building's roundabout, we hopped inside and jetted down Sheikh Zayed Road. I looked up again at the towering skyscrapers I'd come to know so well during the last four years, but they looked different now. Their sparkles had faded, their mystery and majesty diminished. The center of my chest that had once filled with excitement and wonder had been replaced with a ball of anxiety and stress, and whether this was due to the city or to me, I wasn't sure.

Madinat Jumeirah, an artificial souq of sorts, built in the shadow of the world-famous Burj al Arab Hotel, is one of the most popular stops for any tourist in Dubai. It's an over-the-top attempt to blend the rampant consumerism of Dubai with the timeless atmosphere of a Middle Eastern souq, or marketplace, allowing visitors to escape to a far-off world - while being surrounded by what makes them comfortable. What it lacks in authenticity it more than makes up for in brand awareness, with a Cinnabon across from the stall selling tourists tickets to the indoor ski slope at the Mall of the Emirates.

The shop selling authentic abayas and kanduras, the traditional conservative dress of the locals, might close its doors at 8 p.m., but the Belgian beer cafe just down the hallway is open until much later. Serving boisterous expats exotic brews from around the world to the tunes of blasting modern pop music, the allure on a Thursday night was strong. As we wandered through the winding halls of Madinat Jumeirah, the scent of Oud Al Khaleeji Bukhoor wafted through the air at every turn, with its zesty notes of basil, rose, and citrus blending with rich sandal and cedarwood. Found in malls, mosques, and hotel lobbies alike, it is an unforgettable aroma all across the region.

And then we saw the gold ATM.

Casually placed between a photo booth and a cart selling antique postcards and sand art, stood an ATM where we could literally buy gold. With a swipe of our bank card, we could choose between a small gold bar, a necklace in the shape of a camel or the Burj Al Arab, the "World's Only 7-Star Hotel" - a classification that doesn't actually exist.

'Buying gold out of an ATM... What will Dubai think of next?'

It was time for a change. With our chapter in Dubai coming to a close, it was clearly time for a new one, to feel the uncomfortable gap between my life's pages again - unable to read what was next while letting go of what is now behind. Another leap out into the world.

The burnout had built slowly for me as one year turned to two, two turned to four. Anne had been in Dubai for over five years at this point, and after we returned home from our wedding, we started to think about the future and where we'd spend it—where the next breadcrumb would lead. The tumultuous daily life of my production job had ballooned into an unsustainable size, and sleepless nights were filled with panic and rapid heartbeats. I was becoming unhealthy, unwell, and unfit - and my ADHD was back in the passenger seat and trying to grab the wheel. What had once been exciting and new had become a predictable chaos that I could only observe but never seem to control. My mind was more erratic than ever, refocusing endlessly on each new task placed before me, unable to sort, organize, slow down, or prioritize. Each day had new unforeseen issues, challenges so easily overcome if planned for, mixed messages, and poor communications that could quickly turn tiny issues into monumental challenges - all of which I had to fix and no longer had the tools to cope with.

One day it was a Sheikh demanding a last-minute change to a video, which meant stranding out-of-town guests at dinner while I rushed back to the office until 3 am. The next day it would be learning minutes before starting a massive production that duplicate crews had been booked, resulting in last-minute cancellations, full-day rates paid out and professional relationships pushed to the brink. On one of my last shoots, at an oil rig deep in the desert outside Abu Dhabi, the temperature read 136F (58C) on the thermometer our safety coordinator held in his hand, mandating 15-minute breaks in the idling vans just next to us, pumping a steady stream of AC. I was done.

Ironically, the most miserable project I ever worked on while living in the emirate was a campaign for the Minister of Happiness. How telling is that? Plagued with miscommunications, no-shows, creative changes, location moves, and burning the last good faith that remained with the production crews I had built over years, the work environment had dissolved not only into unmanageable, but simply unsustainable.

The glossy sheen of a growing bank account had worn dull, and the lack of purpose in our lives, our work, and our socializing had become clear. People often refer to Dubai as "the city with the golden handcuffs", many becoming so enthralled with the good life and the unconscious push it gives you to show up and show off, that it lulls many into living a lifestyle above their means. This often results in taking out loans and being unable to leave the city, while outwardly projecting material success and dominance.

But life in Dubai was easy, at least the convenience of it all - and the city was safe, the safest I'd ever been in, which made the idea of leaving that much harder. In our three years of living together, Anne never had a key to our apartment. It was never locked, even when we went out of town. Want a single bottle of water from the shop downstairs? Order it on your phone and it'll be there in five minutes. Have an urge for movie theater popcorn but no good movies are playing? No worries, hot, fresh, salty popcorn will arrive directly from the cinema on a motorbike in no time. We'd grown used to the safety and convenience of the emirate, and we now knew these would be elements we'd seek in any place we next called home next - but it wouldn't be here.

And so, in the weeks following our wedding, we made a plan, set a date, turned up the heat on our monthly savings, set a target, and planned to cut the cord on our Dubai chapter as soon as we reached it. A feat easier said than done for many, the daily conveniences and tax-free salaries too comforting to easily walk away from, but we were determined nonetheless, and we were in it together. One goal —and we just had to get there.

But where were we going to go? And wherever it was, would it be home?

* * *

My hands were shaking, and my heart racing. I re-composed the text at least four times as my taxi bumped out of the JLT neighborhood and once again headed for the sandy streets of Dubai Studio City. "Can we meet downstairs for coffee when you get in?" it began. "I have something I need to tell you." My boss was always a couple hours later arriving at the office than I was, so I didn't expect an answer right away. I stared out the window, the hot February sun already showing signs of warming towards the summer months.

'I've done it. No turning back now.'

It shocked me that I'd finally lost the drive to make money without meaning, and I was actually doing something about it.

I'd started a ball rolling which ended with me leaving Dubai – a city where, at one point, I thought I might live forever.

Sitting in the stuffy cab, the hot smell of all the passengers before me still lingering in the warm fabric behind me, I thought about the lack of nature in my life, the monotone existence of tan and brown life in the desert, and the complete absence of any creature as small as a fly. In over four years in Dubai, I don't ever remember seeing a single insect. Never so much as a gnat in the house, a bee buzzing by my ear, an annoying mosquito accidentally making its way into our living room – nothing. And now I couldn't have missed them more.

"Sure Jeff, I'll be there in ten minutes." a text pinged back to me as the taxi looped behind Emirates Hills. Walking into the lobby, hot dust collecting in the corner of the humid, brown tile floor, I nodded my head at the security guard and headed for the coffee bar. Our production team was small, and I was a big part of it, working as a senior creative producer, like a puppet master overseeing all the aspects of creative projects, and doing my best to ensure that all elements went as smoothly as they could. I juggled a lot of balls and kept a lot of plates spinning that most didn't even know about.

'What will they do without me?'

When the doors opened, my boss walked in and made his way through the lobby to me. As he sat down with his coffee, I felt a sense of calm and much to my surprise, when I opened my mouth, I spoke confidently and directly– like my soul was in control, desperate to get me out of there. "My time here in Dubai has come to an end," I said. His response shocked me. "That's great news! We will miss you terribly, but it's always exciting when anyone ejects from Dubai!"

I was taken aback. He'd said it with the same tone a cellmate would use if you told him you were granted parole. He may not be getting out anytime soon, but he was happy for you. He wished you would stay locked in the tiny cell with him, someone else to go through the grueling days, but he genuinely shared your excitement to be free.

My boss was an American too, from New York, and only one of two Americans I met in the Gulf during my four years there. He'd moved there for the same reason I had – an exciting new chapter, following a breadcrumb that led him to the desert as well. And while I didn't know where his next breadcrumb would lead, still too far ahead to see clearly, and he wasn't going anywhere soon. His life in Dubai was complicated, entangled with business, family, and finances. He couldn't leave but was happy I could.

I'd taken my first job in Dubai without knowing a single person in the entire Middle East and with zero experience, history, or knowledge of the region or culture, because it was an opportunity to finally, just maybe, attain some financial stability.

Within six months of leaving that tiny $150 per month apartment in Phuket, alone, single, and unemployed, I was making more money than I ever had, and Anne and I were newly dating. But here I was, nearly 1500 days later, consciously ending this chapter and moving on to the next with a life partner - and money in my savings account for the first time ever.

However, this would also mean a career break at 33, with no idea what would come next, which scared me - but it wasn't nearly as scary as the panic and anxiety I felt when I imagined staying put. I'd learned all those years earlier, on the debris-strewn tsunami-ravaged beaches of Phuket, that happiness doesn't come from money. Happiness comes from meaning and community.

In Dubai, we had little of the former though we enjoyed plenty of the latter. Some of our close friends had moved on from Dubai and on to cities like London, Sydney, Singapore, or Hong Kong and we felt the urge to move on, too. Our community was shrinking, as so often happens in Dubai with transient expats moving on to greener pastures. But we still had friends who felt like family, friends we couldn't imagine leaving behind.

'How can we leave our friends? Are they going to stay in Dubai and thrive? Are we being idiotic?'

But I felt something was missing in my life, or rather something was moving further out of reach, which none of those friends could relate to at all. The American Dream that seemed so shiny growing up had started to grow stale over time - and that pained me greatly. Dubai had so much to give, but only for those willing to give up a lot as well.

I'd heard of people arriving at this same conclusion – that money doesn't buy happiness, but to be honest, I thought they were lying. I'd fortunately never been desperate for money growing up, but I certainly hadn't ever had much more than just what I needed either. The goal was always to get more. Money for a bigger house, a bigger car, a new toy - that was the American Dream the culture had sold me, as if that was the secret to happiness. But what those gentle Thai people had shown me years earlier was finally settling in, and I was getting it. Money wasn't *everything*. It was *one* thing, but there was much more to life, a lot of which was missing in mine at that moment.

Learning the lesson that money wasn't all that mattered to me was a blessing for which I was grateful, but I was infinitely more grateful for the fact that Anne felt the same way. Having access to tax-free salaries and perceived elitism is hard enough for one person to step away from, let alone two – no less at the same time.

To make sure we always remembered why we did it though, forty-eight hours before we took the last bags out of Apartment 907 in Dubai JLT Cluster S, we each recorded ourselves talking for twenty minutes and telling our future selves why we'd had to make this change – to be able to watch in case we found ourselves doubting our decision or regretting the acceptance of paying taxes once more.

I was moving on again, in search of something more, of more adventure, more change, more unknown, the self-medication I'd prescribed myself so many times before. I'd left Washington, D.C. for California, left California for Thailand, Thailand for Dubai, and now Dubai for who knows where. We had no idea where we'd end up, but that was the fun of it—a predictable pattern of unpredictability that was nearly woven into my DNA by this point. Six months, 180 days, of exploring wherever we wanted lay in front of us before we'd run out of money. We had six months to find a home.

But it was also terrifying. Professionally, I was going to have to start over in a new culture and country in my mid-thirties with a noticeable gap on my CV. I was an expat who had been living outside the US now for six years.

'Will I ever go back? If home isn't Dubai, and won't be France or the US right now, where will it be?'

* * *

Know what you are chasing, dig deep, shine light into the corners of your mind, and try to understand what pushes you to make the decisions that define your next move, your next chapter.

You may be chasing love, fame, fortune, adventure, perspective, or none of the above. More often than not, it may be right in front of you the whole time, but if it takes you a trip around the world to realize that, then so be it. May you always find what you are looking for, one way or another, and may you deeply know what you are chasing, sooner or later. May you find peace with what you find, today, tomorrow, and long into the future. May you also gain the wisdom that miles traveled do not equal problems solved and that not all that glitters is gold, even if it comes out of an ATM.

No matter how extensively we travel, our problems have a first-class ticket to all of our adventures and life's chapters - regardless if you try to ignore them. But before Anne and I could leave Dubai, I needed to deal with one of mine—one that had been haunting me for as long as I could remember.

I just never thought that more time at the dinner table would finally solve it.

21

Face Your Flaws: Eat the Cheese, Drink the Wine!

"Wine and cheese are ageless companions, like aspirin and aches,
or June and moon, or good people and noble ventures."
-M.F.K. Fisher

Ste. Maxime, France. April 2018

Being from the South of France, Anne didn't care for Paris much and had only been there a handful of times. She'd made that perfectly clear the day we first met, high up in the HDS Business Center in Dubai. She much preferred the laid-back lifestyle in the south, the cool breeze lifting off the glistening blue Mediterranean, the crisp rosé flowing freely—the good life on the Cote d'Azur. And who could blame her? Once, on a Euro trip with my best friends from high school, we'd planned to end up in Nice but had run out of both money and willpower somewhere around Munich and never quite made it, the allure of beer gardens and hostel happy hours too much for us to abandon. If we'd only known what we were missing on the French Riviera...

A year after the mix-up at the coffee machine in Dubai, on the very day we met, I'd been fired from that job, and shortly thereafter, Anne had quit, just months before the company went out of business for good. It was the worst job I ever had, but the best decision I ever made was to take the leap and dive headfirst into that new chapter in Dubai. And now, a couple of months before we were set to leave the UAE to travel the world, we flew back to France to bring some of our belongings and spend a long weekend with Anne's family.

"À table!" my father-in-law shouts, excitement filling the air. I've heard it hundreds of times now, but the joy of it hitting my ears never wears off. We've already been sitting together for an hour enjoying "apéro" - sampling small bites of French classics, toothpick in one hand, chilled glass of rosé in the other. Two of my favorite phrases in French - "À table!" and "apéro", both revolve around the table–the local religion, especially in the South.

I'm an American. We don't do food well. Our national dish is made of animal parts stuffed between an oblong starchy white bun smothered in ketchup and mustard, more concerned about quantity than quality. Americans have a bizarre relationship with food, but I have an especially complicated one – or at least I did, until I started coming to France and spending time with Anne and her family.

Eating together every night isn't the norm for many families in the US, but it sure was for me growing up. We all had our set places at the oval wooden table in the dining room, like the four corners of a compass, never wavering. I still sometimes reach down when I eat to grab the bottle of mandarin seltzer water that was always there growing up, moist droplets forming a ring at its base on the rust-colored oriental carpet below.

On one night each year, Americans gather for a big, blowout feast that you can place bets and set your clock to. Thanksgiving is a worship of all things gluttonous - and football, of course. The fourth of July is fun, but I only remember the outdoor bar-becues—never a formal meal, usually standing up in someone's backyard with a sloppy joe in one hand, napkin catching the dripping entrails in the other. Christmas was always a big meal or was meant to be, but in our house, it usually turned into more of a lowkey affair after munching on nuts and chocolate around the Christmas tree all day - something I didn't mind one bit. We often didn't have the energy or drive to cook a big meal afterward.

But Thanksgiving - Thanksgiving is different.

Thanksgiving is classically, unapologetically, and grotesquely American - a holiday we celebrate with pride and bulging belt buckles. The smells from the kitchen start wafting through the house before many of us are even awake. All the stores are closed that last Thursday of November, until midnight at least, when they explode open again for the capitalistic orgy that has become Black Friday. It's our holiday, we own it, and we tell ourselves a fairy tale narrative about its origins.

Each family has their unique variations on classic dishes and traditions all their own, but the staples of turkey, mashed potatoes, and pumpkin pie remain across the board - unless you're a vegan, but we didn't have those in the 90s.

And wherever we celebrated, whatever was on our plates, we always kept the same family tradition. One by one, we went around the table and told everyone what we were thankful for, just one thing. It was always a mix of family, friends, and anyone else my parents had welcomed to our table who might have been in need of a warm Thanksgiving feast.

It's a tradition I keep up to this day, although I haven't spent a Thanksgiving in the United States in nearly fifteen years. In 2010, I was in Cambodia eating Thanksgiving dinner with Ryan while we filmed the STIGMA documentary, sharing what we were thankful for over salty beef noodles and chocolate milk. In 2008, I was in Kanyakumari, India - the southernmost tip of the country - sharing curries and naan with Alana and other students from the Brooks Institute after hearing those three words that changed my relationship with religion. It's one of the hardest parts about being an expat for all these years, missing the annual American celebration that is Thanksgiving.

But while Thanksgiving may not exist in France, there is certainly no lack of tradition either.

Before we even sit down, my father-in-law, an ever-thinking and brilliant engineer, has mapped out the best seating order around the table, pairing possible topics and languages spoken by each guest, to maximize enjoyment and conversation potential - an art we lost in America around the time we arrived in Plymouth, I suspect.

From the hundreds of hours I've been lucky enough to spend around French tables, a few things have become clear. The love, passion, and obsession with the food are only eclipsed by the dedication and vast importance of the time spent together, connecting as family and friends, sitting around that table. My French is pathetic on a good day, hardly able to string together more than two words in a sentence, but I would be hard-pressed to ever find a conversation around a French table that doesn't, in some way, revolve around food. It is rare to spend an entire meal without the topic, or memory, of another meal making its way into the conversation.

My mother-in-law is one of the most creative people I've ever met. Each tiny element of the entire meal, from the tablecloth to the napkin holders, the serving spoons to the tiny chocolates served at the end of the meal, a sweet capstone to a pyramid of delicious homemade dishes we've consumed over several hours, is ornately thought out ahead of time, each meal with a completely different theme, color scheme and flavor profile from start to finish. "Ahh, it was nothing, easy," she always proclaims when thanked profusely after such an amazing meal. It's how she shows love.

The ingredients are fresh, the flavors bold and complimentary, and the baguettes come out of the boulangerie oven that morning. The man who sells the cheese, *le fromager*, not only has a passion for each variety, but a university degree in the topic as well. A member of the French Culinary Academy, he presents over 200 cheeses from which to choose. And some of the cheeses are so stinky, so pungent, they are kept in an airtight container and stored not in the kitchen fridge, but in a separate room. Seriously.

The food is respected, sacred even. Certain flavors would never be mixed. The order in which you eat them remains an unwritten code, and eye contact with each person around the table as you all cheer the rosé, rings true for every meal, never wavering. The portions are small, the courses varied, and the pace is slow; life is *good*. Why rush? The concept of "snacking" doesn't even exist in France. Breakfast is at 8 am, lunch at noon, and dinner at 8 pm - nothing in between unless it is a cookie after school for the little ones (at 4 pm sharp, "Le Goûter" as they call it). The idea of sitting on the couch with a bag of chips at 10 am is utterly foreign in France, and downright offensive.

Anne always says to eat like her mother. Beautifully tanned and sun-kissed, she is an effortlessly stylish French woman who hasn't been an ounce overweight in her life but enjoys food every bit as much as I was trying to all those years. "Everything in moderation, including moderation," my mother-in-law says with a sparkle in her eye. Leaning over to me she says "They say to drink with moderation, but I don't know her." followed by a childlike giggle. The mood is endearing and warm beyond belief. We may have been eating and drinking for hours at every meal, but I never remember being too drunk or too stuffed when the meals ended. If I were given an intro to French test, I'd pass the food and drink vocabulary section in a breeze but struggle to conjugate a single verb.

But the food is just a tool that links it all together, a delicious golden thread that weaves itself through the conversations, gently bringing those who sit together closer as the hours pass. While there are always uncomfortable aspects of integrating into a new culture, sitting at the table with my French family is never one of them. However, knowing who, where, and how many times to kiss, hug, and shake hands with French friends, family, and strangers? That will never cease to induce anxiety or make Anne laugh at my endless confusion.

* * *

I must have been around seven when my Mom started her move towards healthy eating. Organic ingredients almost instantly replaced the brightly colored packaging in the cupboard, the sugary name brands I was familiar with substituted for muted earth-toned boxes and ancient grains I'd never heard of like spelt and bulgur. We ate a lot of soups, dark brown bread, and baskets of fruit.

I was already so keenly aware of how different and unique the Waldorf School was compared to the neighborhood schools attended by the kids on my block, and having different food was just another peculiarity of my family. Not even having the same foods in my house as these friends did was yet another indication that I was different, further making it feel like I was unable to blend into their group, or any group.

In high school, I was always first in line at the kitchen for snacks and lunches, quickly grabbing the delicious sugary options they served that I couldn't get at home. Snapple juices, bags of Cheetos, double-chocolate chip muffins. That's when I started racking up the pounds too, and declining participation in more and more high school sports. I remained on the basketball team through my senior year, but I sat on the bench a lot, lacking the motivation to give it my full effort, and it showed.

Six weeks into my freshman year of college, I'd depleted the entire account balance available on my student dining card for the semester - mostly spicy chicken sandwiches, I think. In three years I never even stepped foot in the college athletic center once, for fear I would look out of place, like I had no business being in a gym. I tried running only one time in college, returning to my dorm room without making it half a mile, crossing University Street behind the dorm buildings, and only running halfway down palm tree-lined Campus Avenue before I gave up and turned around.

'I'll go again tomorrow, and at least twice as far.'

It was always tomorrow. I'd always deal with my weight tomorrow, always deal with every single one of my problems tomorrow. But tomorrow just never came. I often felt like someone who had lived through the Great Depression, hoarding junk food whenever I had the chance like I didn't know when I'd eat again.

I'd long since moved out of my parent's house, across the country from Maryland to California, far away from all the healthy and fresh organic foods my mother tried so hard to feed me, yet I still couldn't resist the urge to buy all the junk food possible when given the chance. This need to rebel against my mother's food, the healthy example she was trying to instill in me, and prove I could eat what I wanted, warped my connection with food for decades. Or maybe it was to create a sense of control in my ever-changing life. This challenge led to years of body issues, unhealthy eating habits, and a messy relationship with food that would be out of sync until I started sitting at those French tables with Anne and her family - twelve years after moving away from home.

Sitting at those French tables was almost a religious experience, and if 'God is love', then each reminder that I didn't need to stuff absolutely everything in sight into my fat face must be me loving myself too. What I wasn't aware of at the time was that unhealthy eating habits and portion control issues are also symptoms of ADHD - so maybe it wasn't the fault of carob after all.

Sitting through beautifully endless meals in France, never complete until a long silence indicates that not a single person has one more thing to say, I learned to truly appreciate each bite of food. I learned to slow down and enjoy the act of eating, savor the flavors, and embrace the slow pace of French meals and the intent and purpose behind them.

All it took to redefine my relationship with food was finding an amazing French woman to marry, being welcomed into her family with arms wide open, and clocking hundreds of hours eating delicious homemade French food - eating the cheese and drinking the wine. Easy, right?

French dining is an endurance sport. Filled with laughter, love, connection, passion, and a reverence and respect for the table and what it represents to each member of the family, which I am grateful has been instilled in me.

I will always struggle with a complicated relationship to food, but being able to see other cultures' connections to preparing, eating, discussing, and enjoying it together has helped me tremendously to understand how, why, and with whom we eat - and the power of the human connection it leads to. We eat not only to nourish our bodies but to nourish our souls.

Part of the beauty of travel is being given the opportunity to share intimate moments with people around the world from different cultures, walks of life, backgrounds, and traditions. While most will feel different, foreign, and uncomfortable, if you're lucky, take the time to try and deeply understand them all. Embrace the differences from your own experience and attempt to see something from a different perspective - even something as seemingly innocent as the dinner table. Perhaps it will reveal something to you that helps you to gradually face one of your flaws, to get you ready to take on one of your next adventures. I hope for you that it includes something as delicious as a robust Camembert de Normandie.

Life is short, frustrating, fleeting, and unpredictable, so take the time to eat good cheese, drink good wine, and ponder your relationship with both. Dubai had taught me a lot, both about the world and about myself, but most of all, Dubai had given me the greatest gift yet –a partner.

Anne had become my center, the one person who could ground me, a rock holding me in place so I didn't blow away into the breeze - or too far into my own mind.

Our flight out of the Emirates left bright and early on a hot and cloudless Monday morning in June. Flying direct from Dubai to Seattle, I peered out of the window and glanced at the map flickering on the screen before me and noticed that we were flying directly over the North Pole - ice caps and arctic tundra flickering between the clouds as we floated by. We were en route from one side of the world to the other, and while I'd struggle for years more to understand my relationship with food, I was making progress. Anne was by my side now - Dubai and everything that had come with our journey there fading into our past as we flew forward. It was time to find the next breadcrumb, the start of our next chapter.

As it happened, this chapter started with seeing Mima for the last time, the person who had pushed me to start following my life's breadcrumbs in the first place.

22

Don't Always Live in the Moment: Oh The Places You'll Go

"Every man's life ends the same way. It is only the details of how he lived and how he died that distinguish one man from another." – *Ernest Hemingway*

Ventura, CA, USA. Summer 2003
"Congratulations!
Today is your day.
You're off to Great Places!
You're off and away!

You have brains in your head.
You have feet in your shoes.
You can steer yourself
any direction you choose.
You're on your own. And you know what you know.

And YOU are the guy who'll decide where to go."
Seuss, *Oh, the Places You'll Go!, p.9, 2011*

Mima gave the same book to every one of her grandkids when they graduated from high school—all twelve of us, I think, but I still like to think she gave it only to me. It felt like it meant a little bit more when she handed me that big, colorful book, her neat, curly handwriting just inside the front cover, dated May 2003. If she only knew how seriously I'd take the advice within its pages, though maybe she did all along, and I wasn't about to let her down.

Spending carefree summers as a kid at her beach house in Ventura, CA, I heard such lines recited regularly—Mima quoted Dr. Seuss all the time. Days were filled with magical Swingswang-Swans, Humming-Fish, and Brown Bar-ba-loots fresh in my mind as I ran across the Srickle-sand to the ocean. *Oh, The Places You'll Go* was her favorite though, filled with fantastical illustrations of goofy lands, and every summer with Mima felt just as special and exciting as the pages of that book.

Grandmothers have a way of helping you to dream big, and she was one of the first to instill the spirit of a true explorer in me from as early as I can remember. She'd climb the tallest trees, get lost on the most winding of trails, and let us chew cinnamon gum in the back of her little red convertible, Chanel #5 wafting back through her freshly permed hair. She'd make us pancakes in the shape of any animal we could dream up and let us smother them in bright red strawberry syrup. She lived with more energy than a litter of puppies and was just as curious and unapologetic.

She practiced what she preached, too. On more than one occasion, well into her 80s but claiming to be 10 years younger, she flew overseas alone to work on archaeological digs in the scorching hot desert sun of the Middle East. Spry, classy, and sassy, she retained her youthful energy and fierce spirit right into her 90s. Imagining her living in a kibbutz, surrounded by mounds of dirt, the unforgiving Israeli sun beating down on her permed hair and perfume wafting through the air as she brushed away the dust on ancient pottery makes me smile. "Who on earth is this woman?" the archeologists must have said –, half joking, half in shock at her dedication.

'You have no idea.'

Emirates Terminal 3, Dubai. UAE, June 2018

"Cheers, my love," I said with a grin, champagne glasses clinking with nervous energy. Our bags were packed, carry-on only, backpacks were stowed, and we were off. All our belongings were donated, sold, or stored, our work contracts terminated, residence visas voided, no home address, only the open road. We were free.

"The things we do, my love." Anne said with a sigh, as the fasten seat belt sign illuminated above us.

Emirates flight EK229 left Dubai early on a sunny morning in June, flying nearly 14 hours directly over the top of the world before touching down in Seattle and launching Anne and me on a six-month trip around the world. As I felt the hum of the massive airplane come to life below me and we started to taxi, I thought back on the last four years in Dubai and couldn't help but wonder if the city had gotten the best of me or if *I* had simply gotten the best of me.

'Am I running from the city or running from myself?'

Could I have thrived in Dubai if I'd just developed better

personal skills? If I had introduced some discipline into my life? Maybe those buildings were shinier than ever, maybe the stress was self-induced, and maybe we could have had a great life in the UAE. But as the engines ramped up and our speed increased, leaving this magical and complicated city in the desert behind us, I could only focus on the future and what I could do differently from this day forward.

Anne and I had been working on our itinerary for months, literally counting the days until we boarded that plane on a whiteboard in our living room, crossing off each day after returning from work, marking the time until our exit. We'd plotted the cheapest routes, overnight buses, and bargain flights with layovers in random cities - bonus points if we'd never heard of it before.

And we'd bought travel health insurance specifically for the United States because our global travel health insurance provider refused to cover it. We always needed far more expensive, separate travel insurance for the US - annoying for us, but indicative of another much larger problem back "home". I'd been lucky during all my travels, never once having a major health crisis or injury, and the issues I had encountered - Thailand, South Africa, Chile - hadn't ever cost more than whatever bills I had in my pocket at the time. But the fear of ending up in a US hospital and nose-diving into financial ruin was terrifying.

'How is this the best system? How many people don't go to the doctor because the fear of the cost is more than the fear of getting sicker?'

But Anne and I weren't thinking of danger that afternoon. As we glided by the Space Needle and touched down at Sea-Tac International Airport, we just wanted nature —lots and lots of nature. And silence. Or rather, stillness. That was what we were after. We wanted more of what we first found in Iceland, and now, wherever we traveled, we demanded it. We immediately retreated from the big cities and sought the forests and the mountains, straight through Seattle, heading for the long roads through seas of ponderosa pine trees heading south. If there was a lull, we wanted to be in it, to savor that moment between inhale and exhale.

We had a rental car, which Anne instantly named Petra, for 21 days, a bright red SUV that would safely take us through Oregon, California, Arizona, Nevada, Utah, and Colorado. She would take us to majestic Crater Lake, to the quiet awe of the Redwoods National Park, to the mind-bending edge of the Grand Canyon and the early morning silence of Rocky Mountain National Park, most of these places which I'd be seeing for the first time myself.

In the first three weeks of our trip, we drove 2,361 miles (3,800 km) through seven states and six national parks. Each day was an education in the stunning nature I'd left behind, in my own backyard, to seek the unknown across the oceans. Few places on earth have the natural beauty and biodiversity of the United States.

'Too bad Americans don't have more vacation days to explore all this beauty.'

Each day was a chance for me to appreciate the endless array of scenery in the United States, right when I needed to see it most, reflected beautifully in Anne as she experienced each new place for the first time. I'd needed to step away in order to come back and fully appreciate its majesty all these years later.

Few weeks have gone by since living abroad without someone making a joke about an American president, the circus that is American politics, and asking me what I think about it. "I don't know what to think anymore, to be honest." I often reply. Politics have clouded my entire view of my home country for many years, but seeing the America that was separate from all that - the trees, rivers, lakes, and mountains that couldn't care less about what was going on in marble buildings thousands of miles away, and would be there long after they had all crumbled - made me smile.

I continued to wonder what home really was, if I'd ever call this place home again, and where our next chapter would lead us. I was left to ponder the things I'd left behind as well, the countless roads that had led me to this moment, sitting with Anne in a car she named Petra. I pondered the infinite roads I'd *not* gone down as well – the roads that were never meant to be part of my story at all.

Arches National Park, Moab, Utah, USA. July 2018

With the sun still fast asleep, Anne and I piled into Petra, light t-shirts blowing in the warm pre-dawn breeze as we made our way towards the entrance of Arches National Park. The faded dimly lit "Silver Sage Inn" sign blinked in the rear view mirror as we dissolved into the morning darkness. We were the first people awake on planet Earth that morning and anything was possible. Every minute of the day was ahead of us, and every possible outcome too.

Passing through the welcome gate, we entered the world of hovering giants high above us. Home to over 2,000 natural sandstone arches, this Martian landscape is the stuff of fairy tales. The first hints of daylight illuminated little of the world ahead as we meandered down the lazy two-lane road weaving ahead of us. Deep shadows hung heavy and the gravel popped under our tires as we came to a stop in a remote parking lot. The first to arrive, we started our hike from Wolf Ranch to the famed Delicate Arch, roughly 3 miles (5km) round trip, up the steep, sloping rock face and into the faint hint of dawn light on the horizon. We passed by ancient petroglyphs left by the Ute Indians some three hundred years earlier—mages carved of bighorn sheep, wild dogs, and riders on horseback came alive as our delicate shadows moved beyond them. The scenes reminded me of similar figures etched into the glass cups in the bathroom with the neon green shag carpet, it's almost like I had seen them before.

Rounding the corner to the Delicate Arch, we walked in single file, Anne leading the way, as she has done so much on our adventures, the first striking rays of light escaping from behind her body as she confidently balanced her stride on the narrow path. The bold summer sun growing brighter with every step, we stood at the end of the trail, the massive sandstone arch sloping majestically as it has for over 300 million years before us. The golden tones from the sunrise enveloped every inch of amber rock - a symphony of warm light blanketing everything in its sight.

It felt irreverent not to sit and take it all in—disrespectful to Mother Nature to utter a word as we digested the natural beauty before us, soaking in the silence of natural wonder. Anne grabbed my arm and rested her head on my shoulder as I squeezed her side tightly.

"The things we do, love," she gently whispered into the silence of a new day.

* * *

It has taken me years away to realize the beauty I had to leave behind in the US to find myself. But here I was returning with my partner, my teammate, and being able to explore these places with her was the greatest gift of all. Through traversing nearly one hundred countries around the world, I had yet to find a feeling as exhilarating as showing off the natural beauty of the one I'd come from, the one I'd turned my back on. I was proud, conflicted, heartbroken, and filled with gratitude. But was this "home" anymore? I wasn't sure.

'Will I ever live here again? Will we have children? Will they ever call America home?'

There was no way of knowing yet.

When our Emirates flight had lifted its wheels off the scorching tarmac of Dubai just weeks earlier, I had, somewhere deep in my soul, fantasized that we'd arrive in the US and both fall in love with it - me again and Anne for the first time, as somewhere she wanted to live next, perhaps even the place to raise a family. But despite the beautiful nature, the stunning wilderness, and open roads, there was a tension and strain we experienced in the cities that just didn't feel right.

While revisiting the US with Anne had a profound impact on my renewed respect and love for the natural beauty of the country, it also left me conflicted and torn about where our next chapter would lead us. We had headed straight for nature and the mountains, for the stillness of the empty natural landscapes. But we'd also avoided the major cities as much as possible outside of visiting friends, and that's where we'd likely raise a family if and when the time was right. If and when we decided to do it in America, that is.

We were caught in endless traffic in Los Angeles, got our car broken into, shattered glass crunching beneath our feet as we returned to our trusty ride Petra who'd been a bit beat up. Our credit cards and cash were stolen and used to buy McDonald's, luxury mattresses, and gift cards before we could cancel them. In an instant, we'd been snapped out of the fantasy we found in the woods. Stopping in Las Vegas en route to the Grand Canyon, we were disillusioned by the vacationing masses. No one seemed happy, people were tense. Everyone seemed to be moving in slow motion without knowing where they were going - incessant dings, bells, and whistles surrounding us announcing quickly diminishing bank accounts.

'Could we actually raise a family here?'

Through Seattle, Portland, San Francisco, Los Angeles, Las Vegas, and Denver, each major city felt like a different America than I'd remembered. The never-ending enthusiasm I'd been so proud to carry into the world seemed to have worn off in many we spoke to. The light, cheery, and hopeful attitude the world had come to expect from Americans had been dampened, and people were struggling. The homeless population in each city appalled Anne. She never had seen anything like it. After years away, I couldn't believe my eyes either. While seeing people experiencing homelessness was part of everyday life growing up in Washington, D.C., seeing it now, I realized how extreme the situation had gotten in contrast with how little I had seen overseas.

'Where is the social safety net? How can a country as wealthy as the USA let this many people slide to the fringes?'

We'd just packed up our bags and left Dubai, a country pushing the free market to the brink, a controlled experiment in capitalism unchecked. And we'd left it because of the extreme stress and anxiety the work expectations caused us. And while Dubai didn't have the homeless problem of the US, the factors that led many there were easily recognizable in both places.

I had a lot to think about, a lot to reflect on, and more breadcrumbs to follow before I'd know what to do next. But I felt like I had the tools now, that I was seeing more clearly than ever.

"Oh, the places you'll go!" Mima shouted encouragingly as Anne and I pulled away from the small casita she called home, headed to the next National Park on our journey. She was 91 and I knew this was the last time I would see her. As I stared through the rear view mirror at her waving excitedly with frail arms, thin hair dissolving into the caramel hills behind her, she knew it too.

I didn't know what I was searching for when I started, of course, but she knew that. What was important is that I started, and all along she knew I'd find what I was looking for someday, as long as I just took the first step. I couldn't have been more proud to introduce her to Anne, and while we still didn't know where we'd live, I had found what I was searching for and Mima saw that.

"So... be your name Buxbaum or Bixby or Bray
or Mordecai Ali Van Allen O'Shea,
You're off to Great Places!
Today is your day!
Your mountain is waiting.
So...get on your way!"

Without those seeds Mima helped plant in me, I may never have jumped on a plane to Thailand alone at 20 or accepted a job in Dubai where I didn't know a soul at 30. I wouldn't have gotten lost in Bangladesh or ended up in a leprosy colony in South Africa. And I wouldn't have met Anne, who I now could never imagine living a single day without.

Those glossy pages of tattered National Geographic magazines in the bathroom with the long, green plush carpet were my treasure map, but Mima laid the first breadcrumbs, enticing me to dive into their pages. She gave me permission to roll the dice and take the first steps towards discovering them all.

It is hard to appreciate all the places you'll go without understanding all the places you've been and the impact they have had on your world perspective. At some point, I'd have to find a middle ground between the Las Vegas Strip and desolate natural landscapes scattered around the globe. Home was surely hiding somewhere between the two, I just didn't know where yet.

But what I did know was that I had my partner. Who was the pilot, who was the sidekick, I didn't know. Where one of us ebbed, the other flowed. Where one held back, the other leaped forth.

And as we leapt, we both knew it meant leaving the US, and for me, with a renewed love for all that it could be but a bittersweet sense that it wasn't all there anymore. Thoughts swirling in my mind, we were again boarding a plane, this time to the bottom of the world, or at least it felt like it.

Heading nearly 5,000 miles (8,000 km) south, we were on our way to one of the most unique and unforgiving landscapes on earth.

23

Find Your Partner: The Worst Hotel in the World

"Let's, let's stay together. Lovin' you whether times are good or bad, happy or sad." —Al Green

Salar de Uyuni, Bolivia. July 2018

It was dark when our bus rolled into Uyuni and, to be honest, I don't even remember where we were coming from - a connecting flight somewhere in Brazil, I think. It was just after 6 p.m., but in the Southern Hemisphere that meant the sun set early in July, the middle of their winter. Most of the small shops that lined the few streets that made up this tiny town were closed. Only a handful of stalls remained open, dimly lit by flickering LED lights and a stray lamp post here or there. The streets were quiet. Strung-up lights connected the faint path ahead like breadcrumbs leading us toward our new adventure.

This small Bolivian town in the southwest of the country

served as the popular launch point for visitors from across the globe who were looking to explore the vast Uyuni Salt Flats, the largest salt flats on earth at over 6,200 square miles (10,000 sq km). The result of prehistoric lakes from 40,000 years ago that slowly evaporated over time, leaving nothing but a salty crust in zigzagging patterns as far as the eye could see, Uyuni was simply otherwordly.

Roaming the streets, Anne had preloaded the map to our small guesthouse on her phone, along with the location of the family-run tour company office where we would need to be at 8:00 sharp the next morning. Following her lead, I couldn't help but appreciate the setting I found myself in. Here I was, deep in South America, 12,000 feet (3,600m) above sea level on the crest of the Andes, in a new city, in a new country, following the lead of my trusty travel companion and best friend as we ventured into the unknown once again. We were two peas in a pod, bouncing around the globe together like excited pinballs, unsure of where we'd end up next.

Waking up with the sun a few hours later, we could have zipped up our small bags blindfolded, knowing exactly where every one of our minimal belongings fit. We'd been on the road for nearly six weeks at this point and had rarely stayed in one place for more than a couple of nights. Meandering back through the narrow streets Anne had mapped out, I followed her to a dusty, rusted-out cream-colored Jeep loaded down with canvas bags, dull blue coolers, and water tanks strapped to the roof–the long lost sibling of our trusty vehicle in Sudan four months earlier. Once our bags were tied down on the mounting pile, we squeezed in the back seat and set out into the vastness of the evaporated prehistoric lakes of the Altiplano high plateau. -The Uyuni Salt Flats of Bolivia beckoned.

Sitting cramped in the back seat of that jeep together, I couldn't help but think back to the moment I stepped out of that cab in Bangkok, peering up through the blinding sun to see Anne's huge smile and hands waving frantically on our first adventure together after a pinky promise that surprised us both. I couldn't have hidden the smile on my face if I'd tried.

As the car dropped off the last paved road, the ambient noise in the cabin of the jeep changed to a steady grumble of cracking and crunching, our thick wheels smashing crusty salt with ever-rapid rotations of their heavy rubber frames. The few scattered buildings remaining faded behind us as the dwindling vegetation and color whizzed by, replaced with nothing but hues of cream, ivory, and bone - nearly everything in sight a varied shade of bright white salt.

We spent the morning driving into an ever-expanding horizon that refused to come closer as we all sat in silence, our driver's eyes the only previous witness to this stunning natural phenomenon in the place he calls home. Faintly, as if a mirage, specs of color began to emerge in the distance, and as we came closer, we were quickly surrounded by a monument of flags from around the world sticking out of the earth like tiny toothpicks in an empty sea of crusted white. Beating and rippling wildly in the wind as if they were trying to escape this prison of brine, the dark blues, vibrant reds, and stark yellows screamed through the sky, snapping with each gust of wind. We ate cold rice out of a damp cooler and explored a towering cactus garden placed into this boundless expanse by a playful creator. Watching the sunset that night, a palate of glorious fiery reds and blood orange painted across in the sky, the silence between us came naturally. We were aflush with awe, as we witnessed the stunning display in the world around us.

Curling up within the walls of Palacio de Sal, a hostel of sorts, made entirely of salt blocks, we couldn't help but giggle at where we'd found ourselves. Over one million salt blocks combined to create the floor, ceiling, walls, beds, tables, and chairs of the 12-room lodge, which made for one of the most unique, and downright uncomfortable, places we have ever stayed. Freezing cold, unable to sleep, pounding headaches from the altitude, and a desperate desire for the morning to come, I couldn't avoid the heartfelt recognition that this was what a partner was for. There is no one else in the world with whom I would have wanted to be that miserable, ensconced in such a breathtaking and magical place at the outer limits of our planet.

'At least there's no Justin Bieber.'

* * *

If there was one central theme through all my early solo travels, it was just that: they were solo. I was alone, and I was on my own. I was a one-man band. Backpack on my shoulder, a big dumb smile on my face, and all the youthful exuberance and naivety of a puppy dog. This wasn't intentional, it just so happened that I hadn't found anyone crazy enough to join me - but I sure hoped that one day I would.

For every new chapter I started in my life - moving from D.C. to California, bouncing to Thailand, and then on to Dubai - I was hoping to find this fictional character. As I turned thirty alone on the road in 2014, I began to think that it just may not happen. After all, who was spontaneous and adventurous enough to follow this goofy, enthusiastic American to the far corners of the globe without any direction at all except for the adventure itself?

Arriving in Dubai without knowing a soul, I was newly optimistic that there may be a chance in that vibrant new city, imagining the thousands of strangers I would meet and get to know over my years in this new home. But I could never have dreamed that Anne would be exactly the second person I met in that city, and that we would be married less than three years later.

Within days of meeting each other, I was enthralled. A boisterous, accented, golden-tanned European woman quick to make the first joke, eager for anything, and nothing but fun. Anne was my introduction to both Dubai and to what was possible if you truly are able to find your better half out there on the road.

But Anne wasn't just a happy-go-lucky travel partner—she was also my salvation. Sure, outwardly she was more than I could ever have imagined, a beautiful, light-hearted, goofy person to travel the world with. But inwardly, she calmed me, she brought me down to earth, slowly stopped my frantic spinning, and began to place some order into my universe. She made me want to be vulnerable with her, to share my goals, my weaknesses, and my ambitions, no matter how buried, because we both saw in each other what we could accomplish together. Sometimes one plus one can equal more than two.

Finally, I felt like I had found someone I could share life's great adventures with, both externally on the road and internally in my soul. She was someone for whom nothing was forced and nothing was faked. While Anne may have been cautious or unsure about some of the places or situations we found ourselves in together, she never let that get in the way of the adventure.

Quick to voice her opinion, to make her thoughts known, and to try something new, even if it scared her, she complimented my personality and traveling style perfectly - like peanut butter and jelly, like a baguette and camembert.

The goal of finding a life partner is not to find a copy of yourself but the person with whom you fit together like two puzzle pieces –the mutual recognition that you'll both make the other better, regardless if it is easy or not. This is a balance that must be perfect, with both parties giving and taking equal amounts, both willing to step up and knowing when to push, when to pull, and when to remain calm and motionless. Being with Anne taught me when to lead and when to follow, when to make the decision, and when to rely on her expertise.

While I had vastly more travel experience than she had when we met, Anne was quick to sign up for any new adventure, placing her faith and trust in me to show her the ropes and to ensure we managed to get from A to B. As our relationship - and the miles traveled together - progressed, our unique dynamic began to evolve. Anne was quick to pick up on some of the more reckless travel decisions I would have made on my own and adamant that we implement some form of structure, organization, and thought into how we went about the world - and lived our lives together.

Of the endless qualities I find so magnetic in Anne, her constant striving for more, for better, for progress is perhaps my favorite. "Je ne suis pas là pour boire l'eau des pâtes," she is quick to say, a saying which has found its way into my heart and follows us everywhere: "I am not here to drink pasta water." She isn't here to play around, mess about, or sit in one place. If she wants something, she goes after it. If something needs to be done, then let's do it tonight.

If there is something we want, we go after it, right now, together.

* * *

The sun finally did arrive that frigid July morning in the Salt Flats of Bolivia as we tossed and turned in the hotel made of salt, and with it, one of the most unexpected and memorable travel days Anne and I had spent together yet. Muscles sore and eyes nearly glued shut after cursing the Travel Gods all night, we groaned and moaned as we again packed up our things, chewed on cold bread, gagged down a tin mug of instant coffee, and hit the road stuffed in the back of the cream colored rusty jeep high in the Altiplano desert.

Believing we were heading back to the dusty streets of Uyuni to begin our long bus ride to the cascading capital city of La Paz, we settled in for a long and bumpy ride. To our surprise, we continued towards the horizon, not away from it, and back towards what little civilization we'd come from. We continued to the southwest, toward the border with Chile, and slowly increased our elevation to over 13,800 feet (4,200 m) as we approached Laguna Colorada - the Red Lagoon. This massive 37 square mile (60 sq km) lake is roughly one foot deep with profound rust-colored algae, providing further contrast between the dazzling blue skies and the towering cinnamon-hued snow-capped hills in the distance. Simple, olive-tinted shrubs lay rambling around the edges of this massive pond and, dotting the shores, a huge flock - a "flamboyance" - of brilliantly bold flamingos were following each other around like teenage ravers looking for the after-party. A sea of fuchsia inhaled and exhaled in unison before our gaze.

Standing between me and the other-worldly scene before my eyes stood Anne in all her eclectic glory. Adorned in her eccentric, mismatched travel clothes – Adidas track jacket, multicolored leggings, well-worn shoes, silk scarf covering her head from the dust, reflective chrome sunglasses dotting her face – she perfectly encapsulated everything I could ever have dreamed of in a travel and life partner – and so much more. She took my breath away that day and has continued to every day since.

Find your life partner, spend the time, and do the work to understand what it truly is that you need from another in order to develop into your best self. Get to know yourself so well that you can spot in others the qualities that will make you a better you. Come to know what you can offer and to understand the qualities that shine the brightest within you so that you may share them with a partner, with others, with the world.

No matter the work it takes, when you encounter a potential match, know that if you have found the right person, through struggles, tears, obstacles, and failures, that the triumphs will be that much sweeter and expand your life exponentially beyond what you thought possible.

Life isn't meant to be lived solo; sharing is half the fun.

The desert holds its own magic, a mysterious mix of extreme highs and deadly lows, arid desolation with extraordinary, contrasting beauty all its own – whether in the Sahara Desert of Sudan or the Altiplano of Bolivia. While Anne and I had been on countless adventures the world over, seeing her against the stark backdrop of endless nothingness solidified her wonder in my mind even more. Without a single element on the horizon other than Anne, her magic stood out more than ever.

No matter how stunning a desert may be, there is something about the sight of trees and mountaintops reaching, frozen, into the heavens, that I can never get enough of. The desert is simply no match for raw mountain wilderness—at least not on my treasure map.

But this was *our* map now, and Anne and I were pieces marching to the next space, chasing the next breadcrumb, hoping to find the wisdom we needed to make our upcoming move. The next breadcrumb was going to require quite a leap to catch and would put me face to face with something I had grown up absolutely hating.

The only difference was this time I would be doing it in the Arctic.

24

Try Everything Again: I Really Hate Hiking, But I Can't Stop

*"Deep down, at the molecular heart of life, the trees and
we are essentially identical."*
–Carl Sagan

Hiking used to sound like the stupidest thing imaginable, at least on paper. All you do is walk, more often than not up some sort of steep path with stupid dirt and a stupid view. There isn't a 7-11 around every bend, and cell reception is always spotty. The sun is always too bright, sunscreen stings in your eyes, and if you happen to be carrying water, it's always warm and tastes like plastic.

I swore by all that for years, and can bet I said most of those things out loud at some point, too, but then something changed –especially after our US road trip and the wonder we experienced in all those National Parks. Nature was something we needed in our next chapter, seasons, the rhythm of the year, and daily reminders of the natural world around us. At least one insect flying by from time to time would be nice as well.

It's no secret that exercise releases endorphins and that endorphins make you feel good, but I hadn't ever put the two together consciously and felt the difference for myself. There is a certain amount of physical discomfort you have to put yourself through in order to get to those endorphins, and I was never willing, or interested, in putting in the work to get to the reward. That could be said for a lot of areas of my life over many years. I was never interested in delayed gratification, only instant, which was rarely in my self-interest.

After feeling that spark of energy from the natural world again, it was hard to ignore it. And after spending four years in the sterile desert landscape of the Middle East, it was impossible not to continue chasing the wilderness.

Conflicted and bittersweet feelings still swirling in my gut about our time in the US, and my reflections about returning to it, or not, I was in need of those endorphins that hiking can bring. We'd searched for the most quiet and protected nature in America, and the impacts had been profound, bringing calm to both my mind and body.

So what would we find if we searched for some of the most remote and isolated nature the world had to offer?

Nuuk, Greenland. September 2018

Three months into our trip around the world, Anne and I found ourselves waking up to a cool, but sunny morning in Nuuk, Greenland. After devouring large bowls of hearty granola and thick yogurt dripping with honey, we threw on our backpacks and marched south down the main drag, headed for the nearest bus stop. While waiting, Anne wandered off down a side street, chasing incredibly colorful and intricate graffiti murals dotting the drab and weathered buildings. I struck up a conversation with a weathered local who, when finding out the hike we were about to do, immediately told me to watch for bears. One had come dangerously close to attacking a hiker just a few weeks earlier.

'Wait, is he talking about polar bears? We are in the Arctic after all. Good to know.'

"Is this bus heading to Qinngorput?" I said sheepishly, certain there was no way I had pronounced it correctly as the clunky bus screeched to a stop in front of us. A simple nod indicated the grizzled bus driver had at least half understood what I meant as we took two seats towards the front. Exiting the bus ten minutes later and watching it quickly motor off down the road, Anne and I found each other standing in the middle of nowhere, with only a smattering of brightly colored houses in the distance and a small collection of newly built apartments lining the road. It felt like we were living out of a Wes Anderson movie– "Welp, guess this is it - time to walk," Anne pronounced with a grin as she skipped off ahead of me.

As clouds began to form above us and left only patches of blue sky poking out behind them, we slowly said goodbye to the pavement and hello to the Greenlandic shrubbery and jagged rock formations dotting the path ahead - the endless array of grays and greens masking where one became the other. The lower soil layer in Greenland is permanently frozen, but the native plants have adapted, and their color adds to the unique makeup of this natural landscape. Bright, white puffs of Alpine Pussytoe dot the trail, offset by the delicate flowers of White

Arctic Whitlow grasses.

As the saying goes, Iceland is full of green, and Greenland is full of ice. In the barren and desolate Greenlandic landscape ahead of us, pools of black water lay lurking in the low points and young moss-covered boulders dotted the horizon, some the size of a lunch box, others the size of a box car. Giggling like school children getting away with something, we confidently walked through the imposing scenery and headed towards Ukkusissat; its peak now covered in a dense, wet fog that had quickly encircled and engulfed the natural world around us - like a heavy blanket of moisture that Mother Nature had tossed on the morning.

After nearly two hours of climbing, wedging, hoisting, and crawling up seemingly endless terrain, difficulty increasing with every step, we looked at each other and had a chuckle, a mutual understanding that we weren't going any further. Anne and I have developed a solid and unspoken understanding after all the traveling we have done together. We wouldn't be making it to the top of Ukkusissat, and that was perfectly fine. The moist fog thickened into a constant dense rain. Our bright blue and red jackets were doing their best to keep us warm and dry, but they had reached their limit, too.

Turning back towards Qinngorput, we laughed as we scampered down the trail across the wet rocks and increasing puddles of fresh rainwater lining the landscape. "Hey, I would still rather go hiking in the rain with you any day than sit in an office." I called to Anne, the joys of being out in nature with all its infinite personalities still amusing in the wet and cold, endorphins pumping within me. Arriving back to the slim covering of the bus stop, I turned to Anne and said "Remember that guy we met in town on our way up here? He told me we really needed to be careful of bears."

"Wow, of all the ways to go, a attacked by a polar bear in Greenland would be a good one!" Anne responded without missing a beat.

* * *

Since we began traveling together, Anne and I have planned entire trips around hiking, visiting National Parks, and finding the best mountains and nature to explore when we're anywhere near them −all the time chasing that feeling we get when our bodies are put to work in the silence of nature.

I now have the same reaction fifteen minutes into any hike: "Man, how good is it to use your legs a little and feel your heartbeat?!" Hiking is like a yawn for your entire body, much like yoga but with better views. I can't help but think of my body thanking me every time I put it to use, like it appreciates me pushing myself a little, allowing it to show me that I can handle a bit more than sitting at a desk for eight hours a day and casually strolling on the elliptical machine on Tuesday and Thursday mornings.

Traveling is always about the sensory overload - sights, smells, sounds, feelings, emotions - all make travel so much more visceral than everyday life. But for me, the smells are usually what I remember most. Smells help me to remember home in a strange way, a home I have long left, and a home that in so many ways doesn't exist anymore. A home I am still searching for. A home that is in some ways further from me each day, yet drawing me toward it as well.

The smell of fresh pine trees always brings me right back to the whoosh of air and the overload of smell I'd get opening the screen door of my childhood home during the holidays, fresh Christmas wreath lovingly attached to the door knocker by my mother. Eucalyptus is the scent of my childhood summers and adventures with Mima in Southern California, learning to climb trees and feeling free to roam under the massive trunks of those giant white trees, their bark peeling and collecting on the fresh California grass below. I went for ten years without living in a country that had proper seasons, moving from California to Thailand and on to Dubai. So once we started traveling, I couldn't wait for autumn, to smell the changing seasons, to smell the scent of the falling leaves, the coming rains, and the damp foliage around the city. There is no scent quite like the smell of the frigid air filled with falling snowflakes. It's impossible to describe.

As soon as the leaves started to fall a few months into our trip, our first real autumn together, it instantly brought me right back to the neighborhood parks of my youth; the smell of the changing air filling my nostrils. That familiar eucalyptus smell of southern California is nearly identical to that which I found in southern France, a new home for me since I met Anne and a smell I continue to associate with the feeling of home, family, comfort, and relaxation. And that powerful pine scent? If I get lucky, I pass through a deep wave of that familiar smell on any hike in the mountains, always pausing with a smile on my face when it hits me. I found it in Nepal, Colorado, Croatia, and even found it in Greenland - none of the places where I grew up, but serving in the same way to fulfill a small taste, or smell, of home.

Hiking will remain a cherished pastime for me. From Greenland to Peru, Austria to Jordan, it will always represent the moments Anne and I have felt the most alive while exploring the world together. And it has given me the pause to recognize some of the more subtle elements in my environment, no matter how fleeting, that give me that feeling of home.

Maybe I hike to chase those familiar smells. Maybe I hike to put my body to use and block out my thoughts for just a moment, to bring me calm and silence. Maybe I hike to feel small in the world, and often lost—an important thing to feel sometimes.

Maybe we hike to feel closer to each other without saying a word, because we both feel that same inexplicable pull to the mountains, or maybe we hike because we're both still searching for that feeling of home, and somehow, for whatever reason, when we go hiking, we catch a feeling of something that gives us some of that comfort, as children of the earth, even if it's in a country where we've never traveled before and may never return to again.

Any time I find myself lost in the silence of the forest, the words of Robert Frost always run through my mind. "The woods are lovely, dark, and deep. But I have promises to keep and miles to go before I sleep." I'll never know what he was chasing in his woods, but I have a feeling he found it, and I, too, have miles to go before I sleep while I look for mine. Whatever bond I now have with hiking is a promise I'll always keep as well. It's my body trying to tell me something, and I'd be a fool not to listen.

Take the time to assess the things in the world that you connect with and those you don't. Some of these connections may last a lifetime, and others may change. What I hated about hiking as a teenager, I love now. What I once hated about life as a teenager, I love now.

As you grow older, revisit the feelings, places, and activities that you've built up strong emotional responses to. Who knows, you may discover a new part of yourself that needs to be awakened to help you take your next steps along the path of life. Don't write off the past, don't write off that which used to make you uncomfortable, and don't write off those who used to make you uncomfortable either.

But for all the hiking Anne and I had done to this point, we'd never needed more than a backpack, a half-filled water bottle, and a couple of granola bars. If I was truly going to test my love for hiking, really push myself to the limits and search for the benefits on the other side, I needed to take on a hiking challenge well beyond my pay grade – and there was only one place to go.

It was time to climb the tallest mountain in the world.

Well, most of it, anyway.

25

Know When to Stop: Having a Midlife Crisis on the Roof of the World

"The mid-life crisis is just those times when you're not so into the things you were when you were younger." -Jay Kay

Kathmandu, Nepal. December 2018

The zigzagging, dusty streets of Thamel are alive with adventure nearly 24 hours a day - incense and motorbike horns endlessly filling nose and ears. This popular neighborhood in the Nepali capital is the meeting point for adrenaline-seeking travelers from around the world, most either on their way to or just returning from the majestic Himalayan mountains for which the country is so well known. Eclectic shops lining the tight alleys are filled with used climbing equipment and knock-off North Face jackets, worn-out hiking boots and medications for altitude sickness. In August, I'd turned 34 in Aguas Calientes,

Peru, just a couple of months into our whirlwind trip around the world, and by December, we were piecing together the last bits of gear we'd need to attempt our big trek to Mount Everest Base Camp a few days later. And while birthdays had never been outsized moments of celebration for me, the idea that I'd turned 34 kept gnawing at the back of my brain, because it meant on my next birthday I'd be 35 and *surely* I'd have to have my life figured out by then. No matter how relaxed and laid back the hostel happy hours and reggae cover bands were, listening to a fairly convincing Nepali Bob Marley one evening while sprawled out on mismatched beanbag chairs, my mind kept bouncing back to one thing – on my next birthday, I'd be 35.

And here I was at 34, without a job, on a trip around the world. Once again, I was fleeing the reality that at some point I'd have to grow up and start building a real career, in a real city, where I planned on staying longer than a football season or two if I ever wanted to have a family.

Since leaving the US, I always gauged where I lived abroad by what time I'd have to stay up in order to watch my beloved Washington sports teams lose. In Thailand, it was midnight, and in Dubai, it was 9 p.m. We were moving in the right direction, and anything on the earlier side would be an improvement.

Anytime time I thought of my career as we collected the last of our gear throughout Kathmandu the back of my neck would stand up, and an almost primal terror would grip my gut, an acknowledgment that deep down I knew it this moment would be coming soon. This moment, as we collected the last of our gear through Kathmandu, used sleeping bags, and a 50-liter backpack, was no different. I was 34, for goodness sake. This kind of mid-life crisis should have happened to me at 24, or at least that's what society had told me. Regardless, for once in my life, the next stop was going to need to be where I settled down for at least a few years, and I would have to face the true inner task I'd been putting off for so long – discipline, motivation, a strong work ethic, delaying gratification. Happy hour is only an hour, right? I'd successfully extended it for over a decade.

'Why do I keep moving? What am I trying to find?'

Everyone deals with this deep inner work differently, whether it is to avoid dealing with it or to avoid admitting it exists altogether. I had spent the better part of fifteen years doing the former by simply moving around the globe, hoping the next destination would magically solve it – like a software cleaning program idly working in the background and clearing space on my desktop without me having to do much more than let it run. I thought my problems would automatically sort themselves out if I ignored them long enough, but that's not how it works. As the renowned mindfulness teacher Jon Kabat-Zinn has written, "Wherever you go, there you are."

For me, the avoidance of staying in one place for too long, especially while traveling, allowed me to only deal the most essential tasks required in that moment. I didn't have to think about a career path, about stocks, dental insurance, or a pension plan if I woke up every morning only having to think about the my current needs for the staples of food, water, and shelter.

Finding a family doctor in a new city and finally asking nagging health-related questions left me with both anxiety and panic.

'What if I'm dying? What if I only have a few months left? I might as well enjoy them.'

Memories of my illogical health panic in Phuket on my 30th birthday surfaced in my mind. But more logical questions had been pushed to the back of my mind for too many years..

'*Does this mole look funny? Is this normal anxiety about life or have I been having panic attacks? Is my blood sugar ok?*'

Lukla, Nepal. December 2018

Early the next morning, bulging backpacks slung over our apprehensive shoulders, we nervously sipped instant coffee from styrofoam cups as we found ourselves boarding what was surely the worst plane ever assembled, quick to wonder what we were doing flying from Kathmandu, Nepal to Lukla, literally the most dangerous airport in the world.

Precariously perched in the foothills of the Himalayan mountains, this tiny village is the starting point for any brave soul attempting to summit Mount Everest, the world's tallest peak– a mountain top that we wouldn't even see until we'd been trekking upwards for over a week.

We weren't here to summit Mount Everest, but we were here to hike to her Base Camp, a 10-day round trip trek covering some 84 miles (135 km) and topping out at an elevation of 17,598 feet (5,364 m) - the highest point, if we made it, that either of us would ever have ascended.

Neither Anne nor I, nor our friend Jess, who was brave enough to tackle the challenge with us, were anything close to athletes. Still, we thought, "What would happen if we really pushed ourselves –if we at least took on a year-end challenge that we might very well fail?"

So now here we were, anxious and breathing deeply as the world's worst airplane bobbed like a feather in the wind, just barely hovering over jagged cliffs as far as the eye could see. There was only one on each side, but Anne still found a way to dig her fingernails deep into my hand from the seat behind me, trying to keep cool while internally panicking. The runway in Lukla comes out of nowhere, and if you catch a glimpse of it out of the window as you approach, you'll swear that *this* is surely not where you're going to land.

The runway literally dead ends into a mountain wall that seems way too close, and the entire runway sits at an angle with the steep hill at one end to support the plane's deceleration, and the fast drop off at the other end to spit planes off into the air. The runway simply ends, plunging hundreds of feet below, leaving you hoping the plane has enough momentum to stay afloat. The worst part of the whole trek may well have been just flying in and out of that airport. If you've ever dreamed of doing the trek, don't Google it before you go. And definitely don't Google plane crashes at Lukla airport...

"Pfft, good luck," a gruff female voice stammered as she heaved her large frame up the last step to the village of Lukla from the cascading dirt path below. This was our first look at a hiker returning from Base Camp just as we approached the entrance to Sagarmatha National Park to start ours. I couldn't believe the bitterness on her breath, seeming like she was personally offended that we were just starting to attempt something that she herself had obviously hated.

'Yikes. What have we got ourselves into?'

I've had a handful of moments in my life when I am truly disconnected from it all, when either the location I am in geographically or the situation I'm in physically, demands that I disengage from every single thing in my life except for the core survival instincts we're all born with. Climbing to Everest Base Camp meant only three things – waking up in the morning and sleeping at night in the next village, making sure we brought enough water and found enough food, and ensuring we didn't get lost along the way. That was it. Everything else faded away.

Cell reception didn't exist, which meant neither did Facebook or Instagram. We'd tried to download podcasts before we left, but when you're surrounded by that much pure nature, it's hard to do anything but just listen to the silence and take it all in, repeated inhales and exhales the metronome from sunrise to sunset, while the oxygen levels decreased with each step closer to our goal. We could pay a little extra at each tea house along the trail to charge our phones, but what was the point? This was Mother Nature giving us a chance to step away from all of that for a few days - something we were apparently powerless to do in our everyday lives. We gladly gave in. When was the last time you didn't have the internet for ten days? It was a true gift.

It was mid-December, approaching the holiday season, and deathly cold temperatures were quickly seeping into the high-altitude valley villages where we continued to climb to each day. Phakding to Dingboche, Tengboche to Gorak Shep - it just kept getting colder each night. Since we were going up to such high altitudes, we were required to stop every couple of days for at least twenty-four hours to let our bodies recalibrate and acclimatize to the increasing absence of oxygen in the air. With all the extra time, surrounded by cold and silence, no electronic distraction, and often too exhausted to speak to each other, we were all left with time to ourselves to think, and try to process what we were doing out there.

This was the last great adventure of our trip around the world together. In a week, we'd be in France with family, sitting around the Christmas table sharing our stories and reconnecting with each other, "eating the cheese and drinking the wine". A week after that, we'd be on a one-way flight to Amsterdam in the dark of night, with not so much as a thought about what we'd do there. However, for now, all we had to focus on was getting up this glorious mountain.

Each day was filled with deafening silence and the overpowering feeling of smallness that mountains that size engenders. I'd wanted to find my purpose in life by the end of this trip around the world, wanted to know for certain what direction to follow, which professional path to take for the next installment of my life. We'd successfully ejected from Dubai, but had yet to dial in the destination of where we'd land - flying, for now, through the outer reaches of global space, trying to soak it all in. No amount of layers warm you when it is this cold. Walking up the well-worn creaking steps of our guest house in the Namche Bazaar, we were already well north of 11,000 feet (3,400 meters) and short of breath - what little we had, escaping our mouths and forming wisps of white in front of us as we searched for our rooms. Throwing down our dusty packs onto the colorful bed, they bounced off stacks of thick mismatched blankets, and Anne and I were quick to dig out our sleeping bags and burrow inside them as well in an attempt to get warm. At this altitude, there is a bone-chilling cold that digs into your very core; your only focus is getting warmer, even if only a little. The inside of the room is the same temperature as the outdoors, save for the wind, and the only source of heat in these guest houses dissolves an arm's length from the wood stove at the center of the common area.

After hours of tossing and turning, finally seeing a streak of faint blue in the endless night sky confirmed a few hours later, that morning was soon to arrive. Fighting the feeling of desperately having to pee but aware of the soul-crushing cold if I were to exit my blanketed tomb, we slowly braced ourselves, braved the elements and emerged from our sleeping bags and tugging on a third pair of socks, adjusting the wool hats we'd slept in, and fought through semi-frozen toothpaste to clean our mouths. We were ready to take on Day Four, and our goal was the Tengboche Monastery some 3,280 feet (1,000 m) higher; it would take us all day.

Hot chai tea is more appreciated on a morning like this—any hot liquid a welcome sensation inside otherwise freezing skin and bones, a zen-like moment as you look down and deeply feel your body enjoying the simple pleasure of warmth seeping through your frigid limbs. Quick to scoop rock-hard peanut butter into my mouth and wash it down with undissolved electrolyte powder, we filled our water bottles, heaved our packs up and over our backs, and headed out in silence, only the sound of shuffling hiking boots on well-worn stone following behind us.

The blue sky looks different up this high. Maybe it's the contrast with the jagged peaks, maybe it's the altitude, maybe the clarity that the lack of noise, light pollution, or chemicals in the atmosphere brings. It is stunning. It's the same sky I've seen every day of my life, but it just looks different up this high.

Steadily traversing the tapering cobblestone streets of Namche Bazaar, we headed up. Up the small streets, up the steep steps, up the narrow hillside. With each foot forward, the buildings grew further apart, and by the time the sun pierced the edge of the mountains that lay before us, warm light cascaded down the endless path ahead. The view we saw was nothing but pure nature in a multitude of layers filled with different colors, shapes, and personas.

At my feet, bone-dry latte-colored dust swirled around the tattered edges of my cheap hiking boots. A few steps further ahead, dotting the path around each turn, lay the weathered twigs and twisted roots of wind-worn shrubs holding on to their last remaining green leaves. The towering pine trees that had guided our way up much of the cavernous path for the first few days were now mostly behind us, the greenery reducing its presence the higher we climbed, with the gaps between clusters of trees growing larger with every diversion in the path. Looking ahead at the horizon, the tree line lay visible on the exposed faces of the great mountains before us, the variety of gray, white, and black mingled through the mountainous shapes in layers, fading into the distance. Shadows, silhouettes, and silence danced in mystery. Capping the scene was that magical blue sky, the darkest and most saturated blues contrasting abruptly with the thin snow-white outlines, marking the frigid edges of the peaks in the distance. So stark was the difference that my eyes were truly unable to process what they were witnessing, having little reference to make sense of it all.

My own breath, increasing in struggled gasps with every step, was the only soundtrack to the engulfing silence encompassing everything around me, providing a heavy comfort like a weighted blanket. There was only the path ahead, only forward, only progress. And my mind, for once, was clear, quiet, and empty.

On Day Eight, feet moving in slow motion for the last few hundred feet, we took our final steps, arriving at Everest Base Camp around lunchtime. Dueling emotions filled the air. I was giddy with excitement and on the verge of tears. The camp lay barren, devoid of any evidence that anyone ever based any campsite here. A small collection of piled gray rocks marked the spot, tattered prayer flags in red, green, blue, and yellow flapped violently, strung from side to side.

The irony of Everest Base Camp is that there is no peak at all, no summit, no stunning view down below. It is just the starting point north to the true peaks towering high above. Protected in a valley surrounded by giant masses of stone above us, we marveled at how far we'd come - and at how much further the zenith of this great mountain lay above us. As I stood there, I remembered one of the earliest issues of National Geographic I had found in that bathroom with the neon green carpet from October 1963, the 75th anniversary issue. The cover showed the back of a climber with bright yellow boots and a backpack, surrounded in a sea of white snow as he trekked vertically towards the peak ahead, the American flag proudly planted atop with the title "Six to the Summit: How We Climbed Everest." I put down my backpack, removed my thick gloves, and, hands shaking with exhaustion, reached in and unfolded two full-sized canvas flags, one American, one French. Draping the stars and stripes over my shoulders, I felt like a gold medalist at the Olympics, and a rush of accomplishment and pride overcame me.

We had done it. We had conquered a trek we thought we had no business doing. We started with one step and refused to stop until we got to the last one. If we could do *this* together, we could do anything. We chuckled to each other, tears filling our eyes, grins as big as bananas. "The things we do, my love," Anne whispered from her cocoon of scarves. "The things we do."

There was only one thing left to do now. Turn around and walk back.

* * *

What I found in those mountains was a haunting emptiness, a hollow nothingness within the still and silent peaks that constantly surrounded us. I'd wake up in the morning, stand outside in the -13F (-25C) in awe that it was even possible to be there - right there at that moment - and just tried to take it all in, to etch it into my brain so I'd never forget it. The mountains didn't provide me with answers; they provided a mirror. I woke up and looked out at these mountains every morning for a mere ten days. The same mountains that had been looking at each other every morning for over 50 million years.

When you take everything, it allows you to realize how much you have. When all you do is walk every day with 26 pounds (12kg) on your back, up and down mountain valleys as the oxygen in the air slowly decreases to 50% of what it is at sea level, it's easy to have one of those *epiphany* moments. It's almost cheesy.

But it was throughout those 85 miles (135km) that I realized I didn't need to find some sacred clarity in those mountains, some secret road map to where my career, and life, would lead next. Rather, my epiphany was that I already had within me all of the tools I'd need to figure it out.

It was time to stop, and that was ok. Time to stop jumping from country to country, from job to job, and from one thread to the next. Time to stop jumping all together, and embrace being *grounded*.

I had my best friend right there next to me the entire time, often leading the path up the Himalayan floor in front of me, and in all that we'd gone through, all we'd experienced, all that we'd walked towards and walked away from, we'd always figured it out together. As long as we were on the same page, conscious and aware of all that we had, whatever happened would work itself out in a beautiful unveiling of the next chapter of our lives.

I often thought back to that bitter woman we encountered on our first day, what her story had been, and how this trek had helped, or hurt, her perspective on life. I'll never know, but I hope that she eventually found something as magical as I did buried in those mountains.

When asked to give travel advice, I've spent years telling people, "Take the leap and the world will catch you, I promise." It was time I took my own medicine and seriously trusted that the world would give me exactly what I needed when I needed it most.

But for me, the next leap wasn't a leap at all, but rather the absence of one - and being okay with the stillness that came with it. And so, with Anne by my side, and knowing we could figure it out anywhere, life in the Dutch capital sounded as good a spot as any for our next phase of life to begin.

Prior to moving to Dubai, Anne had studied in the Netherlands and although I'd only floated through it on that boisterous Euro trip with high school friends so many years ago, I loved the idea of Amsterdam.

For years, my only memory of exploring Amsterdam was standing on the stairs of the Anne Frank House with my buddies and knocking on the door as a Dutch man on a bike sped by, shouting with a chuckle, "I don't think she's home, boys!" We'd been looking for the Anne Frank apartments and were too dumb to know the difference. Returning to the Netherlands to live would be a whole different experience. And maybe I could finally read her diary.

We were in search of a city that valued a work/life balance and championed the raising of independent, strong, resilient children. These were the foundations of the American Dream

I had been sold growing up, and I was determined to find out if they actually existed. Which country was still living like the Golden Age of America with 1950's prosperity? Wherever we stopped, we would be taking a gigantic hit to our salaries and paying taxes for the first time in the better half of a decade.

The Netherlands felt like a pretty good bet, and we had to start somewhere.

* * *

Know when to stop, know when to take a break, and know when its time to pause and take stock. Know when to take the seeds of perspective, wisdom, experience, and the lessons you've collected throughout your journey and begin to plant them around you.

The adventure of travel is in collecting all the seeds, but the wisdom is in knowing when, and where, to stop, so that you can watch them grow.

But before we settled down, I still had one more breadcrumb that had been nearly impossible to find no matter how hard I tried, as silly as it sounds. At the top of my Adventure Travel Bucket List was the chance to land in a new country without having any idea where I was - a feat I'd always thought was impossible.

However, I now had just the person by my side who could help me pull it off.

26

Never Stop Exploring: Clueless at 30,000 feet

"Live in each season as it passes; breathe the air, drink the drink, taste the fruit, and resign yourself to the influence of the earth." –
Henry David Thoreau

Destination Unknown. August 2019

"Where are you flying?" the friendly Dutch immigration officer asked with the monotonous tone he'd used a thousand times already this morning. "I have no idea..." a huge grin across my face, his attention immediately shifting, eyes darting up to meet mine. "My wife planned this trip and won't tell me where we're going." He wasn't amused, but wasn't rude either, more perplexed than anything. It wasn't an answer he heard often.

Scanning the cropped QR code I presented on my cracked iPhone screen he glanced at his monitor. "Hah - hope you brought a gun." he said half-jokingly as he tossed back my passport. "Enjoy your trip."

'*Where on earth is she taking me?*'

Stumbling into the crowded Terminal 1 at Schiphol International Airport in Amsterdam, I had no idea which way to go. Anne simply refused to tell me where we were going. It had been months, but now our bags were packed, and I was only told to pack light–just a backpack, to be ready for summer weather and to spend most of our time outdoors. After a certain point, I had taken it upon myself to not try to find out–a mission to see how far I could get and a golden opportunity for my Adventure Travel Bucket List.

'*Can I make it through the airport? Immigration? Can I make it through take off AND landing?*'

Traveling like this had been on that bucket list for years - my ultimate travel fantasy to walk off a plane in a new country, completely unaware of where I was with new smells filling my nostrils and alphabets I'd never seen before me as my only clues.

Schiphol is the third busiest airport in the world, with nearly 1,400 daily flights carrying over 70 million passengers direct to 266 destinations in 86 countries - and I had absolutely no idea which one we were going to. As we followed the signs towards gate D44, I pumped my music up, kept my head down, and miraculously boarded the flight without ever seeing where we were going.

Landing shortly after 10 pm local time, I'd kept my head down throughout the 1,022 mile (1,656km) journey for fear I'd see a travel guide on the seat across from me or a t-shirt that would give our destination away. Wheels squeaking to a halt, the loudspeaker crackled to life "Ladies and gentlemen, welcome to Tirana''. We were in Albania, and I had no clue until the plane had rolled to the arrival gate. Mission accomplished!

'Wait, why did that immigration officer tell me to bring a gun?'

Over the next few days, Anne and I explored an entirely new country together, one which I knew literally nothing about except for false stereotypes based on every bad guy in Liam Neeson movies. What we found was an extremely warm and welcoming culture and people, a part of the world that is simply blank in the minds of many. I knew little about its troubled history aside from it being just that, troubled, and didn't know the language they spoke, the foods they ate, or the god they feared.

We were evidently in Albania to hike the "Peak of the Balkans" trail, or at least a portion of it. A beautifully meandering 119-mile (192 km) trail through Albania, Kosovo, and Montenegro, only a sprinkling of tourists visit the Dinaric Alps of South Eastern Europe. Seatbelt sign dinging off, Anne was quick to inform me that we'd be doing a roughly 31-mile (50 km) section of the hike, including the stunning scenic pass from Theth to Valbone, traveled by very few outside a dedicated circle of well-worn travelers.

'31 miles? Is she crazy?'

Since moving to Amsterdam I'd been hitting the gym, doing everything I could to finally lose weight, but 30 miles was more than we'd ever hiked in two days. It was an A-B hike, starting in one town and finishing in another on the other side of absolutely massive mountains.

'What if we don't make it? What's our Plan B?'

We didn't have one. I'd taught Anne well, and she knew we'd just figure it out. Arriving in the ancient city of Shkoder, one of the oldest in the country and home to the Rozafa Castle built in 168 B.C., we had some learning to do. "Wait, who are these people, who ruled here?" I pondered aloud to Anne. "Maybe I can help?" a friendly voice chimed in from behind us.

"Inhabited first by the Illyrians in ancient times, Greek colonies were slowly established along the coast." the young Albanian man told us, his young daughter tugging at his tan shorts. We learned that in the 2nd century BC, the Roman Republic annexed the region, and after its fall, it became part of Byzantium. "The Kingdom of Albania was formed in the 13th century!" he said, "before being ruled by the Ottoman Empire for nearly 600 years until it declared independence in 1912." Listening intently, already overwhelmed, I was nevertheless fascinated to hear more. He continued, "In 1939, the Kingdom of Albania was invaded by Italy, which renamed it "Greater Albania" before it became a protectorate of Nazi Germany during World War II. Following the war, the People's Socialist Republic of Albania was formed, which lasted until the fall of communism in 1991. And here we are."

'Holy hell, is this guy a teacher? There's a lot more to this place than Liam Neeson. How have I made it to age 35 without ever knowing a single thing about Albania?'

Sitting on the banks of Lake Shkoder, the largest lake in the Balkans, we laughed about ending up in Albania while eating fish that came straight from the water beside us. Italian bleak, flathead mullet and carp served charcoaled and bare on worn plastic plates.

"The things we do, my love" Anne smiled at me and said. "The things we do." I smiled back.

The main roads in Albania are well maintained, for the most part, but once you get off the highways and up into the beautiful, almost secret, mountains, they slowly turn to rubble, some to dirt, as you meander up the winding mountain passes pocked with shrubs and lined with sheep.

Anne picked the "Peak of the Balkans" trail because of the remoteness, knowing I'd love escaping to the mountains, away from the cities and crowds one would encounter on a weekend getaway in Venice or Paris. "I just saw the mountains and the water, it looked like a classic Jeff and Anne adventure," she said with a grin.

Crossing over a knee-high stone wall, we were certain we had missed the turn and ended up in someone's yard - and we were correct. An older Albanian man appeared across a large field and slowly walked toward us, his aged wrinkles and warm smile becoming more and more defined as the sun brought his face into focus from under a withered and tattered leather cap. As with so many of my encounters with strangers when lost on the road, no words were exchanged. It was obvious we were lost and he knew exactly where we were trying to go. Turning his back and waving his arm in a welcoming gesture he invited us to follow him through his field, over a fence, through a clearing, under thick brush covered in thorns, and finally up a well-trodden and dusty steep path. Continuing into an increasingly narrow valley between two densely covered mountainsides, we followed this warm stranger, excitement building within us both. He must have been in his 70s and was as spry as a mountain goat.

Thanking him as best we could, after sharing a bruised banana and a firm handshake, we continued up the path where a poorly hand-painted sign appeared. Barely able to make out the words "Blue Eye", years of harsh weather and dust having chipped away and worn the paint right off the wood, we veered down into the depths of the forest.

The Blue Eye is a natural swimming pool formed by a freezing cold waterfall coming directly from the Black River—water so cold you'd swear it was seconds from freezing. The hike in was on a harrowing and endless path that took us through valleys, rustic farms, and ultimately to one of the most remote and stunning watering holes we'd ever seen.

Descending into the canyon valley, we came across a magnificent turquoise stream and knew we must be getting close. Its depths were so saturated with color that it looked out of place beside the dull hues of gray and brown surrounding it. Chasing the illuminated stream toward its source, we heard the calming sounds of babbling water ahead, and as we rounded one last boulder, we saw the breathtaking sight. The Blue Eye, a tranquil and stunning deep pool of water, spiraling shades of blue circling its dark center, truly lived up to its name—a gushing waterfall on one end with jagged rocky cliffs surrounding it on three sides. A reward unexpectedly finer than we had anticipated when we'd started the trek hours earlier, this is what we traveled for.

As we arrived at the water's edge the only other people there were walking by us on their way out and, for a time, we had the entirety of this hidden natural wonder to ourselves. Stripping off our mud-caked hiking boots and dust-stained brown socks we dipped our toes in the utterly frigid water. We had no towels, it was getting dark, and we had a long hike back up the valley to our homestay - but I just couldn't miss the opportunity.

"You'll never regret a swim!" I could hear David saying in my mind. First, the water was only to my knees, then to my thighs, the water so impossibly cold that it felt like knives stabbing my legs, warning me of danger ahead. When the water hit my belly button I was past the point of no return, and my chest took in an involuntary gasp of air - time to plunge. With a grin on my face, I let go, submerged my sunburned frame, and felt as though all the blood in my body was dancing under every pore.

We stayed with local families and ate homemade cheese from

their goats, fresh eggs from their farms, honey from their hives, and bread from their ovens. We slept under old wool blankets in drafty rooms as we continued our way up the nearly vertical trails and paths to the stunning Valbone pass, one of the most jaw-droppingly beautiful peaks we had ever seen. I didn't have any idea such a place even existed. I had never seen it in a guidebook, website, or on a travel blog. It felt like we had discovered the 9th wonder of the world. "What other secrets are out there?", I said to Anne as we steadied ourselves against the strong breeze, balancing on the pass between stunning 360-degree mountain views.

* * *

This is why I travel. This is why, when given the chance, I'll continue to board planes to unknown countries. There is no greater feeling than knowing that you are in an utterly unfamiliar part of a world but have all the sights, smells, foods, and locals to teach you all about it. Once again, I dare you to find a place in the world where a local isn't kind enough to show you around and and excited to tell you all about their home. All you have to do is ask—or often, just smile.

I travel to feel small. I travel to remember my place in the world and to be constantly reminded how little I know about the planet on which we all live. Anne and I were in our 43rd country together, in an area of the world we knew nothing about. This was the same electric feeling we'd felt on that first morning together in Bangkok, the same feeling we'd chased around the world, waiting to see if it had an end, which we had yet to find.

No matter how much you travel, no matter how far you explore, no matter how much time you spend on the road, there will always be entire countries, tribes, villages, histories, and cultures you know little about, and that is the beauty of travel.

Just like people, places change too. Some start off foreign and uncomfortable but grow to feel like you've known them all along. Others, as I was soon to find out, felt immediately like home – even if I'd never been there before.

27

Finding Home: Pot Smoke, Poffertjes, and Prosperity

*"You can never go home again, but the truth is you can
never leave home, so it's all right."*
—— *Maya Angelou*

Ubud, Bali, Indonesia. November 2018

In late 2018, a few weeks before we set off to hike up that big
ole mountain in Nepal, Anne and I arrived in Bali, Indonesia. We
had carved out 6 weeks to recharge and cross paths with various
traveling friends before embarking on the final adventure of our
trip around the world. After a couple of days of relaxing and
exploring the dramatic, cliff-studded beaches near Uluwatu on
the southern tip of Bali, we headed inland to Ubud, long known
to be a hippie-flocking magnet for those looking to explore their
own interior, deep in the jungles of this tropical island.

Walking down the main street, something just felt familiar.

Maybe it was the Southeast Asian backpacker vibe that reminded me of my early days in Thailand and brought those memories of excitement and wonder flooding back. Maybe it was the growing sounds of insects in the air that reminded me of hot sticky summer nights growing up in Maryland. Whatever it was, it just felt right, and I had to smile. There is no better feeling than arriving somewhere you've never been in your life and feeling *at home*.

But it was remembering an old text my friend David had sent me a few weeks earlier when he learned we were going to be in Ubud that really made the difference. "If you have the chance, go to the Ubud Yoga Barn, super heady spot," it said. The Yoga Barn is an institution in Ubud that has welcomed thousands of impassioned yoginis and health-conscious travelers for nearly twenty years. No matter your alternative style, you'll find a fix for it at the Yoga Barn whether you're looking for a yoga class, detox retreat, womb awakening seminar, biodynamic yogurt bowl, chai latte or an ayurvedic colon cleanse—they have it all.

While the colon cleanse and womb awakening weren't quite for me, I went to sunrise yoga classes nearly every day while we were in Ubud spending my mornings sitting cross-legged on an array of cushions in the Yoga Barn cafe. I would check email, edit new What Doesn't Suck videos - "48 Hours in Serbia", "Great European Road Trip" - and apply to jobs in cities around the world, but especially in Amsterdam. The whole time I was there, I felt utterly and completely at home - high up in the Indonesian jungle. It wasn't obvious at first why it felt so familiar, but the longer I stayed the more obvious it became.

The turmeric in the latte reminded me of my mother's cooking, the font used for all the hand-carved signs was the same as above the door at the Washington Waldorf School I walked under each day from the age of 6 until I turned 18, and the smell of the incense reminded me, somehow, of the halls of the kindergarten where I spent my early years.

Anne, however, didn't share in all my excitement. It wasn't that she didn't love the Yoga Barn, but it just didn't strike those same chords for her, which made it even more special, in a way. I connected with this place in a deeply personal and unique way. This didn't need to be a shared experience. This was an experience for me, a déjà vu back to my "home" while being very far away from my actual home, which now consisted of feelings and sensations, with nothing physical remaining.

Those friendly Indonesian faces - so different from my own - in a culture so varied from what I grew up with, still radiated the feeling of home for me. It finally made me realize that indeed, no matter where you are in the world, it is the feeling of home that you take with you and not the four walls which surround it. The more you travel, and the longer you are away from the home where you physically grew up, the easier it is to recognize these things. Home isn't just a place; home is a feeling.

Amsterdam, Netherlands. March 2019

It's a crisp morning in Amsterdam, and Anne is still sound asleep in the bedroom of our tiny apartment on Wakkerstraat. We've been married just over two years and live on a quiet neighborhood street lined with 100-year-old Dutch row houses just a 15-minute cycle from the center of the city. It's been four months since we left the buzzing vibes of Ubud, Bali, and two months since we traded in carry-on for carry-out, amidst the madness of trying to settle in a new city. Some bricks on our building are black as soot, some dirty mustard, most a deep clay brown - all with crisp white trim lining the window panes and door frames. We don't own much, just our clothes really-and a few suitcases, laptops, and a French press, but we're happy.

Nestled on the eastern side of the city, the Oost neighborhood is a bustling mix of youthful energy, hip cafes, and true Dutch 'coffee shops' for those looking for that special kind of buzz. Oosterpark, a sprawling thirty-acre English garden-style park with a meandering pond, remnants of a windmill, and a curious flock of bright green parrots hopping between the trees acts as the community gathering spot. A weekly market envelops the heart of a neighborhood just a block away, the streets lined with stalls selling everything from freshly squeezed juices, wheels of famous Gouda or Edam Dutch cheeses, and, of course, poffertjes, delectable mini Dutch pancakes coated in a generous layer of hot butter and dusted with clouds of powdered sugar.

The sun was rising earlier and earlier each day as winter slowly released her tight grip on the country with back-to-back warmer afternoons increasing each week, and the signs of spring were beginning to appear in this next chapter of our lives. In the months leading up to our arrival in Amsterdam, we had spent our days exploring with only our backpacks. Ancient Arabian cities one week, freezing Arctic tundra the next, vibrant Incan villages after that. Days filled with carefree afternoons on steamy Thai rooftops and careless nights in lively Lebanese seaside cafes. There were no days of the week—only seasons, and every night was a Friday. If I thought my ADHD was bad, my hyperactive travel disorder was even worse, but there seemed to be a glimmer of calm on the horizon because no matter where we were, there was always one question in the back of our minds:

'Could we live here? Is this a place where we could settle down and raise a family? Is this home?'

The night Anne and I landed in Amsterdam, gusts of wind and sideways rain greeted us outside Schiphol Airport at 2 a.m. It was day 180, the last day of our trip around the world - twenty countries on four continents. Our passion for adventure travel, discovering the world around us along with new parts of ourselves and each other, had fueled us to hop from country to country in search of the feeling that told us to stop. A feeling that told us it was time to find '*home*' - a home I'd been seeking for nearly two decades.

In the weeks since we arrived in Amsterdam, we eased into the city, living into every aspect of Dutch life that we could, and for the first time in these many months of our travels, we didn't feel the urge to up and leave for the next destination. My mind had stopped spinning so quickly, and something was changing. The Dutch way of life rubbed off on us. It meshed quickly with what we were looking for and made us feel comfortable. The Dutch spoke impeccable English, championed an active lifestyle, which resulted in us walking or biking nearly everywhere, and they held a 6 pm dinner absolutely sacred, with many busy parents leaving work before 5 pm to collect the little ones and make an evening meal. The Dutch were direct, no-nonsense, and to the point. We always knew where we stood, and problems seemed to be solved quickly and efficiently. We were less than a two-hour flight to Anne's family, and after spending most of the last decade in Asia and the Middle East, the East Coast of the USA now felt like it was practically within shouting distance.

Most importantly, NFL football started at 7 pm most Sunday evenings, so I could finally watch Washington lose all their games live.

Thinking back to our whirlwind 180-day trip around the world, it felt good to be in one place for longer than a weekend, and in a city that made us feel warm and welcomed. A city and a culture that made us feel like we could do better, be better versions of ourselves, and thrive. It made me think of a travel monologue we've all heard endless times but which had now taken on a whole new meaning. "Should we experience sudden pressure loss in the cabin, stay calm and listen for instructions from the cabin crew. Oxygen masks will drop down from above your seat. Place the mask over your mouth and nose.... make sure that your own mask is on first before helping others."

It was time to take care of myself, and ourselves, time to fully turn inward and do the hard work. For now, we had decided to make Amsterdam our home. Buying a house is one thing, but making it a home is another. And while the coziness and feeling of home is protected by four walls and a roof, the soul of the home is made up of those in it - and whatever version of themselves they bring inside it. If I wanted to be the best version of myself, I still had some work to do, no matter how uncomfortable it made me. As the weeks turned to months, my mind continued to slow down, and while what I found was uncomfortable to confront, at least it was clear. It was finally time to put all the pieces together, each one a crucial pulley in a delicately balanced dance I was learning to master within my mind.

All the breadcrumbs I'd collected from around the world that had given me both inner and outer perspective had to be organized and archived, and as I started to piece them all together, to understand where I'd been, more and more memories of chance encounters and wisdom from strangers on the road, especially older travelers, came flooding back to my mind.

And as Anne and I prepared to revisit America once more,

we didn't anticipate that we'd come face to face, over pints of raspberry ale, with some of those strangers who would make us uncomfortable, too - grandparents who wanted to make America great again.

28

Respect Your Elders: MAGA Grandparents and Banana Cream Pie

"Young people, you need the wisdom of age, just as some of us older ones need your enthusiasm for life."
– Ezra Taft Benson

For years, I was scared to go down into the basement of the house I grew up in. The dark seemed just a little darker down there, with more unknown corners hidden behind bookshelves and boxes than anywhere else in the house. When my mother would ask me to run down and bring up a box of Christmas tree decorations or a carton of milk, I would turn off the lights on my way back up and then sprint around the corner to the light - the feeling of the dark engulfing me from behind.

I was unfamiliar with the dark, a primal feeling of fear too innate to separate myself from this early in life. The little flags hanging from the ceiling would always be the last thing I'd see in the basement before flicking off the light, their various multi-colored cloth textures and shapes slightly moving in the air as I slipped back up the stairs to safety.

If you think it's odd that I collect masks and money from around the world, you should meet my Dad. He collects flags, sand, and rocks. For years, lined up on his bathroom window sill would be rows and rows of empty film canisters filled with sand, rocks, and pebbles - each with a tiny handwritten label naming the exact location and date he'd collected each one. But the flags, the flags were all kept in the dark basement. Floating high above me, each one expertly stuck into the corners of the ceiling tiles creating a vast swath of fabrics and symbols.

I knew little about most of the countries– for some, I couldn't tell you their names to this day - but from an early age, I looked up at these flags, aware that each was from a completely different culture with its own stories, histories, languages, foods, and wisdom. I'd like to say I was most interested in wisdom, but I barely knew what that was back then.

What I did know was that the amazing distant worlds I had discovered on the pages of those dusty National Geographic magazines in the bathroom with the neon green shag carpet had all come from these countries. These flags were more crumbs on my treasure map, and I was about to follow two of them in polar opposite directions.

Phuket, Thailand. August 2013

Steve was a classic Aussie bloke, overly friendly, with a loud welcoming voice you could hear a mile away, and a smile that never faded. He loved a good pint and a good tune. He'd lived in Phuket for a couple of years before I moved into a little apartment on Patak Road, snaking behind the popular resorts on Karon Beach just a few hundred meters down the road. He owned Roadhouse, an all-wood, open-air, Aussie-style steakhouse. Rarely busy, live music played almost every night. I spent many fun nights there with Steve and his Thai girlfriend, Porn, enjoying good food, good company, and meeting a trickle of strangers passing through Thailand on their holidays.

It was here, exactly one year before the crisis of my 30th birthday in that tiny apartment, sitting on one of the high stools at the bar and sporting a shiny forehead from the August humidity, that I met an older couple whose accents were just foreign enough that I couldn't quite place them. They spoke perfect English, and though their names were long forgotten before I woke up the next morning the conversation I had with them that night had a great impact. "You must go to Lapland!" they exclaimed excitedly. "You'll absolutely love exploring Finland if you love to travel so much - our home is a magical place."

Over the next hour, they spoke at length about Finland, their culture, history, and the great love and respect the people had for each other and for nature. Not only did Finns value nature, but human life as well, a societal rule that championed childhood development, public safety, community assistance, free higher education, and above all, happiness. Finland has even been named the "Happiest Country in the World" for a shocking seven years in a row. As an American, this was all completely foreign to me. I'd heard of these utopic European wonderlands where all people were taken care of, where quality of life was at its highest and people were truly happy, but I couldn't process that they actually existed.

'But... isn't America number one?'

303

Growing up, I believed America stood for these principles and was leading the world towards accomplishing them, no matter how hard or long it took. But have other countries already achieved this? Was the race already won by a small country in the north of Europe? All I knew about Scandinavia was that everyone paid extremely high taxes, but did this mean they went to making life better for everyone too?

I had to get to Finland to find out for myself, to understand if these high-functioning societies were all they'd been cracked up to be.

Salla, Finland. March 2014

I didn't normally drink coffee, but boarding the plane from Berlin, Germany to Helsinki, Finland, I needed one. It was just so damn early, and would be pitch black outside for hours more. Not even leaving the airport in the Finnish capital before connecting to Rovaniemi - a tiny town in Finnish Lapland - I jumped on a bus to Salla, a town so remote that their slogan is "...in the Middle of Nowhere". Helsinki already sits at the top of the world, the second most Northern capital city (Reykjavik is #1), but Salla was another nearly 800 km (500 mi) north into nothingness.

Finnish children are regularly listed among the happiest in the world too, with no homework or fear of walking home alone. Other Scandinavian and Northern European countries are also always high on the Happiness Index list by the UN Economic Forum for the best quality of life, the safest, and most content citizens - all with some of the highest tax rates on earth. These countries may all have dark, long winters, but they seem to be on to something.

Finnish Lapland has a population of only 179,000 - but over 200,000 reindeer roam the endless natural landscapes here. And then there were all those stunning images of the Northern Lights I saw on the floor in the bathroom with the long, neon green shag carpet when I was growing up. Many of them were captured right there above the Arctic Circle, in the middle of nowhere. I still didn't know why I'd come exactly, but it felt right. I'd followed the advice of elders I'd met along the road, so there must be something to learn.

Listening to that older couple I'd met in Phuket a few months earlier had awakened a curiosity in me about their country –a curiosity and excitement I'd rarely gotten from movies, magazines, or billboards. Hearing a couple, about the age of my grandparents so passionately talking about their lives and all that Finland meant to them left me feeling like I owed it to them to experience it – the older generation passing down their wisdom to the younger ones. I felt both guilty and excited that I knew nothing about Finland. Half of the excitement was in exploring a new country and the other half was in blindly trusting the words of older strangers who saw a childlike wonder in me.

And in my constant search for home, for belonging, I had to find out what was behind these happy people. An older couple who had lived fulfilling and vibrant lives with the health and vitality to travel well into their 70s and bump into a lost wanderer like me at a roadside joint in SouthEast Asia must have more figured out than I do.

My toes were starting to tingle as I stood outside the small wooden cabin I was staying in, a matchbox structure buried in the shadows of towering, snow-dusted pines. From within their shadows, a middle-aged woman slowly approached me and asked if I wanted to visit a real Finnish sauna. Her cabin was a short distance away but nearly invisible within the army of trees. She was warm, friendly, a loving Mom type, and welcomed me to join her at a local spot her family had been going to for years.

I went back inside the warm cabin, grabbed my bathing suit and an extra pair of socks, and jumped into her light blue 90's station wagon, disappearing down a thick pine tree-covered road, fresh snow covering everything in sight - dim yellow headlights as our only guide. My intuition was fired up, and although I had my guard up, this wasn't Malaysia, and there was no Otto in sight....

'Trust the locals, they'll show you the heart of their country.'

I thought we were going to some sort of a community center, a busy indoor neighborhood pool in the small center of Salla, but we continued driving further and further outside of the city, making friendly conversation, as my excitement and curiosity grew with every turn - no repeating yellow billboards to be seen. Eventually, we arrived at what looked like a small campsite. The only building in sight was somewhat modular, and the only light was a dim porch light that came into view as our headlights shut off. Two small buildings connected to each other —one round with a pointy thatched roof, the other a small rectangular shed building sprouting off its side. Faint moonlight glistened off nearby water just beyond the small buildings.

'Are we at a lake?! It's March and it's pitch black.'

Once inside I realized the circular room was the sauna itself, hot steam escaping into the pitch-black night from its vaulted ceiling, and the offshoot was the changing area. Peering out the fogged-up window, I saw we were in fact on the banks of a pond, only about 25 feet (8m) from the water's edge. While the entire pond was frozen solid, these locals had chiseled off blocks of ice in a small area on the banks, about 4ft by 4ft, and connected a hose from the building to keep the water moving so the surface wouldn't freeze over. You know, so they could go ice swimming, in water that Mother Nature was intent on turning into a sheet of ice.

'Never regret a swim... am I about to regret this one?'

Over the next couple of hours, I sat in the sauna with a collection of elderly Finnish couples, each caught in their normal evening routine of rotating rounds of hot sauna followed by a polar plunge. Each was as naked as the day they were born. Too shy and ashamed to strip down to nothing, I awkwardly sat in my bathing suit next to them. Over 100 billion humans have lived before me, each one unique and utterly the same, and yet I still felt more uncomfortable than ever in a body I'd often described as "cottage cheese stuffed in a pillowcase." But here I was, out of my comfort zone again, doing the work as best I could, and that felt like progress.

I thought they were all insane, but they encouraged me to join them and after some hesitation, I was going back and forth showing them how to make snow angels on the snowy banks. Tiptoing gingerly to the water's edge I dipped a toe into the utterly frigid water with a combined 300 years of elderly Finns cheering me on, smiling, half submerged in the painfully cold waters of Lake Ruuhijärvi. There was no other option for me, I could only go in further, endless tingly icicles stabbing my skin the further I stepped. When I could no longer feel my shins I had to move fast or I'd panic and back out. As my waist went under, I could feel my heart racing, and as my chest was absorbed into the black waters, the air involuntarily left my lungs in a gasp fit for a horror movie. But I'd done it, finally floating up to my neck, an awkward smile on my face as I looked around the faces smiling at me, seeking some sort of recognition.

Yes, it was dark and freezing, yes I was only in a bathing suit, and yes I exited that water feeling absolutely more alive than I had in months. I felt like I had newly generated blood coursing through my entire body. I also felt a profound appreciation and understanding that life can be lived with beauty, health, energy, and passion without being boastful or shouting from a mountaintop. And then I bolted back to the scorching embrace of the steaming cedar box before I lost feeling completely.

These Finns were definitely on to something.

As I peeled back on my layers of thermal, flannel, and thick woolen socks, I smiled, thinking of the Finnish couple I had met in Phuket who were the entire reason I was here, and imagined them doing the same with their friends. The warm glow of the sedan headlights illuminated our little swimming hole as we backed out of the woods, and that grin remained on my face for the rest of the evening. Another spontaneous travel experience, another gift from the Travel Gods, another local willing to show me theirs if I showed them mine.

In the few days I spent in Finnish Lapland, I went snowshoeing in the silent mountain forests, stopping only to appreciate the silence and drink fresh elderberry tea. I drove sled dogs deep into the wilderness, ate sausages over an open fire, tried reindeer skiing, slept in the woods, ate horse meat, and searched for the Northern Lights. Their elusiveness drew me back to Scandinavia for years to come, playfully continuing to push me to explore these countries that excited me so much.

Taking the 10-hour overnight train 500 miles (800km) back down to Helsinki, I was filled with an appreciation and love for an entire country and culture I'd known nothing about, and wouldn't have, without the random advice of two friendly and wise grandparents I happened to strike up a conversation with on the other side of the world. That chance encounter changed a lot of things for me, igniting a passion and deep love for Scandinavia and the countries nearby that hold the same ideals for the protection and support of human life at their core.

Two Harbors, Minnesota, USA. June 2019

Neither Anne nor I had been to Minnesota before, one of the five remaining states in the US I had yet to visit – so when a good childhood friend, another of Rob and Alice's children actually, announced he was getting married in Minneapolis in June 2019, just months after we'd settled in Amsterdam, we were quick to book our tickets with a couple extra days before the ceremony to get lost in the woods – a theme which had become utterly predictable in our lives at this point. The chance to explore more nature, American nature, was too good to pass up.

We decided to stay in the little town of Two Harbors. You'd drive right past it without thinking twice on your way from Duluth, Minnesota to Thunder Bay, Ontario, but it suited us just perfectly. We had a little rental car, a cooler we'd filled with beef jerky, string cheese, and Vitamin Water, and found a cheap roadside motel close to the entrance to a few national parks. This was our happy place. Quickly parking the car and throwing our stuff in the room, we headed out on foot to explore the tiny town of only 3,500 residents nestled on the shores of mighty Lake Superior. Betty's Pies, Gooseberry Falls, and the Split Rock lighthouse were the main attractions in the area. We weren't expecting all that much, to be honest, but it was charming, and there was a brewery.

"You don't look like you're from around here?" said a soft, friendly voice. Turning around, we saw an elderly woman and her husband, classic American enthusiasm with stereotypical warm Minnesotan charm and accents. "If you can, go to Betty's Pies. They have the best fish and chips anywhere, and the pecan pie is to die for!" For all we knew, this was old Betty herself. More likely they were just a random couple on the street who saw two strangers, wanted to make us feel welcome, and who gave us a good laugh as we sauntered down the road.

The sun popped out for only a few minutes that afternoon, but being mid-June on the shores of beautiful Lake Superior, we immediately grabbed our beers off the long wooden counter and took them outside to one of the sprawling wooden tables partially bathed in the warm afternoon light.

"You two don't look like you're from around here?" a kind older woman said as she stepped outside the taproom into the warm afternoon breeze.

'Again? What is it with these people?'

This was beginning to be a theme - a laughable, friendly, classically Midwestern American theme. "Nope!" I said, happy to engage with another friendly local and excited to demonstrate further to Anne that all Americans are unapologetically friendly, sometimes to the point of absurdity.

'This! This is what I miss about America! I want more of this!'

"My name is Ann, and this is my husband Phil." she said with a smile, politely extending her hand to greet us both. Ann and Phil invited us to their table to join them and another older couple, all grandparents in their 70's, spending a warm June afternoon at the brewery in Two Harbors, Minnesota, just like us.

Over the next two hours, we experienced one of the most

surreal and profound connections we've ever had with strangers we met while traveling. Right-wing, Trump-supporting, Republican, middle-of-America conservative grandparents - and Anne and I, a liberal, social democratic leaning, Eurocentric younger couple sitting side by side with them, all drinking Summer Raspberry Wheat Ale together.

We couldn't have been more different, but we instantly connected. I probably would have been appalled and offended, instantly discounting anything these people would have posted or commented about on social media if we'd met on the internet, but no screens were separating us now, only a smooth wooden table speckled with warm June sunlight dancing around us. We talked about religion, politics, abortion, marriage, and children, all the things you aren't supposed to talk about with family, let alone strangers. We talked about their farms way up North on the border with Canada, about their adopted children, their grandchildren, and their views on drugs and teen pregnancy.

These two couples, as warm and welcoming as our own grandparents, could not have been further from anything I identify or associate with, but here we were, utterly enjoying our time connecting. Phil bought another round, and his lovely wife Ann quickly got out her phone to show us pictures of their grandchildren and livestock. (I'm not sure which they loved more...)

We talked about travel, and the cities we'd all been to. All six of us had been to Venice, I remember that much. Sitting with nearly 90 years of marriage between these two couples, we asked them for advice. Phil paused, gathered his thoughts, and reaching across the table, grabbed his wife's hands. "She's my best friend," he said through quickly forming tears. A burly, Republican farmer from Minnesota was reduced to tears while talking about his partner to a young couple they'd just met.

We disagreed vehemently on nearly every topic, but there was mutual respect. It was like the pause button had been pressed, the yelling between sides had been frozen for an afternoon, and we all relished the opportunity to interact with the other side, observing each other like wild animals on the plains of the Savannah without the goal to attack one another, slowly drawing closer. The conversation was unpredictable, at times uncomfortable, eye-opening, and in the end, reaffirming that all people really do want the same things - to be healthy, happy, and loved, even if we disagree completely on how to get there. It felt like we'd all been through years of therapy together.

Finishing the last of our raspberry ales we all stood up, feeling the weight and impact the afternoon had on us all, and we couldn't help but take a picture standing together behind that big, smooth wooden table bathed in June sunlight. Looking back at that photo, you'd swear we were all family. Ann clutching Anne's arm like a doting grandmother, Phil and I grinning from ear to ear like we were about to head out on a weekend fishing trip. We didn't exchange information, or phone numbers or find each other on Facebook. They went their way and we went ours, but we left with a deep feeling of mutual respect. Heading by foot up Highway 61 back to our hotel, Anne and I were at a loss for words, the reverberations of our human connection buzzing in our bones long into the night. Pure, raw, honest human connection.

* * *

I've not always been open and excited to talk to strangers. The thought of striking up a conversation with someone next to me always brings me right back to that feeling of running up those dark stairs in my childhood basement - the deep-seated feeling to flee, to not feel vulnerable or exposed by the small talk.

I think back to my Dad's flag collection, hanging there from the white ceiling tiles, each flag with thousands of stories hidden behind each fold. Stories to be discovered by heading out into the unknown and talking to strangers, many of whom have gained a lifetime of wisdom and insight worthy of my respect if I was willing to give them the chance to share it with me.

There is a lot of wisdom out in the world, especially among our elders, so stop and talk to them if you get a chance. I don't remember if my Dad had flags from Finland or Minnesota hanging in that basement, but I like to think he did. I also like to think that the conversations and time spent with those older couples in Thailand, Finland, and Minnesota, spread years apart, might make them smile, too, when they think back to the time they stopped to chat with a couple the age of their grandchildren who they met as they were traveling around the world.

If you're ever in Two Harbors, stop by Castle Danger Brewery and talk to a few friendly strangers yourself. Try the raspberry ale, too, if you're there in the summer months, and if nothing else, go to Betty's Pies just up the road - the banana cream pie is truly to die for.

I like to search for wisdom when I travel, often hidden in the most unexpected places, behind the most unexpected faces. And often, it's not something you can actively search for as much as something you actively open yourself up to. The world is made of an invisible pattern of infinite lifetimes of gained wisdom, dying off silently without being shared. The earth has wisdom too, if you listen closely enough.

Now that I could see more of my puzzle and more of the wisdom I had been seeking, I needed to start putting the last pieces together, and fast. The time to put them all to use was quickly approaching, because soon Anne and I would have more to care for than just ourselves.

29

Becoming an Adult: Nitrous Oxide and Savasana

"Focus on the good and the good gets better." - Abraham Hicks

Silver Spring, Maryland, USA. April 2001

One late afternoon while I was in 10th grade, my father's best friend stopped by our home. Dr. Klein was an ever-friendly middle-aged doctor, a bald head almost as shiny as his smile. Somewhere during the exchange I'd been roped into, I'd drifted off, thoughts of escaping to the downstairs TV filling my head, when the conversation suddenly zeroed in on me. I was caught off guard.

"Jeff," Dr. Klein said, as my eyes refocused. "Life is about collecting experiences. We're all born with a huge empty sack that we carry around on our backs, like Santa Claus —light at first, with nothing to show anyone. But slowly, as we go through life, we collect more and more experiences - some good, some bad, some funny, some sad - but they all go in that sack so we can share them with others someday."

I was far too young to digest the depth of that comment at the time, but it has stayed with me all these years. No matter where I am in the world, whenever I have a funny experience, a frustrating encounter, a scary accident, or a happy coincidence, I often think of Dr. Klein - that sack on my back, one more experience to carry around with me, and share with others one day when the time is right.

It's comments like those, although likely forgotten before Dr. Klein left our house that afternoon, that can stick with you the most. I hope Dr. Klein knows that his passing advice to an inattentive 16-year-old has traveled the world over- that my sack of experiences has slowly been filled with tidbits from around the globe, and that I am now sharing them.

Amsterdam, Netherlands. July 4th, 2019

The summer sun in Amsterdam rises absurdly early, the sky starting to lighten well before 5 am. The sun had also set well after 10 p.m. the night before too, on one particular night when we stumbled out of the dance club at 5 a.m. It was nearly full daylight, which was unsettling – a depressing, nearly soul-crushing, mildly humorous surprise. It was the first all-nighter we'd pulled in years, and it would be the last for many years to come.

'Another life experience for my Santa Claus sack...'

I knew we'd gone out too hard, but we had friends in town and the excitement got the better of us. We hadn't made many friends in Amsterdam yet, so we were excited to go out and experience some of the wildness everyone knows is only hidden behind a thin curtain in the Dutch capital, but we'd also gotten a bit too carried away.

The club had a nitrous oxide bar of all things - how does that even exist? We felt old, but not as old as the drug-fueled 50-year-old Dutch couple with whom we kept a long and deep conversation going on the dance floor for some reason. Perhaps it was our feeble attempt to connect with locals in our newly-adopted home.

Sure, it wasn't ideal, but it's hard to break through to any new culture, let alone one as closed off as the Dutch can be. We desperately wanted to connect with the Netherlands, but we just didn't know how. A blurry night out at a club surely wasn't our best attempt, but it was an attempt nonetheless. The next morning we suffered a brutal hangover – our last one for a very long time, it would turn out.

That was on a Saturday morning, and when Anne rang the buzzer to our building the following Monday evening after hot yoga, I was still reading the text message she had sent earlier.

"Well, that was interesting. I just full-on cried during savasana."

We'd finally the wall. We'd mutually hit that point in our lives where we wanted something different, something more. We were ready for a change, a new adventure.

"What are we doing?" Anne said, with a steel resolve I knew she meant from deep down but had rarely seen in our nearly five years together. "Why are we doing this to our bodies and pretending we aren't? How can I go to yoga to find peace, relaxation, health, and clarity and then take it all away from myself the next weekend?" For the next year, neither of us had a single drink – not because we set a goal to, but because we just really didn't feel like it. To do something every day for a week used to be nearly impossible for me, but to take on a monumental challenge like this for an entire year slowly built a certain confidence in me that if I could just get started and keep the momentum building, I could do anything. The ADHD that once ruled my mind was no longer in the front seat, it was holding on for dear life from the backseat as I navigated forward, firmly in control of the steering wheel.

For years, I used alcohol as a crutch, a life vest to keep me afloat in social situations, because my first instinct was to retreat if I felt uncomfortable or out of place. With a beer in my hand, and another one an arm's reach away, I had something to hide behind, something to give me a bit of the confidence I lacked, something to make me forget how uncomfortable I felt in my own body most of the time – and something that slowed down my mind enough to allow me to think. But growing up meant facing the hard things head-on and embracing the struggle.

Somewhere around Day 30 of that year, I turned 35 during a weekend trip to Paris and felt the best I'd ever felt. Food tasted different, and better, than ever before. It was richer and the flavors deeper, but maybe that's to be expected when you're eating fresh pastries, bright-eyed and energetic, at 7 a.m. in Paris.

On Day 110, we celebrated Anne's 29th birthday. We'd spent her last three birthdays traveling, two of which she either completely or mostly missed because we were in an airplane. This year, we were in our cozy little apartment in Amsterdam, and it was a regular autumn morning. I got up earlier than she did and made a quick pot of coffee in our dimly lit kitchen, the skies still pitch black.

I pulled out the handful of small gifts I'd wrapped for her and stored them under our wheeled guest bed in the living room - a book, some yoga pants, spices she liked from Trader Joe's –nothing fancy. Years of travel had formed habits of not collecting things. The chocolate chip pancakes would be a good touch, though albeit not much of a surprise to her. But when she walked out of our bedroom, I was excited nonetheless. We were finally celebrating Anne's birthday on the ground, in our own apartment, and we'd finally stopped moving.

With a funny look in her eye and a wrapped gift bag dangling from one hand, she walked over to the stove. "You know those places where it's a tradition for the birthday kid to give a present as well? Well, that's what we have here," she said with an excited smile. She opened her presents first, tearing through the gift paper in seconds; she was really flying through them. Although she was mildly impressed and thankful for my small gifts, I wasn't sure where her impatience was coming from. Then she handed me the small bag.

Reaching in, I could feel something that looked like a wash-cloth, but what I pulled out first would change my life - our lives - from that moment forward.

I didn't know if one line or two on that test strip meant pregnant, but the look on her face followed by the tears that instantly fell from my eyes told me everything I needed to know. "You're going to be a Dad," she said. I don't think we've ever hugged so much, both in tears, standing in our pajamas on that dark, cold October morning, as I discovered that the washcloth was actually a tiny onesie, while the chocolate chip pancakes started to burn in the pan behind us - smoke filling our tiny apartment.

Stunned and giggling, we celebrated in muted excitement together before she left for work that morning, planning to meet at our favorite steak restaurant in the city center for dinner that night to celebrate both her birthday and this news of the just-revealed adventure that lay ahead of us. By the time I arrived to meet her that evening, I had a surprise for her as well.

Anne had received a job offer 6-weeks after we moved, but I'd applied to over 200 jobs since we arrived in Amsterdam nine months earlier and had only been offered a single interview. After weeks of phone screenings and interviews, I had finally received the call that very morning, that I was being offered the job – from the only company I'd even heard back from.

I knew the day we landed in Amsterdam that without structure, a job, routine, friends, social groups, professional connections, or sports clubs I had to do my absolute best to implement the strictest daily regime I could to ensure I survived what I hoped would be just a few weeks until I landed on my feet. I had collected the tools from around the world, tested, failed, and learned how to harness my brain to work for, not against, me – but now I had to put them all into practice.

I sat in our tiny apartment in Amsterdam for nine straight months applying for jobs and trusting the process, all the time thinking back to that tiny apartment in Phuket and all I had been through in it. Those sixty-eight days alone and in solitude had given me the tools to cope with this challenge, and I was determined to prevail.

'Maybe I just need to get out of tiny apartments.'

Sitting cozy in a dimly lit back booth that night at the restaurant reminded us both of the dark booths at the British pub in Dubai where we'd spent so much time, and where we'd hatched our plan for 'What Doesn't Suck?', our first real adventure, five years earlier. And here we were, about to start another. I reached into my jacket pocket and pulled out a crumpled brown paper envelope and handed it to her – one final gift on this memorable day. Reaching inside, she pulled out a small wooden keychain revealing a typical Dutch canal house. She instantly knew what it represented, and we both teared up and ordered ribs and carrot cake to celebrate.

We could finally think about buying a house and making it a home. But had we found *home*?

Leaving the US seven years earlier, I never thought I'd settle outside its borders, buy my first house anywhere other than Colorado or California. Never thought my children would be born internationally. But the more we explored the Netherlands, the more we found ourselves thriving. The Netherlands scored number one in the Quality of Life index, a mix of cost of living, purchasing power, healthcare index, and even commuting time. In a country with twice as many bicycles as people, we happily traded in hours each day in rush hour traffic for cycling to and from the office.

Most employers in the Netherlands offer 25 paid vacation days with a mandatory "13th month" equivalent to 8% of your annual pay – you know, to help pay for your summer travels. Healthcare isn't free, but it is heavily regulated, easily affordable, and mandatory for all. Yes, taxes are high, over 50% for some, but the subsidized, excellent education, public safety, maintained infrastructure, and accessibility to a high quality of life is worth it. Better yet, and most importantly, the sacred 6 pm dinner hour spoke volumes. No long working hours, and no emails through dinner and bedtime – a true work–life balance.

'Isn't this the American Dream? Isn't this the finish line we're all trying to get to?'

And for us, especially, standing with tears of joy moist on our cheeks this morning, raising children was at the front of our minds. I thought back to Finland and all I had learned there years earlier about their culture and how happy the people had been and remembered Finnish kids were rated the second happiest in the world.

Who was number one? The Dutch.

Joshua Tree National Park, California, December 31, 2019

Heading out California State Route 62, Anne and I had our road trip playlist blasting as we both mumbled the words to Country Road, endless swerving yellow lines vanishing into the horizon along the desolate desert highway before us. Two hours outside of Los Angeles the high rises and traffic smog had slowly been replaced by sweeping scenes of dry brush, faint mountain outlines on the horizon and the silhouettes of 1,200 wind turbines dotting the landscape providing all the power for the entire Coachella Valley. Anne was 13 weeks pregnant and the morning sickness that had plagued her for weeks had finally diminished.

The sun was fast dissolving the boundary between sand and sky, the amber light of the dusty clouds fusing seamlessly with the honeycomb haze rising from the road ahead. 2019 was in her final hours and we were sprinting towards Joshua Tree National Park to watch her come to a close amidst the iconic natural landscape.

"Sunset is 4:45 today guys, better hurry up. It gets cold quick out there." the friendly park ranger advised as she handed us a park map and a receipt to throw on the dashboard as we entered the park. Speeding down the winding road we were parked and had only minutes to spare, our feet crunching on the thin layer of ice and snow in splotches over the sand. Marching towards a large pile of boulders the size of school buses, Anne and I scrambled to the tallest peak and sitting in silence watched the year come to a close arm in arm wondering what excitement and adventure 2020 would bring as the sky gently bruised purple and pink before it went to sleep.

Sitting atop those rust-colored boulders in Joshua Tree National Park, the thin layer of snow surrounding the base of the odd trees dotting the horizon in every direction, I was surviving my thirties and coming through them a better person than when I started them in that tiny room in Phuket, crying into a bowl of mustard and chicken. And I was 100 pounds (45 kg) lighter too, still working off a few McChickens' from the early 2000s, but finally able to get the weight off after a little hiking, discipline, and seeing less than fifty choices of cereal at the grocery store in Amsterdam.

Little did we know as we returned to the park the next morning to watch the sunrise that the world would never forget 2020, humanity only weeks away from a pandemic we'd never forget and a period in all our lives where the feelings of isolation, loneliness, depression and despair would plague nearly all of us. A time period where the tools I developed in that tiny Thai apartment alone for sixty-eight days would become crucial to Anne and I surviving what would be one of the most transformational periods of our lives.

* * *

Returning home to Amsterdam to start 2020, I was a couple of months into my new job as a creative producer - a job that required precise details, complex tracking, budgeting with far more zeroes than made me comfortable, ruthless organization, high-stakes problem-solving, and clear prioritization. A nightmare set of skills for the Jeff of old but I was finally equipped with the cheat codes to my brain collected from all corners of the earth to handle them well. Anne and I soon found out we were having a baby girl, and we finally had an offer accepted to buy our first home - a modern Dutch row house with three bedrooms, a back garden, and a small open kitchen. We could finally get a dog, and a crockpot if we wanted to. We were starting to form roots, a deep connection to a new place, in a new country neither of us had ever called home but was starting to feel like one. This would be the fifth place we'd lived in together, and finally, one that we might spend more than a few months in.

And on day 365, exactly one year to the day after we stumbled out of that club at 5 am and decided we wanted more, Stella was born.

A few months later, the frost-long melted, bright-colored tulips had come and gone and the summer air was warm and weightless. Endless paperwork had been filled out with perfect detail as Anne and I emptied our pockets into a dull plastic bin and passed through security at the American Consulate in central Amsterdam. Our infant daughter strapped to Anne's chest, she poked her huge curious eyes above the edge of the baby carrier.

Staring through the thick glass at the stoic consulate official inspecting all the paperwork it had taken weeks to collect and prepare, he flicked through robotically as I held my breath. All the forms were there, I triple-checked. My high school and college transcripts. My elementary school doctor records. Two copies of the Consular Report of Birth Abroad application - both written in black ink, not blue. He flicked through them all, moving paperclips around and reorganizing as he went. Then he paused, glanced up, and looked at me humanly for the first time when he saw her birthday. "Born on the 4th of July, huh? Nice." He nodded, like two guys passing each other in the gym. Subtle, sure, but a sign of respect and acceptance. Absurd to think I had anything to do with it, but I swelled with pride nonetheless.

"Congratulations, Mr. Johns. You have successfully transferred your American citizenship to your daughter. We'll begin to process her American passport and you'll receive an email when it is ready for pick up."

Tears filled my eyes. Red, white, and blue bald eagles soared through my blood. I was caught off guard by my emotions, my American patriotism surfacing against my will hidden right below the surface. I was proud at that moment. Proud to be an American. Proud to have passed along the same to my daughter, and proud that after going out into the world with no idea where it would lead me here I was standing in the Netherlands with my French wife passing on all I could of the American Dream to our firstborn child.

Life is complicated and messy - hardly a straight line from A to B, endless twists and turns on each of our treasure maps. Standing outside the US Consulate in Amsterdam that sunny afternoon I was filled with both joy and a bittersweet feeling. I'd passed on my American citizenship, but a passport is just a collection of stamped-together papers.

But how could I ensure my American *spirit* came along with it? And how could I do all of this if we were settling into life in the Netherlands? Settling in so much that we were buying a house with plans to remodel it, a house we'd soon learn had a gripping history as well.

And what was more, how were we going to finish it all before our family grew any bigger?

30

Take Time to Reflect: Nazis and the Auto Body Shop

"The privilege of a lifetime is being who you are."
– Joseph Campbell

Haarlem, Netherlands. October 2022

At the end of 2021, Anne and I placed a bid on a house in Haarlem, a small historic Dutch town of 165,000, halfway between Amsterdam and the Dutch beaches of Zandvoort and Bloemendaal and a short 15-minute drive to both. Amsterdam had been our home for three years, our first daughter had been born there, and we'd blended into Dutch life, but we hadn't found the community we were so desperately seeking - the connective tissue that truly makes a place feel like home. But in Haarlem, we knew people. It was a city filled with young families, so we took another leap - a much smaller one than we were used to, but a leap nonetheless.

Looking online at photos of the house was odd – impossible to picture. The entire ground floor was bare concrete and drywall, with tool benches and car parts stuffed everywhere. Two car frames sat at the ends of the huge open room, one on stilts.

'Is this a house or an auto body shop?'

But once we stepped inside, we understood. The entire ground floor had indeed been a car shop since the 1970s and was a bakery and pastry shop thirty years before that. First opening up to sell bread and fresh pastries during World War II, the potential history intrigued me, and I found myself scouring the internet and local Dutch business archives for any information I could find from the time we first saw the listing online.

The kitchen and living room were on the next floor up with small bedrooms above that, but it had so much potential. With thoughts of an open kitchen, large living room, exposed beams, and wooden panels, we envisioned a new home for our growing family – a place we could design from scratch.

"I'm not here to drink pasta water," Anne said. We placed a bid that afternoon.

A couple of months after we moved in, I sat down in that concrete jungle, the walls insulated in some places with nothing more than thick cloudy plastic. I was wearing a beanie and could see my breath.

'We have a lot of work before this house will be a home'.

"Tap... tap..." Prying out my earbuds, I thought I was hearing something and decided to ignore it – probably someone selling something at the front door, but I stood up to answer it anyway. "Goededag." the older Dutch man said as I slowly opened the door. Standing beside a woman I assumed was his wife, both appeared to be in their 70s and were sweet, charming, and as warm as any grandparent has ever been. "Sorry, ik spreek maar een beetje Nederlands." I stammered slowly, waiting for them to switch to English knowing that most Dutch speak better English than I do. "Ah of course," the kind gentleman said. "Do you know the history of this house? That it used to be a bakery?" he said with a smile.

"Ah yes, I did know that - we just moved in a few months ago, and I have been looking through the records for any old photos!" I beckoned them inside as they waved to an idling car parked just down the street. The woman, who I learned was the man's sister, had been hesitant to knock, not wanting to bother anyone who lived in their old home. "We grew up in this house." The woman said. "My sister was born in the small bedroom upstairs."

Sitting in the cold air of our empty ground floor they told me the story of their family. Their father had bought the house from a man named Jan Joosten, a Dutch resistance fighter who had worked two jobs to support his growing family. He worked during the day at this house, right where we stood, in what had been a busy pastry shop and bakery at the height of World War II. At night, he would distribute the underground resistance newspaper De Trouw (The Truth). On the weekends, he would organize American baseball games on the streets in front of the large white corner house, which would draw a crowd that allowed men to come in and out with stacks of newspapers hidden under their clothes.

By the spring of 1945, Jan was unable to keep the bakery afloat and sold it and the home above to the father of these septuagenarian siblings and moved a couple of streets away as he welcomed his sixth child, a daughter. A few weeks later, his home was raided, he was caught hiding in an upstairs closet, dragged outside by Nazi soldiers, and arrested - carted away to Amsterdam with others from the Noord-Holland Domestic

Armed Forces. On April 15th, 1945, he was murdered by firing squad and thrown in a mass grave with 19 other resistance fighters in the dunes of Overveen, a five-minute drive towards the sea from the house - just three weeks before World War II ended. He was 39 when he died, the same age I am now.

"I don't remember much about this house, I was too young," the woman carried on, "but there was one story my mother always told us before she died."

On the top floor of the home is a small bedroom with a slanted wall and a slanted window. All the rooms up there have slanted walls, but this room is the smallest – the size of a walk-in closet. When we moved in it was the perfect size for a baby crib and a small changing table. Little did we know that the room had served the same purpose nearly a century before, maybe longer.

"My older sister was born in this house during the war, and my parents had an old wooden crib in that small bedroom at the top of the stairs." she began. "My parents housed Polish soldiers fighting the Germans during the war. They gave them bread from the bakery downstairs and a place to sleep. They were rowdy, stank, and had foul mouths, but they made us feel safe." she continued. One day, her mother had heard her youngest baby screaming from the small room at the top of the stairs but the crying suddenly stopped before she could climb up to comfort her - Dutch stairs are notoriously steep and short, nearly like a ladder. Two of the gruff Polish soldiers were upstairs at the time, and she panicked, thinking something had happened, imagining the worst. Rushing up to the room, she approached to see these two soldiers standing at the crib, one holding the young child in his arms, gently swaying her back to sleep and humming a Polish folk song under his stale breath.

Through broken Dutch and hand gestures, he explained, as

tears formed in his eyes, that he was a parent too, his infant daughter left at home when he'd been called to join the war effort. The bright white yarn of a newborn blanket representing the innocence of the world, and the tattered and worn chestnut uniform he proudly wore representing all he was doing to protect it. A father being a father to a child in need in the middle of a war – the most human of actions at the most inhumane time in modern history.

I adjusted the beanie on my head, itchy on the side just above my forehead. A silence lingered in the cold air of the ground floor – the weight of the story just told sitting between us. "Thank you for answering the door, I'm so happy I knocked. Enjoy the home." the older gentlemen said as they turned around, not wanting to take more of my time, unaware of the impact the last ten minutes had had on me. Waving as they rounded the corner out of sight, I closed the old wooden door and stood motionless. I was struck not only by the history of the building our family now called home, but at the complex layering of human stories that crisscross and pile up across time. Of course, this building had a story from World War II. It was built in 1906, after all. Most of the houses around us did, too, small row houses packed like sardines in crooked rows for blocks in every direction. Each one is a century old, no doubt each one with a century's worth of stories to tell.

Later that night, as I stood in that tiny room with the sun setting outside, slanted window behind my head, a small crib tucked in the corner, and our daughter in my arms, I felt consumed by the stories of those who came before me. Generations of human struggle had passed through this space, the air between these four walls we now call our home. A soldier missing his family as he fought Nazi troops. A mother tending to a newborn during a terrifying time. A baby unaware of the turmoil surrounding her, her entire life journey ahead. And nearly 80 years later, another infant girl in the arms of yet another doting father going to sleep in the same home, her entire life ahead of her, waiting for the wisdom of the generation before her to help guide her journey, too.

The lives, stories, struggles, and triumphs of every human that has come before us encircle the globe like a complex, invisible, golden web. Some are tangled and knotted, others cut short, some stretch for miles in only one direction - spread out like treasures for anyone who takes the time to look and listen. They lay unseen, unbothered, and slowly, as the decades pass, many are lost to time. Once again, talking to strangers, kind Dutch grandparents who knocked at our door, wisdom wasn't lost that day, but found. Jan Joosten and his story live on in our home and hardly a night passes that I don't think of those soldiers comforting a crying baby in the room where we now do the same - human stories on top of human stories.

Haarlem, Netherlands. March 2023

It's a freezing Friday morning, colder than normal for March, even in the Netherlands. My phone buzzes on the countertop as a calendar reminder pops up on the cracked screen. "10 Years an Expat." The house is quiet, our eldest daughter is at daycare and our youngest daughter, just two weeks old, basks in the comforting warmth of Anne's neck on the well-worn couch. The once cold concrete floor, filled with plastic walls and car parts, has been transformed into our home, finally finished enough to move into just a day before Margot arrived. An open living room and kitchen, a play area for the girls, a coffee corner for tired parents - a home I had found, a home we had found, a home we had created.

'I can't believe it's been a decade, ten years of my life. Over a quarter of my existence abroad. Married to a French woman I met in Dubai, living in the Netherlands with two children who will speak English, French, and Dutch.'

'How did this happen?'

I thought back on the ten years since I'd left the US, since I packed up all my dusty travel trophies, crammed them into a storage unit in Long Beach, and boarded a one-way flight to Bangkok. It made me think of everything I missed, the little meaningless things, too. I missed the look of a crisp dollar bill in my hand, overly friendly strangers at gas stations, and the brands on the shelf that I grew up with. Everyone spoke English to me, with no need to stumble through Arabic, Thai, French, or Dutch to explain I didn't speak any of them, at least not very well.

But it also made me reflect on what the US had lost since I left a decade ago, and how it had changed since I started traveling twenty years ago when I boarded that airplane alone with a one-way ticket to the other side of the world without a clue what I'd find except carnage from a tsunami.

* * *

I love the Netherlands. We deeply love living here and the opportunity for the high quality of life it has given us. But I don't love it more than the United States, at least emotionally. Life here may not be as exciting as living in a city like Dubai, a tropical paradise like Thailand, or as glamorous sounding as Los Angeles but for now, for today, none of that matters – only the peace and quiet to bring our girls gently into the world where we can be present and healthy for their first years.

It's been over five years since we landed in Amsterdam on a dark and stormy January night, and if I'm honest, I'm surprised we're still here. After all the searching, all the travels, all the possibilities of finding home on the road, I thought we'd spend a year or two here and move on like we always had, like I always had – but we're still here. And we're not alone.

Ironically, many of our friends here are also Americans, all young families, all who left the US in search of a better life abroad – some of the 75,000 who obtained EU visas in 2022. One family from Minnesota experienced live shooter drills, complete with fake blood, in their kindergarten classrooms which was the final straw in their decision to bring their two little ones to the Netherlands. Another faced the same in Florida, where a black man was shot to death with his young children in the car by an angry white man because he accidentally parked in a handicapped spot. Some are from Chicago, others from Atlanta, Michigan, or New York – all searching for their American Dream across the pond.

My entire journey, whether I've known it or not, has been a love letter to the American Dream, an unconscious attempt to prove to myself that life was best lived under the stars and stripes. And that's the thing about a dream, it has to be kept alive to continue existing. The second we stop remembering it, repeating its details, and sharing it with others, it slowly slips further and further out of reach and becomes a distant memory.

Isn't this what the American Dream is all about, anyway? The mindset that anything is possible, the idea that with hard work, motivation, and planning, you can achieve the best for you and your family? Sure, I was raised to believe that it meant a life in the US to achieve those things, but there aren't any rules – only the dream, and the spirit to chase it. America gave me the vision of a life well lived with all my needs met, a beautiful family to live it with, and the means to enjoy it all together - but most of all, the enthusiasm to find it, wherever that may be.

So search for that dream. Search high, search low, search within you and around you. Search for it in others, search for it in your past, and search for where it will lead you in your future.

For Anne and me, for our girls, for today, that dream is alive and well in the Netherlands.

31

Epilogue

Copenhagen, Denmark. September 2023

"How about Copenhagen?" Anne said, Margot softly sleeping in her arms. It was a perfect fit. "You and Stella would have so much fun." A one-hour flight, direct train to the city center, charming amusement park steps away, a hotel with an indoor swimming pool and cargo bikes for rent - the Danish capital had it all.

"What do you want to do first, kiddo?" I said, peering up awkwardly as Stella sat transfixed on my shoulders, staring at the stage ahead. Tivoli Gardens is one of the oldest amusement parks in the world, turning 180 years old in 2023, and I had decided that before the end of my six months of paternity leave, I would take her on our first Daddy-Daughter adventure.

We walked in the gates promptly at 11 am when they opened and had the entire day to explore. Though just barely 3, Stella was the boss—I was just along for the ride. Her eyes were as huge as the caramel apples swirling behind us as she sat on my shoulders, watching young girls just a few years older than she was, dressed head to toe in bright costumes and twirling to the music. Frozen with delight and wonder, the smile never faded from her face.

We spent eight hours in that park, eating popcorn, riding the train, two merry-go-rounds, and her first roller coaster. We visited the arcade and the aquarium, flew in little airplanes, ate pancakes for lunch, and too many ice cream cones to tell Maman about. That night, we had pizza and apple juice for dinner. Stella couldn't stop laughing, and neither could I.

Walking through the city center the next morning, backpacks on us both, we held hands as we crossed the bridge over the sprinkled rows of train tracks below leading to the central station. The grip of her small hand in mine, she skipped along the sidewalk and peering ahead, pointed excitedly at the swinging movement of the twisting roller coasters starting their daily ritual anew. "Kijk Daddy, ik did this yesterday," she said with glee. "We did!" I responded with a smile, as we continued walking. "Thank you Daddy... for this." she said with the next breath.

I paused, picked her up, and engulfed her in my arms, tears filled my eyes as I squeezed her tight hoping she wouldn't notice for fear she'd think something was wrong. This was it, I was living in the moment I had searched nearly twenty years to find. Twenty years spent gathering every single life experience I could to share with my kids one day, and in five little words a rush of contentment and peace came over me. I finally felt like I had armed myself with the perspective and experiences to provide life advice to my children - and for once, my mind was calmed by just being in the moment, with no need for danger, unknowns, or adrenaline.

This was a new adventure now. This was What Doesn't Suck, this was getting on a plane to a new destination, and this is why

I'd done all those things in the first place. This was the American Dream, more alive and well than I ever could have imagined.

'I won't fear what I don't understand. What you are to be, you now become.'

It had finally happened, the mantras inked on my chest, manifesting themselves in front of me in ways I could never have dreamed of right when I needed them most.

Happy, healthy, and smiling, the sun glistened off multi-colored buildings as we waltzed through the buzzing streets of a once thriving 800-year-old Viking fishing village as Stella and I logged some of our first adventure memories together.

For the first time since pouring through the dusty pages of those National Geographic magazines on the bathroom floor with the four-inch neon green carpet, I felt true contentment. The compulsive urge to jump on the next plane to anywhere had vanished, the desperate panic to see it all at once was quiet. I had become the explorer and had the stories to prove it, even adding specs of white to my beard in recent months. It was time for a much more important adventure now–to use the power of a harnessed mind to serve me and my family going forward.

As we landed back in Amsterdam that evening, Anne stood beaming in the Schiphol Arrivals terminal with Margot strapped to her chest–the same doors we walked out of five years earlier on a freezing dark January night–as Stella ran screaming through the crowds to them both. Exhausted, filled with love and gratitude for what we had, and ready to start the week ahead, we clasped hands and followed Stella as she bounded up the moving escalator in front of us giggling, her small backpack bouncing awkwardly behind her - golden curls heading in every direction from her perfect little head.

"The things we do, my love," Anne said through a satisfied

smile.

"The things we do." I whispered back.

* * *

It's been twenty years since I boarded that Cathay Pacific flight from Los Angeles, bound for Phuket just weeks after the 2004 Tsunami, and I could never have imagined all that has happened since. I've stepped foot in nearly 100 countries on six continents, half of them together with my best friend, had experiences I could never have dreamed up in my wildest fantasies, seen things too incredible to believe, and met strangers who left lasting impressions on me forever, whether they know it or not.

Granna has passed away, Grandpa many years earlier, and that house in Salt Lake City with the four-inch, neon green, shag carpet has long been sold—home to a new family now, but I think of it often. If the new owners are halfway sane, I imagine their first thought was "This 1970s carpet has got to go - who puts neon green, shag carpet in a bathroom?" and it makes me chuckle.

The glossy National Geographic pages stacked on top of each other in the cupboard of that bathroom, long since discarded, provided a treasure map for me. They sparked a fascination within, seared images into my developing mind that I would spend years seeking to uncover, to see in front of my own eyes, convinced they held the experiences I was so desperate to discover.

But what those images really were, were clues to the life

lessons I'd find within their scenes - the moments, people, and conversations I'd have along the way, while searching to find them. They were the immigration officer at the airport in Tajikistan, the brilliant young boy on the train in India after that awful bus ride, one-eyed Otto in Malaysia, the Muslim woman in the village in Bangladesh, the old man on his farm in Albania, the MAGA grandparents in Minnesota. They were the wrong moves at the right times, the true instincts, the gut feelings, and the wild chances I'd grow to appreciate so much, just waiting to be found throughout my travels.

It took me years of compulsive traveling around the globe - on airplanes, up mountains, down dark alleys, and jumping into the unknown - to realize that my sack of experiences is overflowing. Now it's time to go through them all, place meaning on those I can, and build the lessons they taught me into my life going forward. For some people, those lessons come naturally. For me, they involved a lot of jet lag and a hyperactive mind that needed to experience them as intensely as possible before that mind could be tamed.

In late 2021, I finally took Anne and Stella to Silver Spring, Maryland for the first time to see where I grew up. We drove by the Waldorf School and the Mormon Temple, by the parks and hangouts where I spent so much of my youth, and to the first house I called home. The new owners graciously let us in, let me explore, and told us how much they loved it there. The front step where I stood waiting for the carpool while pretending to smoke a twig still has a huge chunk missing from its side, the same worn blue carpet leads downstairs and the old off-white refrigerator still sits idling in the basement, just beyond the stairs I'd run up, afraid of the dark, with the flags waving gently behind me. But this place was just a skeleton now, a shell of the home I spent so much of my life looking for abroad. It isn't my home anymore, it's theirs. My home is right next to me, with two giggling and curious daughters and a wife who has given me everything I could have ever wanted and so much more.

My parents have lived in Ecuador for over a decade now and are the happiest they've ever been, more passionate and fulfilled than ever. And my sister, Julia, is still in Boston, now married. The decision to stay there was already written long before she made it. Her husband, as the Travel Gods would have it, is a French teacher. And our family is more connected now than ever, even if our WhatsApp conversations span three time zones on three continents.

Like my parents, Mr. Petrash is now in his 70s, still an educator, shepherding curious children and adults through the roller coaster that is understanding yourself through education. For over 30 years, he has given each one of his students that same fierce dedication, eye contact, and complete attention, and I'll bet it has stuck with each and every one of them as well.

When the global COVID-19 pandemic hit in early 2020, John Krasinski, made famous for playing Jim on the American version of "The Office", made a YouTube show highlighting all the good things going on in the world. Focusing only on the random acts of kindness, the smiles and laughs amidst a sea of doom, watched nearly 100 million times, these videos shined a light on the best of humanity, and he called the show "Some Good News". It wasn't me, but it made me smile to know that someone had finally made "The Good News". I just never thought it would take a pandemic to get there.

And that storage unit just off the freeway in Long Beach? I finally cleared it out, having spent over $11,000 to keep my things stored for a decade – the proof that I existed in this world.

Now this book has become the proof that I existed, the proof that we existed, the proof that I went out into the world and experienced all that I could to pass along to my children one day.

The small office where I'm typing these last words holds trinkets of my journey here, finally shipped over after their long hibernation in Long Beach. A tattered label curls off a badly beaten-up bottle of white wine I salvaged out of the ruins in Bangtao Beach after the tsunami nearly two decades ago. My ticket on The Rocket, the steam paddle boat in Bangladesh, swirling Bengali letters furled across it, hangs framed on my wall. A poster for "STIGMA" hangs above a row of books next to a mismatched collection of masks and stacked-up currencies, all breadcrumbs tracking my journey.

Since that pinky promise in the fall of 2014, Anne and I have traveled to nearly fifty countries on five continents across nearly a million miles together, and I'd do it all over again in a heartbeat. And after the birth of "What Doesn't Suck?" in that cozy back booth in Dubai, Anne and I have filmed over 100 travel videos together that have been watched some 15 million times. Hopefully, they can live on through the vast galaxy of content on the internet for people to stumble on long into the future. But the main reason we made them was for us, for our future family, our kids, to show them that Maman and Daddy were cool once, to watch on Christmas morning and get a chuckle out of together.

During the Revolutionary War, the American Dream was at times flickering, in danger of being snuffed out altogether. But it was the French who appeared with a crucial backup of supplies, ammunition, and naval support to stave off the British. And in the end, as it turned out, my quest for the American Dream needed a little help from the French, too.

I took more risks than most to find it, and left it all to chance, but the Travel Gods saw me through in the end. The treasure map left by one grandmother, the breadcrumbs to follow left by the other, the permission of supportive parents to explore them all to see what I'd find, even if they knew I'd have experiences they never did. Experiences they knew would shape me, and turn me into a man, and experiences they were confident the strong upbringing they gave me would ensure I made it out in one piece.

My unconventional journey started at a crossroads between a fringe religion pushing me one way and alternative education pushing me in another, to find my true self and never stop searching for it. It's been nearly 30 years since my Mom tossed those Ritalin pills down the toilet, and while she was confident I would find my own way to learn to harness my mind, she had no idea the journey around the world that quest would take me on, and I could never be more grateful to her for trusting whatever it needed to be.

Now, decades later and 3,800 miles (6,200 km) across the globe, the two sides of my split childhood ideologies have rejoined. I happily walk our daughters to a Waldorf daycare just two blocks from our home. Stella speeding ahead on her little bicycle, Margot strapped to my chest, huge eyes looking up at me with wonder. I finally understand what my Dad was trying so hard to impart to me all those years earlier, through the only religion he knew.

'God is love. How did it ever get more complicated than that?'

More than anything, I want my children to know that the goal of every adventure I have taken around the world has been to get to know myself better, so I can pass on my experiences and life lessons to them, knowing they'll also have to go out into the world to live their own stories, make memories and capture their own life lessons. Their search for independence and meaning is just beginning, in an environment that will support them in finding it, and maybe they'll even step onto an airplane and head into the unknown alone one day as well. After all, 85% of solo travelers are female, so they'll be in good company.

Who would have thought that a hidden cupboard in a basement bathroom covered in four-inch neon green shag carpet, would have been where I found my love of travel? This book is a love letter to those travels, to all travel, to all I have met along the way, and to the feelings and understanding those travels have awakened.

Sitting in a scalding sauna several mornings each week, sur-rounded by a handful of impossibly naked Dutch grandparents, I can only smile - for this book is a love letter to the Netherlands too – a country that has provided not only a quality of life I spent years searching for, but a loving, secure, and safe foundation for our growing family.

It's a love letter to my family, both French and American, who gave me the space and freedom to go out and have these experiences in the first place, armed with the tools to never get so carried away that I couldn't reel myself back in. Before I jumped out into the world, my parents gave me two gifts for which I will always be grateful. They gave me the best version of their own life experiences, based on their upbringings and lessons learned along the way, with all the love and attention for me to try and understand what they each had to offer. And they gave me the freedom and support to head out into the world and find my own when I needed them most - a lot easier said than done when your lost teenage son wants to buy a one-way ticket to a natural disaster on the other side of the world.

It's a love letter to my friends, from Acorn Hill to Waldorf, to MHC, Redlands, Brooks, and abroad – for putting up with my adventures and staying connected along the way, even if years sometimes slipped by between hugs. It's a love letter to photography, to my camera, to anything that has helped me capture moments and freeze them in time, whether in one fame or a million strung together. It's a love letter to America, for giving me the adventurous spirit to explore the world like my forefathers before me, armed with an enthusiasm for life so unique to the red, white, and blue.

And it's a love letter to my wife Anne. Without her adding the clarity, love, and focus my life needed, this book would never have been written. I wouldn't have had the confidence to write it. I wouldn't have had the confidence to do many of the things we've accomplished together. And I wouldn't be striving as hard to be my best self for her and for our girls.

Lastly, it is a love letter to my daughters, so that they too may be inspired to travel the world and see what they can find out about themselves however they see fit, whether down the block or across the globe. And if they ever want to know why Maman and Daddy left Dubai, they can watch the videos we recorded explaining why – which I've still never watched.

So never regret a swim, eat the cheese, and drink the wine. Take the leap and the road less traveled. Follow the spark, trust the locals, and respect your elders. Never stop exploring, take time to reflect, and know when to stop. Travel fast, think slow. Life is beautiful, live it loudly. Live it boldly and never give up your search to understand it fully.

Life has no obligation to make sense, and the beauty of it is that it rarely does, but if you can get lost in the sweet spot in between, you may find some answers, too – or at least create some good stories.

Author's Note

It's hard for books to get noticed these days. Whether you liked Jet Lag Junkie or not, please consider writing a review on **Amazon** or **Goodreads.** It would mean the world to me. Happy travels!

Scan below to rate and review "Jet Lag Junkie" on Amazon

SCAN ME

About the Author

Jeff and Anne met in Dubai in late 2014 and quickly began travel planning, taking weekend adventures, and exploring the most unique places they could find. Their adventure travel blog, What Doesn't Suck?, took off quickly, and over the next five years, it developed a loyal following from around the world. Popularized by their "48 Hours in..." series on YouTube, they produced over 25 episodes to help inspire travelers to get out of their comfort zone and see the world. All episodes are available for free at **www.youtube.com/whatdoesntsuck**

They currently plan their adventures from Haarlem, Netherlands where they live with their two daughters. They can no longer travel with just a backpack.

You can follow them on social media **@whatdoesntsuck** or on their website **www.whatdoesntsuck.com**